THE AMERICAN BAR ASSOCIATION

LEGAL GUIDE FOR
AMERICANS
OVER 50

THE AMERICAN BAR ASSOCIATION

LEGAL GUIDE FOR
AMERICANS
OVER 50

RANDOM HOUSE REFERENCE

NEW YORK   TORONTO   LONDON   SYDNEY   AUCKLAND

Copyright © 2006 by The American Bar Association

All rights reserved under International and Pan-American Copyright Conventions. Published in the United States by Random House Reference, a member of The Random House Information Group, a division of Random House, Inc., New York and simultaneously in Canada by Random House of Canada Limited, Toronto. No part of this book may be reproduced in any form or by any means, electronic or mechanical, including photocopying, recording, or by any information storage and retrieval system, without the written permission of the publisher. All inquiries should be addressed to Random House Reference, Random House Information Group, 1745 Broadway, New York, NY 10019.

RANDOM HOUSE is a registered trademark of Random House, Inc.

Please address inquiries about electronic licensing of reference products for use on a network, in software, or on CD-ROM to the Subsidiary Rights Department, Random House Reference, fax 212-572-6003.

This book is available for special discounts for bulk purchases for sales promotions or premiums. Special editions, including personalized covers, excerpts of existing books, and corporate imprints, can be created in large quantities for special needs. For more information, write to Special Markets/Premium Sales, 1745 Broadway, MD 6-2, New York, NY 10019 or e-mail specialmarkets@randomhouse.com.

Visit the Random House Web site: www.randomhouse.com.

Man's jacket lapel with cigar in pocket photo credit:
Christian Zachariasen/PhotoAlto/Getty Images

Manila folder photo credit:
Burke/Triolo Productions/Brand X Pictures/Jupiterimages

Library of Congress Cataloging-in-Publication Data is available.

Second Edition

10 9 8 7 6 5 4 3 2 1

ISBN-13: 978-0-375-72139-7

ISBN-10: 0-375-72139-8

American Bar Association

Robert A. Stein
Executive Director

Sarina A. Butler
Associate Executive Director, Communications Group

Mabel C. McKinney-Browning
Director, Division for Public Education

Katherine Fraser
Series Editor

STANDING COMMITTEE ON PUBLIC EDUCATION

Alan S. Kopit
Chair

AUTHORS

Charles P. Sabatino, Director;
Erica Wood, Assistant Director;
Stephanie Edelstein, Leslie Fried, Lori Stiegel, Associate Staff
Directors; and Ellen M. VanCleave Klem, Researcher

Commission on Law and Aging
American Bar Association
Washington, D.C.

REVIEWERS

Thomas D. Begley, Jr.
Begley & Bookbinder, PC
Moorestown, New Jersey

Rochelle Bobroff
AARP Foundation Litigation
Washington, DC

Eric Carlson
National Senior Citizens
Law Center
Los Angeles, California

Gene Coffey
National Senior Citizens
Law Center
Washington, DC

W. Scott Welch
Baker Donelson
Jackson, Mississippi

David Williams
Vanderbilt University
Law School
Nashville, Tennessee

CONTENTS

FOREWORD

Robert A. Stein, *Executive Director, American Bar Association*

When American families are asked to describe their legal needs, the topics that come up repeatedly are housing, personal finance, wills and estates, family and domestic concerns, and employment-related issues. The goal of this book is to give helpful information about all of these legal issues from the perspective of one of the fastest growing segments of our population—people over the age of fifty. The book is designed to help you make informed decisions on how best to handle your own legal questions, whether you are contemplating retirement, retired, or trying to assist older friends or your parents.

The books in the *American Bar Association Legal Guide* series are designed to provide information about the law in plain, easy to understand language. This book provides information on the range of options that can be used in solving everyday legal problems. We hope this book will help you negotiate some of the legal issues that arise as you age; we also hope that it will help you feel more comfortable with the law generally, and will remove much of the mystery from the legal system.

As the largest voluntary professional association in the world and the nation's premier source of legal information, the American Bar Association is in a unique position to provide authoritative guidance on legal issues. The ABA also provides support for lawyer referral programs and pro bono services (where lawyers donate their time), so that finding the right lawyer and receiving quality legal help within your budget is an attainable goal.

This book was written by staff of the ABA Commission on Law and Aging, who drew on a broad range of experience to write about the many legal issues faced by Americans over fifty. The authors were assisted by ABA members—including lawyers and academics—who reviewed the manuscript. Their contribution is invaluable because they have experience in dealing with legal issues that affect older Americans every day; their perspectives and expertise make this a better book.

The ABA's Standing Committee on Public Education provided oversight for this publication. The programs, publications, and resources of the ABA Division for Public Education are designed to educate the public about the rule of law, and ensure that people understand and participate in our legal system. Public education and public service are two of the most important goals of the American Bar Association. Through publications, outreach, and our website (www.abanet.org), the ABA strives to provide accurate, unbiased legal information to our members, to the media, and to the general public.

Robert A. Stein is the Executive Director of the American Bar Association. He was formerly dean of the University of Minnesota Law School.

INTRODUCTION

Alan S. Kopit, *Chair*
ABA Standing Committee on Public Education

According to the U.S. Administration on Aging, in 2004 there were 36.3 million people in America over the age of 65. If you think that's a lot of people, you're in for a shock—the population of older Americans will more than double by 2030, to 71.5 million people. What's behind the increase in this segment of the population? It's simple: people are living longer; and the people who were born in the post-war baby boom are reaching retirement age. As America's population ages, cultural, economic, and legal changes will follow.

There is a growing recognition that the law is crucial to the social and health needs of older persons and their families. In this book, you will find a wide array of laws directly addressing the legal needs of older people. You'll find up-to-date information about Social Security, Medicare, Medicaid, and other government programs. We discuss how the law affects health care, housing, and pension rights. You'll find information about ways to save time and money by planning your estate, and ways of assuring that your wishes will be followed in the event that you're incapacitated. We've also provided information on grandparents' rights, the rights of people with disabilities, and the special concerns of older consumers.

But this guide isn't just for older persons. It's of tremendous help to *families* of older people. They, too, are involved in helping parents (and maybe even grandparents) plan for and navigate their later years. Often, in the course of this planning, they begin to think ahead and plan for their own retirement. This book can help younger people get a head start on checking their Social Security benefits, evaluating their pension options, and taking all the other steps they need to take in order to ensure that their futures will be secure.

NEW AND IMPROVED EDITION

This book is a complete revision and update of an earlier book in the *American Bar Association Legal Guide* series. We've expanded on some important material from the first edition, and broken the book into shorter chapters. We've also taken into account all the changes in the law, and added a new chapter on marriage and divorce.

This book was authored by the expert staff of the American Bar Association Commission on Law and Aging, and benefits greatly from their expertise and experience in dealing with issues of aging. Their manuscripts were reviewed by ABA members and other lawyers from across the country who are experts in their fields. The entire project was completed under the guidance of the ABA's Standing Committee on Public Education. Together, we've worked to provide you with easy-to-read information that will help you understand the law that affects older Americans. Our goal is to help you spot problems before they become major—when they're easiest to handle.

WRITTEN WITH YOU IN MIND

We've made a special effort to make this book practical, by using situations and problems you are likely to encounter. You won't find legal jargon or technicalities here—just concise, straightforward discussions of your options under the law. Each chapter opens with a description of a real-life problem that shows the practical ramifications of the subject. Within chapters, you'll find sidebars with the following icons:

- ▶, which share practical tips that could be of benefit to you;
- ⓘ, which signal key additional information;

- ⚠, which warn you about potential pitfalls that you can navigate with the right information and help;
- 🗐, which give clear, plain English definitions to legal terms;
- ( ), which highlight experts' responses to practical questions, giving legal information that may help you as you grapple with similar issues within your own family.

You'll find two additional features at the end of each chapter:

- "The World at Your Fingertips," which contains tips on where to go for more information if you'd like to explore a topic further.
- "Remember This," which highlights the most important points that the chapter has covered.

One word of caution: when reading this book, and other books in the series, keep in mind that these books cannot and do not pretend to provide legal advice. Only a lawyer who understands the facts of your particular case can do that. Although every effort has been made to present material that is as up-to-date as possible, laws can and do change. Laws can also vary widely from one jurisdiction to the next. If you are thinking about pursuing legal action, you should consult first with a lawyer; to find one, contact a bar association or lawyer referral service.

With that in mind, this book can help you to make informed decisions about a wide range of problems and options. Armed with the knowledge and insights this book provides, you can be confident that the decisions you make will be in your best interest.

Alan S. Kopit is a legal-affairs commentator who has appeared on national television for more than fifteen years. He is chair of the ABA's Standing Committee on Public Education and is an attorney in private practice with the firm of Hahn Loeser & Parks, LLP, in Cleveland, Ohio.

CHAPTER 1

Divorce and Remarriage

The Implications of Love Later in Life

Mary and Bill have been married for twenty-five years. Early in their marriage, they were inseparable. But now, for one reason or another, they have drifted apart. Bill and Mary have made the difficult decision to divorce. Mary is concerned about health insurance, because she is insured through Bill's employer. Bill's priority is keeping his pension so that he will be comfortable during retirement. What can they expect and how should they proceed?

When older adults divorce, remarry, or live with a partner, there are many special legal issues to consider. This chapter addresses some of those issues. It begins with a discussion of divorce, including the division of property and debt. It then discusses some of the implications of remarriage for older adults. The chapter concludes with a discussion of the legal issues relevant to people who are living with a partner to whom they are not married.

DIVORCE

Deciding whether to divorce may be the most important decision of your life. If you divorce, you will need to navigate a number of emotional, financial, and legal issues. The financial impact of divorce can be particularly significant for older adults; unlike most young adults, many older adults have fixed incomes and limited opportunities to increase their financial assets. This section discusses some of the legal issues that all couples face during divorce, with a focus on issues that may be particularly important for older Americans.

Dividing Property and Sharing Debt

There are two different types of property in every marriage. **Nonmarital property**, which is also referred to as **separate property**, includes property that a spouse brought into the marriage and kept separate during the marriage. It also includes inheritances and gifts received and kept separate by one spouse during the marriage. **Marital property**—also referred to as **community property**, though subtle differences exist between the two—is defined somewhat differently by different states. Generally, marital property includes property and income acquired during a marriage. Wages earned, and homes, furniture, and cars purchased during the marriage are all usually considered marital property. Most older Americans are likely to be divorcing after a lengthy marriage. This makes it more likely that the bulk of their property will be marital property.

If there is no premarital agreement, a husband and wife are generally free to divide their property in accordance with the laws on division of property at divorce, or as they see fit. Each party usually keeps his or her separate property, and the parties divide the marital property. To facilitate division of property, they may enter into what is called a **marital settlement agreement**. A marital settlement agreement is a contract between a husband and wife that divides property and debts and resolves other issues of a divorce. When a husband and wife reach a marital settlement agreement, they can take the agreement to court, where a judge usually will approve it after a short hearing to make sure they understand their rights. Some states with simplified divorce procedures might not even require a hearing if the husband and wife agree on everything stated in the agreement.

However, if parties cannot agree on how to divide property, they may need to ask a court to divide the property. The laws of dividing property vary from state to state. As a starting point, however, most states allow parties to keep their own nonmarital property. Courts have the power to divide marital property between the parties. One party does not have an automatic right to keep marital or community property in the event of a divorce.

PREMARITAL AGREEMENTS

Assuming it is valid, a written **premarital agreement** (also called a **prenuptial agreement**) acts as a trump card in the division of marital property. By entering into a premarital agreement, the wife and husband waive their rights to have a court consider the usual cluster of factors that determine property division. Instead, the parties determine in advance how their property should be divided in the event of a divorce. Couples can also enter a **postmarital agreement** (also called a **postnuptial agreement**), which deals with the same issues but is entered into after the couple is married. Courts generally look more critically at postnuptial agreements; premarital agreements are preferable.

Any couple consisting of one partner who is older or wealthier than the other should consider entering into a premarital agreement. To ensure fairness and enforceability, each partner should retain a different lawyer to represent him or her when drawing up these agreements, and each should make a full disclosure of his or her assets.

Premarital agreements also have important effects on estate planning; for more information, see the "Remarriage" section later in this chapter.

Retirement benefits accumulated during the marriage are marital property, and are therefore subject to division in a divorce. Retirement benefits that were earned before the marriage, or that will be earned after the marriage, are not subject to division.

When a divorcing couple wishes to divide retirement benefits between them without incurring a tax or penalty, they seek certain domestic relations orders from a court, depending on the type of retirement plan. These orders recognize a spouse's right to receive all or a portion of the benefits payable to a participant under a pension plan.

Most plans offered by private employers honor Qualified

COMMUNITY PROPERTY STATES

There are nine community property states: Arizona, California, Idaho, Louisiana, Nevada, New Mexico, Texas, Washington, and Wisconsin, as well as Puerto Rico. In community property states, all property acquired during marriage is jointly owned, regardless of how the title is held. For example, if a husband buys a car with his own wages during a marriage, and holds title to the car in his name only, the car would still be considered the joint property of him and his wife from the time the car was purchased. In some community property states—for example, California—there is an automatic presumption that in the event of a divorce, community property will be divided equally between the parties.

Domestic Relations Orders (QDROs). Military, state and municipal governmental plans allow for marital division of retirement benefits under different rules and procedures. To find out how marital distribution is available under your or your spouse's plan, contact the plan administrator.

Health-Care Planning

When going through a divorce, it is important to address health-care planning; health insurance and medical bills may be among your most significant expenses. When a couple divorces, the family health insurance policy—if any—may no longer cover both spouses. The policy will only cover the spouse who purchased the policy or who acquired the insurance through active employment or retiree health insurance benefits. Children covered under a family policy generally will still be covered after a divorce.

However, a federal law passed in 1986—the **Consolidated Omnibus Budget Reconciliation Act**, also known as **COBRA**—requires most employer-sponsored group health plans to offer divorced spouses of covered workers continued coverage at

SOCIAL SECURITY RETIREMENT BENEFITS

Although Social Security retirement benefits are not property and are not subject to division in a divorce, they are considered income and thus deserve consideration when a couple divorces. If you divorce after at least ten years of marriage, you can collect retirement benefits on your former spouse's Social Security record if you are:

1. at least age sixty-two, and

2. your former spouse is entitled to or receiving benefits.

You can also collect survivor's benefits as a widow or widower if:

1. your divorced spouse dies, and

2. the marriage lasted ten years or more.

Benefits paid to a surviving divorced spouse who is sixty or older will not affect the benefit rates for other survivors receiving benefits.

Often a dependent spouse receives alimony until age sixty-two, when it is assumed that Social Security benefits start. However, the amount of Social Security received at this age could be about 25 percent less than what would be received at full retirement age. To find your full retirement age, visit *www.ssa.gov/retirechartred.htm.* Chapter 3, "Social Security and Other Government Pensions," provides more information about Social Security benefits and eligibility.

group rates for thirty-six months after a divorce. The worker's divorced spouse must pay for the coverage.

A divorced spouse who wishes to take advantage of COBRA should act as soon as the divorce is final. He or she should contact the human resources or personnel department of the covered worker's employer to learn the steps the spouse must take. Generally, the divorced spouse must act within sixty days after the divorce decree becomes final; continued coverage is not automatic. Under COBRA the employer has up to fourteen days to provide an explanation to the divorced spouse on the right to

TALKING TO A LAWYER

Q. *My spouse and I have decided to get divorced after thirty years of marriage. I had a stroke twenty years ago and have ongoing mobility issues, which I worry will become more serious as I get older. Can I address payment for ongoing medical needs in our marital settlement?*

A. Yes. When preparing your request for spousal support, provide sufficient details of your insurance costs and medical expenses and your inability to pay them. Your spousal support payments should be increased to cover your ongoing medical expenses.

—Answer by Holly Robinson,
Legislative Counsel Committee, Salem, OR

continue coverage, after which the spouse has up to sixty days to choose to continue coverage. The employer must advise what coverage is available, its cost, and when payments must be made, as well as any steps that must be taken to establish eligibility for the health insurance. Some state laws also provide for extended coverage for divorced spouses in some circumstances.

Tax Considerations

There are several complicated tax consequences of divorce, and the majority of people need the advice of a tax professional during the divorce process. A certified public accountant (CPA) can help you to project the tax consequences of divorce, including:

- capital gains tax due on investments that may be sold;
- taxes on the withdrawal of pension plans, Individual Retirement Accounts (IRAs), annuities, and profit-sharing, savings, and other retirement plans;
- deferral or payment of taxes after selling a marital residence; and
- the difference between your new "single" tax bracket and your old "married" tax bracket.

HEALTH-CARE AND FINANCIAL-PLANNING DOCUMENTS

Too often, people are so busy with the process of divorce that they forget about other aspects of health-care and financial planning—including the revision of wills, trusts, powers of attorney, and health-care advance directives.

But such revision is critical, especially if the law of your state does not automatically remove your spouse's responsibilities under these documents upon divorce. When you get divorced, be sure to change your will, any trusts that designate your former spouse as a beneficiary or trustee, health-care planning documents, and life insurance policies that name your former spouse as a beneficiary. If you have a lawyer assisting you with your divorce, he or she may be able to help you do this.

Generally, if you transfer property to your spouse as part of a distribution of assets under a final divorce agreement, there will not be any tax consequences to either of you at the time of the transfer. However, if you receive payments from your spouse's retirement plan pursuant to a QDRO, you will have to pay taxes on it, unless you roll the payment into an IRA. It will then be taxed when it is distributed to you from your IRA.

Courts may consider some of these tax consequences when dividing property. For example, suppose the sale of a house or the sale of stock as part of a divorce will necessitate the payment of capital gains tax. A court may be inclined to award extra property to the person who will have to pay that tax, as compensation for the added expense. Conversely, if a property settlement results in a tax benefit, the person receiving the benefit may receive less property as a result. In order for a court to consider tax consequences, the consequences usually must be immediate and specific; courts generally will not speculate about possible tax consequences that may occur several years in the future.

The court can also divide tax liabilities, but if one party does not pay his or her share of those liabilities, then the IRS may hold both parties liable. There are exceptions, however. For example, if the liability arises from circumstances about which one spouse had no knowledge (e.g., failure to pay business-income-related taxes), an exemption may arise for the innocent spouse under the so-called **Innocent Spouse Doctrine**.

In general, fees paid to your lawyer are not tax-deductible. However, fees paid to a lawyer for tax advice and for the production of taxable income—including, in many cases, alimony, are tax-deductible.

REMARRIAGE

The legal issues associated with remarriage are complicated, particularly for older adults. Remarriage may affect alimony and Social Security payments, as well as the assets of each party. In addition, if you have children from a previous marriage, you may wish to work with a lawyer in planning your estate, in order to ensure that your assets are distributed to your children after your death.

Estate Planning

If you are in a relationship in which both you and your spouse have children from a previous marriage, you might want to arrange things so that your own money goes to your own children, and your spouse's money goes to his or her children. However, some people are surprised to learn that the law usually does not permit one spouse to cut the other spouse out of his or her will. If a husband or wife dies and his or her will makes no provision for the surviving spouse, or conveys to that person less than a certain percentage of the deceased spouse's assets (the percentage varies by state), then a widow or widower can **take against the will**. This means that he or she can choose to accept the amount allowed by law (usually a third or half of the estate) instead of the amount bequeathed in the will. The surviving spouse doesn't have to take against the will; if he or she chooses not to do so, the property is bequeathed as stated in the will.

This **elective** or **forced-share provision** is troubling to many people considering second marriages late in life. Recent revisions to the Uniform Probate Code have adopted a sliding scale for widows and widowers who take against a will: the longer the marriage, the higher the elective share. This means that if a marriage lasts only a few years, the percentage taken by the surviving spouse could be quite low, minimizing one source of worry for older couples. However, as of this writing, fewer than half the states have adopted even a portion of the suggested code.

What about a person who has a living trust instead of a will? In some states, spouses aren't automatically entitled to a share of living-trust assets. In those states, one spouse might be able to disinherit the other. Your lawyer can tell you more about the law in your state.

Another way to prevent a spouse from taking against a will is to execute a premarital or postmarital agreement in which the partners voluntarily give up the right to a statutory share of each other's estates, and agree on how much (or how little) of the other's estate each will inherit. Such agreements usually supersede statutory set-asides for spouses. Thus, upon his or her death, a spouse can leave assets directly to his or her children through a will or will substitute (such as a trust).

QTIP Trusts

Providing for children from different marriages may conflict with tax planning. The marital deduction allows spouses to leave their entire estates to each other without paying taxes. But what if you and your spouse have children (especially grown children) from other marriages? You might naturally prefer that your biological children receive more of your estate than your spouse's children from a previous marriage. But your spouse might not agree with your wishes—and if you leave your entire estate to your spouse, he or she makes the final decision about how to dispose of the property after you're gone.

That's why certain families use QTIPs. The **qualified terminable-interest property trust** allows you to leave your property in trust for your spouse, but the property goes to whomever you wish after your spouse dies. You still get the marital deduction, your spouse gets to live off the income from the trust, if sufficient—and, depending on how the trust is written, may be able to access the principal as well—and your children get the property upon your spouse's death. But here's the problem: no one else can benefit from the assets in the trust until your spouse dies, which might not leave other family members enough money for their comfort until then.

As of 2006, if you have a large enough estate, you can leave up to $2 million tax-free to your children—or in a credit shelter trust for their benefit on your death—and put the rest into the QTIP trust. If your estate is smaller, you may want to buy life insurance, with the proceeds going to your children on your death.

Mutual Wills

Mutual wills provide another option for couples with children from different marriages, or for couples who want anyone other than a surviving spouse to inherit property. Such wills specify that each spouse leaves all property to the survivor, who after death will leave specified property to the friends or relatives that the other designates. But be careful: Use of mutual wills might jeopardize the marital-tax deduction, and may also involve issues of contract law that vary from state to state. Moreover, one spouse might be able to change the will after the first spouse dies. Seek professional advice before using mutual wills.

Life Estates

If you want your surviving spouse to be able to live in the family home, but want to make sure that the house will ultimately pass to your children, a life estate is an option that may suit you. A **life estate** is a property interest in which the recipient (the **life tenant**) gets to use the property only for as long as he or she lives, at which point the property passes to a third party (or occasionally reverts to the grantor's estate). While in the possession of the life tenant, the property can't be sold or substantially modified.

You can provide for a life estate in your will, but check with a lawyer before doing so; such property conveyances can be quite complex. A better method may be to leave the family home in trust for your spouse so long as he or she is able and desires to occupy it.

Life Insurance

Life insurance is another tool you can use to distribute assets among children from different marriages. You can set up an irrevocable trust for your children that will ultimately be funded from the proceeds of a life insurance policy. You pay the premiums, but the trust actually owns the policy. When you die, your children receive the benefits from the trust tax-free, while your spouse gets the rest of your estate.

Trusts

The versatility of trusts makes them useful instruments for allocating assets among different families, because you can set up separate trusts for the children of different marriages, or even for each family member.

Social Security Benefits, Retirement Benefits, and Alimony

Remarriage can result in the loss of financial benefits like Social Security, alimony, and retirement benefits to one or both spouses. For example, if you are widowed and remarry before the age of sixty you typically cannot receive Social Security survivor's benefits based on an earlier marriage unless your later marriage ends, whether by death, divorce, or annulment. If you are widowed and you remarry after age sixty (or fifty if you are disabled), you can still collect benefits based on the work record of a former deceased spouse.

TALKING TO A LAWYER

Q. *I'm a sixty-five-year-old widow, and I'm contemplating remarriage. But I'm worried that I might lose the pension that I receive from my late husband's employer. Is it likely that I'll be able to continue receiving that pension if I remarry?*

A. Survivor's benefits in a private pension plan do not terminate on remarriage of the surviving spouse. Certain government or military retirement plans do contain remarriage penalties.

—Answer by Kathleen Vetrano,
Vetrano & Vetrano, King of Prussia, PA

When you reach age sixty-two or older, you may get Social Security benefits on your work record, or on your spouse's record when your spouse becomes disabled or retires. You will receive the higher benefit. If you remarry and your new spouse dies, you will be entitled to receive widow's benefits if you were married at least nine months, with certain exceptions to the rule.

If you have children who are receiving Social Security benefits based on the work record of your former spouse, your remarriage will have no effect on the benefits paid to your children.

In most states, alimony also terminates upon the remarriage of the supported spouse, unless the divorce agreement provides otherwise.

DOMESTIC PARTNERSHIPS AND COHABITATION

Many older adults live with a partner because they choose not to get married, or are unable to do so. If you are unmarried and live with a partner without any written agreements or advance-planning documents, you face several legal risks. For example, if one partner has medical problems, the other partner may not be permitted to visit or have a role in making medical decisions. Likewise, if one partner becomes incapacitated, the other partner may not have any right to make decisions in the incapacitated partner's interest. If one partner dies without a will, the surviving partner may not have any rights to property.

If you live with a partner to whom you are not married, you should consider preparing several documents to make sure that you and your partner have the rights, privileges, and protections you need, including a health-care advance directive, a durable power of attorney, and a will. More information about these documents is provided in Chapters 5 and 7. You may also want to consider entering into a **domestic partnership agreement**, also known as a **cohabitation agreement**. A domestic partnership agreement is a contract that describes how you and your partner will handle property and assets while you are together, and what will happen if the relationship ends. Because divorce laws do not apply to unmarried couples, the agreement can be an important form of protection for both partners and can provide guidance if you and your partner split up. Since some states do not recognize the validity of domestic partnership agreements, it is recommended that you consult an attorney in your area.

THE WORLD AT YOUR FINGERTIPS

• Another book in this series, the *American Bar Association Guide to Marriage, Divorce & Families*, has more information about all the areas touched upon in this chapter. The book is available from the ABA Web Store, at *www.abanet.org/abastore*.

• The Family Law Section of the American Bar Association publishes several handbooks on divorce. Handbooks include: *Illuminating Answers to the 200+ FAQs: Frequently Asked Questions About Divorce—A Client Manual*; *Surviving Your Divorce and Beyond*; *Divorce Forms: A Handbook for Clients*; and *ADR Options: A Client Handbook*. Contact: American Bar Association,

Section of Family Law, 321 North Clark Street, Chicago, IL
60610; (312) 988-5145; *www.abanet.org/family/home.html.*
- To find a lawyer who specializes in matrimonial law, contact
the American Academy of Matrimonial Lawyers (AAML). Members of the AAML are experts in divorce, prenuptial agreements,
property valuation and division, and alimony. Contact: AAML,
150 N. Michigan Avenue, Suite 2040, Chicago, IL 60601; (312)
263-6477; *www.aaml.org.*

REMEMBER THIS

- You will probably need to divide marital property—including
a home, investments, and retirement benefits—during a divorce.
- It is important to plan for access to health care after a divorce.
- The tax consequences of divorce are complicated, so you
should talk to a tax professional if you are contemplating divorce.
- If you are planning to remarry, there can be several legal
consequences. Take the time to plan your estate and secure your
finances before remarriage.
- If you are unmarried and live with a partner, you should consider drafting health-care advance directives and durable powers
of attorney. These documents will ensure that each person has
the right to make health-care and financial decisions if the other
person becomes incapacitated. Both parties should also draft
wills and set out their wishes regarding distribution of their
property.

CHAPTER 2

Grandparents' Rights

The Law on Visitation and Kinship Care

Ed and Louise have lost contact with their grandchildren, who are aged nine, eight, and six. They have learned that the kids were placed in foster care as a result of drug abuse and neglect by their mother. The children were separated in foster care, and their mother was later killed in an auto accident. Can Ed and Louise use the legal system to reunite all of the children?

Today, many grandparents are family caregivers—sometimes by choice, sometimes by default. With the responsibilities of caregiving come legal questions and problems. Consider a few actual examples:

• Two children have been living out of state with their father and his girlfriend since their mother died. Currently, the children's father does not allow the grandmother visitation with the children, and has threatened her with physical violence.

• Due to their mother's drug and alcohol problems, two grandchildren (a six- and four-year-old) have been living with their grandparents for two years. The landlord has threatened eviction if another grandchild moves in.

• When a woman left her spouse because of his mental problems, abuse, and drug use, her parents allowed her and her child to live with them. According to the grandmother, the mother simply "left the child with us while she did her own thing. The father ended up sexually abusing the child when he got time with her, so child protective services and the guardian ad litem recommended that we have custody of the child." The grandparents incurred $10,000 in attorney's fees and $5,000 in counseling bills, and had to take out a second mortgage to cover their expenses.

As demonstrated by the examples above, the issue of grandparents' legal rights and responsibilities arises in two very different contexts. The first relates to visitation between grandparents and grandchildren who are in the custody of their parents or others. The second relates to kinship care, when grandparents become the primary caregivers for their grandchildren because the children's parents are unable or unwilling to care for them.

GRANDPARENT VISITATION

Broad changes in American society underlie the rise in grandparent visitation disputes. The divorce rate has skyrocketed, and post-divorce acrimony between parents often results in the severance of contact between grandparents and grandchildren. Moreover, increased mobility has undermined the close relationships that used to exist among extended family members.

Traditionally, the **common law** (the law derived from judicial decisions) denied grandparents the right to visitation with a child over a parent's objections. Parents were deemed to have complete control of their children, and courts refused to interfere with their decisions except in extreme circumstances. But with the graying of America and a greater willingness to litigate family matters, some state legislatures have redefined the rights of grandparents, giving them access to the courts to enforce these rights.

If you are seeking visitation with your grandchildren, consider whether litigation is your best option. Grandparent visitation disputes are painful and disruptive for children, their parents, and their grandparents. Going to court may intensify the emotional issues and create problems for the grandchildren in particular. Litigation is emotionally wrenching, costly, time-consuming, and may not yield desired results. Consider counseling and mediation as first steps.

State Statutes and Visitation

State laws usually spell out who may petition the court for visitation privileges, the circumstances under which they may do so, and the standards courts use to decide whether to order visitation. Since state statutes vary, this section will discuss general trends rather than specific provisions.

In 1998, Congress passed a law mandating that a visitation order granted to a grandparent in one state be recognized in any state where the grandchild is living.

Who May Petition for Visitation

Most state statutes permit grandparents to petition for visitation. These laws reflect the belief that the grandparent-grandchild bond is unique and precious, and that grandparents are uniquely qualified to provide roots and a sense of identity to their grandchildren—particularly when they have been instrumental in the child's development. Some states have extended the right to petition for visitation to great-grandparents, aunts, uncles, siblings, and even nonrelatives with whom a child has a close relationship. These are all people who may be able to lend stability and support to a child. The laws do not make granting visitation automatic—they simply give grandparents the right to *ask* for visitation.

However, courts in other states have ruled that grandparents may not access the courts to gain rights to visitation with their grandchildren. The rights of grandparents vary greatly from state to state, according to the state where the child in question lives. Grandparents denied access to their grandchildren should consult a lawyer to find out whether their state courts permit them to go to court to obtain visitation rights.

When a Grandparent (or Other Third Party) May Petition

Most state laws set forth the specific circumstances under which a grandparent may seek visitation. The most common of such circumstances are the death of a parent and the divorce of a child's parents. Courts may also allow grandparents to seek visitation when a parent is incarcerated, when a child is born out of wedlock, or when a child has previously lived with the grandparent. A few statutes list no specific circumstances in which grandparents may seek visitation, leaving the issue to the discretion of the court.

The Standard for Deciding Whether to Order Visitation

Most state laws provide that the court must decide whether visitation is in the best interests of a child. This emphasis on judicial discretion parallels the provisions of most child custody and visitation laws. Numerous statutes also list specific factors the court should consider, such as the prior relationship between the grandparents and the grandchildren, the mental and physical health of the parties, and the preference of the child, if the child is old enough to express a preference. Sometimes courts will even consider the willingness of the grandparents or other relatives not to denigrate the parents to the child.

The United States Supreme Court considered the issue of grandparent visitation in the case of *Troxel v. Granville*. In that case, the parents of the father sought visitation with their grandchildren following the father's death. The children's mother was willing to let the grandparents have time with their grandchildren during daytime hours one day per month, but the grandparents wanted overnight visitation two weekends per month. When the grandparents did not receive permission for the visitation they wanted, they filed suit under a Washington state law that allowed "any person" to seek visitation at "any time." In June of 2000, the Court ruled that the Washington law was unconstitutional as applied by the trial judge in that case, because it violated the mother's **due process rights** to make decisions concerning the care, custody, and control of her children. While the Court did not define the proper standard to be used in deciding grandparent visitation cases, this case has nonetheless influenced legislatures and trial courts to use more specific and careful standards for such cases.

Following *Troxel*, some state courts have continued to allow grandparent visitation in accordance with the best interests of the children in question, but many others have not. Numerous state courts have held that grandparents may be granted court-

DUE PROCESS RIGHTS

The term **due process rights** refers to established rules and principles for the protection and enforcement of private rights in legal proceedings, including the right to notice and the right to a fair hearing before a tribunal with the power to decide the case.

ordered visitation rights only if a parent is unfit or the grandparent has previously raised the child. Such courts have focused on whether the child will be harmed by the lack of grandparent visitation. In a few states, appellate courts have not ruled at all regarding whether state grandparent visitation laws are valid. If you are seeking visitation with your grandchildren, consult with a lawyer to find out about the law in your state.

Visitation Following Adoption

A majority of state statutes specify the effects of adoption on grandparent visitation. Under state adoption laws, an adoption completely terminates the legal relationship between a child and his or her birth parents. But what happens to the relationship between the child and his or her biological grandparents? Most courts have said that adoption also terminates a child's relationship with the parents of his or her birth parents. This interpretation makes sense when strangers adopt a child. But when a stepparent or close relative adopts a grandchild, many state laws provide that adoption does not automatically rule out grandparent visitation rights. This situation commonly arises, for example, when one parent dies, the child's surviving parent remarries, and a stepparent adopts the child.

Mediation of Grandparent Visitation Disputes

If you find yourself in the midst of a family dispute over visiting your grandchildren, you may want to consider mediation.

THE "INTACT FAMILY" SITUATION

Should grandparents be awarded visitation when the child is part of an intact family—that is, a family in which the child's parents are still married, and the parents and children reside in the same household? No state statutes specifically allow grandparents to seek visitation when the nuclear family is intact. Some state laws are general enough to allow grandparents to seek visitation when the child lives with both parents, but it is extremely rare for a court to grant visitation against the parents' objections under those conditions. The decisions made by fit parents about what is in their children's best interest will generally not be questioned by the court without evidence of parental abuse or neglect.

Mediation is a means of resolving disputes that emphasizes communication, privacy, and self-determination. The parties get a chance to explain their feelings and needs, and to listen to the other side. Since the parties fashion their own resolution, they can be creative, and they tend to stick with their agreement. Most importantly, unlike going to court, mediation doesn't harden positions and feelings in such a way that a successful resolution becomes difficult or impossible to achieve. Mediation is quicker, cheaper, and less emotionally painful than litigation.

Consider mediation at an early stage of the dispute. The longer the dispute goes on, the more likely it will become that tensions will heighten and positions will harden. Moreover, mediating the dispute prior to a court hearing will save the parties, and especially the children who may be called to testify, the agonizing emotional experience of undergoing a trial involving sensitive private matters—including the need to "choose sides."

Mediation may be available in your community through private mediators, community justice centers, or a mediation program affiliated with the courts that may be geared specifically towards family law matters. Judges refer many child custody and visitation disputes to mediation as an alternative to trial, and in some court systems referring visitation cases to mediation is mandatory.

KINSHIP CARE

Kinship care providers are non-parent relatives who are the primary caregivers for children whose parents are unable or unwilling to care for them. Today, the number of kinship care households in the U.S. is skyrocketing. These caregivers are most often older relatives, particularly grandparents.

Legal Relationship with the Child

Many kinship caregiving arrangements are informal: parents and grandparents agree that the grandparents will care for the children for a time, or the parents leave the children with the grandparents and do not return. A grandparent caring for grandchildren should consider establishing a formal legal relationship with them. This will make it easier for the grandparent to register the child for school, obtain medical and dental treatment, apply for public benefits, and get health insurance for the child.

 THE STATISTICS ON KINSHIP CARE

According to the 2000 Census, over 6 million (or one in twelve) children in the United States live in households headed by grandparents and other relatives. In many of those homes, a grandparent is the sole or primary caregiver. This type of situation is particularly prevalent in urban areas, but anecdotal evidence suggests that the incidence of kinship caregiving is increasing in rural areas as well.

State laws spell out the legal authority a grandparent may obtain. In some states, a grandparent must petition a state court for custody. In other states, grandparents seek to become guardians. Adoption is another, more permanent option. Some states allow other variations on these legal relationships, such as permanent guardianship, open adoption, and de facto custodianship. If you are raising your grandchild and wish to apply for legal authority over the child, find out the options in your state. Learn which court makes these decisions, and whether you can go through the process without a lawyer. This can be a particularly difficult process for grandparent caregivers.

In some situations, the state may step in to protect a child from abuse or neglect by parents. When a state child welfare agency believes that a child is in danger, the agency may go to court to seek custody of the child and permission to remove the child from the home. Grandparents may play a role in these proceedings, possibly as the reporter of abuse, or as a witness, or as a potential custodian of the child. If the state removes a child from his or her parent, the state generally retains legal custody, and the relative may qualify as a foster parent, entitling that relative to foster care payments. (See the next section of this chapter, "Financial Support for Kinship Care," for more information.) Court actions in which abuse or neglect are alleged have different names in different states: care-and-protection cases, dependency actions, children-in-need-of-services (CHINS) cases, and many others. Find out how your state handles abuse and neglect cases, and what legal authority you can obtain when your state's child welfare agency is involved.

Many families prefer not to get involved with the court system. After all, court cases require money, time, and energy. In addition, families may not want to change a child's legal relationship with his or her parents, especially if the caregiving arrangement is temporary. In some cases, grandparents may temporarily care for grandchildren to prevent the state from becoming the children's legal custodian. Grandparents sometimes take this step to ensure that family members retain decision-making authority (such authority may be lost if the state intervenes.) Informal caregiving arrangements often are more attractive than dealing with the courts—especially in comparison with adoption, because adoption permanently terminates parental rights. Nonetheless, formalizing the relationship between grandparents and grandchildren can facilitate access to important benefits, such as financial assistance.

Financial Support for Kinship Care

Eligibility requirements for public programs are complex and often inconsistent, and sometimes even work at cross-purposes.

 OBTAINING SERVICES

If you have not obtained a court order giving you legal authority to care for your grandchild, how can you obtain services from school systems, hospitals, welfare offices, and other agencies?

It is often not clear whether a parent can authorize a person to have this kind of authority for a child. Some states have mechanisms to enhance your authority without limiting the role of the child's parents. For example, about half the states and the District of Columbia have enacted medical-consent legislation, under which a child's parents can authorize another adult to obtain medical treatment for their children. The parents need only sign a simple document, and health-care providers must honor the authorization. At least eleven states now have educational-consent laws, allowing informal caregivers to enroll children in schools.

Some new laws address the tragic situation of parents who have chronic, debilitating, or terminal medical conditions. Under recent **standby-guardianship laws**, such a parent may designate a guardian for his or her children in advance, and that guardianship will take effect when the parent dies, becomes incapacitated, or feels that he or she is no longer able to care for the child. At least twenty-two states have now passed standby-guardianship laws.

TALKING TO A LAWYER

Q. *My husband and I have lost contact with our grandchildren. We recently learned that the kids have been separated and placed in foster care due to drug abuse and neglect by their mother. Can we seek custody of the children and reunite them?*

A. When children are placed in foster care, the state takes custody of the children and works to reunite the children with their parent or parents. Grandparents seeking custody should contact the state foster care agency to request that the children be placed in the grandparents' home. Grandparents can also request that the children's legal custodian be changed from the state to the grandparents. However, if the parents' rights have not been terminated, then the courts will consider whether granting custody to the grandparents violates the parents' rights.

—Answer by Rochelle Bobroff
AARP Foundation Litigation, Washington, DC

Obtaining benefits can be daunting. Here are some benefits for which you and/or your grandchildren may be eligible:

• **Temporary Assistance to Needy Families (TANF)** is the federal welfare block grant program, which replaces the former Aid to Families with Dependent Children (AFDC) entitlement program. You and your grandchildren (or your grandchildren alone) may qualify if you fall within certain income limits. States have some flexibility in deciding whether and how to apply new federal mandates that impose work requirements and time limits in cases where TANF benefits go to the caregiver. To find the rules in your state, contact your local welfare department or area agency on aging.

• **Social Security dependents benefits** are available to any child under eighteen whose parent is collecting retirement or disability benefits, or whose parent is deceased and was fully insured at the time of death. Also, children being raised by grandparents may qualify for dependent benefits based on a grandparent's work record. A child would qualify if:

(1) the child's parents are deceased or disabled; or

(2) the child's grandparent died, so long as the child was legally adopted by the grandparent, and the child's natural parent was not living in the same household and making regular contributions to the child's support at the time the grandparent died.

These requirements are complex, and you should obtain detailed eligibility information from the Social Security Administration.

• **Supplemental Security Income (SSI)** provides financial assistance to low-income elderly, blind, or disabled individuals, including children. SSI is a federal program, although states may supplement the benefit. Grandchildren can qualify if they are blind or disabled and meet the income and asset requirements. You may also qualify if you are a low-income elderly, blind, or disabled person. Grandparents may apply for SSI on behalf of their grandchildren. If a child qualifies, the grandparent can serve as the child's representative payee, so that checks will be issued to the grandparent on behalf of the child. You cannot receive both TANF and SSI; SSI benefits are generally higher.

• **Medicaid** provides medical assistance to elderly and low-income people who are blind, disabled, or part of a family with dependent children. Grandchildren who qualify for TANF or Supplemental Security Income (SSI) are normally eligible for Medicaid. In addition, some children whose family incomes are too high to qualify them for TANF or SSI but who have substantial medical needs may qualify. You do not necessarily need legal custody of your grandchildren to prove that you are caring for them. (See Chapter 9, "Medicaid and Long-Term-Care Insurance," for more information.) If you have difficulty obtaining these benefits, you may need a lawyer or other advocate to help you. (Chapter 15 can provide you with more information about finding a lawyer.)

• The **Children's Health Insurance Program (CHIP)** provides insurance coverage for uninsured children in families with incomes too high to qualify them for Medicaid. The law targets uninsured children in families with incomes below 200 percent of the federal poverty level. However, states have a great deal of flexibility in establishing eligibility rules, payment rates, and other aspects of the program. Most states will not count the income or assets of a grandparent or other relatives in determining CHIP eligibility.

• **Food stamps** are monthly coupons that can be used to purchase food. Their value is based on the number of people in the household and the household income. For purposes of food stamp eligibility, grandchildren cannot qualify as a separate household. You may apply for food stamps at the local food stamp office. Again, you do not need legal custody of the children to obtain food stamps.

• The **Earned Income Tax Credit (EITC)** is a special benefit for low- and moderate-income working people, including grandparents raising children. This tax credit program, administered by the Internal Revenue Service, provides grandparents with a cash payment even if they do not owe any taxes. In order for a grandparent to qualify, earned income must be below a specified level, which changes yearly. The actual amount of the credit is a percentage of your earned income. To apply for the EITC you must file an income tax return. You will need to prove that your grandchild is a qualifying child, based on age, residency, and relationship. The child must be under the age of nineteen (under twenty-four if he or she is a full-time student), or permanently and totally disabled. The child must have lived with you for at least six months, and must be a biological or adopted child, a descendant (for purposes of EITC eligibility, a grandchild counts as a descendant), a stepchild, or an eligible foster child. Again, you do not need legal custody of your grandchild to qualify for the EITC.

APPLYING FOR BENEFITS

Here are some practical tips to keep in mind when applying for public benefit programs:

- Be prepared to visit the public benefits office more than once, and be prepared for long waits.

- Bring documentation with you. You might need your grandchild's birth certificate; your son's or daughter's (i.e., the child's parent's) birth certificate; Social Security numbers; proof of income for household members; proof of assets, such as bank statements and deeds; documentation of household expenses, such as rent receipts and utility bills; and documentation of your role as a caretaker relative, such as a power of attorney, signed statements, or court papers.

- File the necessary application as soon as you can, even if you need to come back to the Social Security office with more documentation. Generally, your benefits will be paid retroactively from the application date.

- Do not be discouraged if you encounter unfriendly or unhelpful caseworkers or a lot of red tape. Keep your eye on the goal!

- Get legal help if you run into problems. Contact your local legal services office, law school clinic, or bar association for information about free or low-cost legal assistance.

- Help applying for the Earned Income Tax Credit (EITC) may be available through AARP's Tax Aide program or Grandparent Information Center.

- **Foster Care Payments.** Another source of federally supported direct payments is the foster care program under Title IV-E of the Social Security Act. Foster care payments made under Title IV-E are substantially higher than welfare benefits, but to receive them the children must be placed in state custody,

HOUSING ISSUES

Grandparents living in rental housing may run into problems if they add grandchildren to their households. If you live in subsidized housing for the elderly, you may lose your eligibility when children move in to your home. If you live in other types of public or subsidized housing, you may become ineligible for your current rental unit because your family size has increased. Even in private rental housing—for example, a seniors-only apartment complex—your landlord may try to evict you. If you are threatened with eviction, consult a lawyer. Laws may protect you from eviction because you have children in your household. The landlord may not be following proper eviction procedures, or a public-housing authority may not be complying with regulations. A lawyer may be able to help you work out a satisfactory arrangement.

and foster parents who are related to the children must meet state licensing requirements. Some standards, such as specifications that the home must have a certain number of bedrooms, may be difficult for economically disadvantaged relatives to meet. In recognition of the importance of placing children with family members, some states have waived some licensing requirements for kinship caregivers and have provided support services to supplement monthly financial payments.

• **Guardianship subsidies.** Some states offer programs that provide a monthly subsidy payment to grandparents and other relatives who obtain legal guardianship of the children they are raising. Generally, the state provides such payments for children who have been in state custody and are receiving care from a relative for some minimum time period. Many states use federal funds under TANF or other programs for guardianship subsidies. Some states (such as Missouri and Louisiana) offer similar programs that do not require a child to have been in state custody.

• **Adoption subsidies.** Special needs children who are adopted out of foster care may be eligible for a subsidy under the adoption assistance program established by Title IV-E of the Social Security Act, or under a similar state program. Keep in mind that the definition of "special needs" may vary from state to state.

THE WORLD AT YOUR FINGERTIPS

• The Grandparent Information Center at the American Association of Retired Persons (AARP) provides general information and publications. The Center keeps a listing of support groups and other resources around the country. Contact: AARP, 601 E Street, NW, Washington, DC 20049; 1-888-OUR-AARP (1-888-687-2277); *www.aarp.org/families/grandparents/gic*.

• Generations United's National Center on Grandparents and Other Relatives Raising Children educates policy makers and provides resources on kinship care issues. Contact: Generations United, 1333 H Street, NW, Suite 500 W, Washington, DC 20005; (202) 289-3979; *www.gu.org*.

• Your state or local agency on aging can help identify services and support for grandparents with a variety of needs. Look in your local government listings under "Aging," or call the National Eldercare Locator at 1-800-677-1116 to find the agency on aging nearest you. You can also search the database of the National Eldercare Locator online through their website at *www.eldercare.gov*.

REMEMBER THIS

• All states have enacted legislation enabling grandparents to petition for visitation with grandchildren. However, some state courts have invalidated these laws so that grandparents cannot sue for visitation. Talk to a lawyer to find out more about the law in your state.

• Grandparent visitation disputes are painful and disruptive for grandchildren, their parents, and their grandparents. Going to court may intensify the emotional issues and create problems for the grandchildren in particular. Consider mediation if you find yourself in the midst of a family dispute over visiting your grandchildren.

• Kinship care providers are non-parent relatives who are the primary caregivers for children whose parents are unable or unwilling to care for them.

• If you care for a grandchild, you may be eligible for federal or state benefits.

CHAPTER 3

Social Security and Other Government Pensions

Information for You, Your Spouse, Your Ex-Spouse, and Your Children

Bob is sixty years old and his health is poor. After working his entire adult life in a variety of jobs, he is thinking about retirement. He has some savings and investments, he has paid Social Security taxes, and he knows that some of his employers had a pension plan. What kind of income can he expect in retirement?

Most financial advisors say that when you retire, you'll need about 70 percent of your preretirement earnings to comfortably maintain your preretirement standard of living. But under current law, if you have average earnings, your Social Security retirement benefits will replace only about 40 percent of your preretirement salary. This means that you'll need to supplement your benefits with a pension, savings, or investments. For people without significant income or assets, the federal Supplemental Security Income (SSI) program and other public benefit programs such as veterans' benefits and federal or state housing subsidy programs may kick in.

One important change in today's work world is that people no longer retire at a well-defined or fixed point in time. Instead, more people are choosing to continue working full- or part-time well into their seventies and eighties. Nevertheless, you have to be retired or disabled in order to be eligible for most pensions and many of the other programs discussed in this chapter.

This chapter begins with an overview of Social Security and SSI benefits, and moves on to discuss the various tax breaks available for seniors.

SOCIAL SECURITY

The Social Security Administration (SSA) administers Social Security, the country's most extensive insurance program for older and disabled people and their families. Benefits include payments to:

- retired workers who have reached at least age sixty-two;
- spouses and dependents of retired workers;
- divorced spouses of retired or disabled workers;
- workers who become disabled;
- spouses and dependents of disabled workers;
- survivors of deceased workers; and
- divorced spouses of deceased workers.

Over 95 percent of American workers are eligible for some form of Social Security benefits, including household and farm workers, self-employed persons, most employees of state and local government, and some federal workers. A separate federal program, Railroad Retirement (which is integrated with Social Security), covers railroad workers. Social Security retirement beneficiaries age sixty-five and older, or those of any age who receive disability benefits, may also be eligible for Medicare. (See Chapter 8, "Medicare and Private Health Benefits," for more information.)

Social Security programs are complicated, and the laws and regulations governing them can change. Contact your local SSA office for information about Social Security benefits or to ask specific questions about your own case (contact information is listed at the end of this chapter).

Qualifying for Benefits

To collect Social Security, you must meet two qualifications. First, you or the worker on whose account the benefits are paid must be **insured** under Social Security. The simple rule of thumb is that forty quarters of work (ten years) in covered employment will fully insure a worker for life. However, there are some exceptions to this rule, so do not assume you are ineligible simply because you have performed fewer than ten years of covered work. Second, you must meet requirements for the particular benefit—that is, you must be the appropriate age, or be able to prove disability or dependence on an insured worker, or be the survivor of a deceased worker.

Payment Levels

Social Security benefits provide only a floor of protection. To be financially secure in retirement, you will need other sources of income, such as a pension or income from savings, to maintain your style of living. If Social Security is your only source of income, look into eligibility for SSI or veterans' benefits, described later in this chapter.

The amount you receive from Social Security depends on how much money you have earned over your lifetime, your age at retirement, and other factors. Every year, approximately three months before your birthday, the SSA will send you a form, "Your Social Security Statement." This statement lists your annual accredited earnings and the amount of your estimated retirement and disability benefits. Check the statement carefully to make sure your employers have been correctly reporting your earnings. You can also obtain this statement from your local SSA office. Call SSA toll free at 1-800-772-1213, or file your request through the Internet at *www.ssa.gov*. Social Security recently added a Retirement Planner to its website. Located at *www.ssa.gov/retire2*, the Retirement Planner includes an online calculator that allows you to estimate your retirement benefits using numbers you provide. Once your benefits begin, you will receive annual cost-of-living adjustments at the start of each calendar year.

The maximum benefit for a worker retiring at age sixty-five in 2006 is $2,053 per month. The average monthly benefit is $1,002.

WHAT IF MY WAGES WERE WRONGLY REPORTED?

You have approximately three years from the year your wages were earned to correct most mistakes in your earnings record. However, there is no time limit on correcting an error caused by an employer's failure to report your earnings. You can fix these mistakes any time, but you will need proof. A pay stub or a written statement from the employer will do the trick. You will need to obtain form OAR-7008 ("Request for Correction of Earnings Record") from the Social Security Administration.

Retirement Age

For purposes of collecting Social Security, for many years people were considered fully retired at age sixty-five. Today, however, only people born in or before 1937 are considered fully retired at age sixty-five. The full (or "normal") retirement age for those born between 1938 and 1959 has been raised gradually over the past few years. For those born in 1960 or later, the full retirement age is sixty-seven.

You cannot receive full retirement benefits until you reach your full retirement age, although you may receive early retirement benefits after you turn sixty-two. If you retire before reaching your full retirement age, your monthly benefits will be reduced for as long as you receive them. Conversely, if you choose *not* to retire at your full retirement age, you will earn **delayed retirement credits** for each month you continue to work without receiving retirement benefits, and your monthly benefits will be higher when you do decide to receive them. The annual delayed retirement credit percentage varies from 3 percent to 8 percent based on your year of birth.

Retirement Earnings Test

What happens if you continue to work after you begin receiving retirement benefits? Until December 1999, if you were between

AGE AT WHICH A PERSON MAY RECEIVE FULL SOCIAL SECURITY BENEFITS

Year of Birth	Full Retirement Age
1937 or earlier	65
1938	65 and 2 months
1939	65 and 4 months
1940	65 and 6 months
1941	65 and 8 months
1942	65 and 10 months
1943–1954	66
1955	66 and 2 months
1956	66 and 4 months
1957	66 and 6 months
1958	66 and 8 months
1959	66 and 10 months
1960 and later	67

the ages of sixty-two and seventy and receiving benefits as a retiree, dependent, or survivor, you were allowed to earn only a certain amount before your Social Security retirement benefits were reduced. This was known as the **Retirement Earnings Test**. In 2000, a new law eliminated the Retirement Earnings Test for people retiring at or above full retirement age. For example, if you were born in 1943 and you retire at age sixty-six (your full retirement age), you will receive full benefits no matter how much you earn.

However, there is still an earnings test for people who retire when they are younger than the full retirement age. If you retire from full-time work before you reach your full retirement age but continue to work part-time, your early retirement benefits will be reduced when your earnings exceed a certain limit (called the "retirement-earnings-test exempt amount"). There are actually two limits, adjusted automatically each year. A lower exempt amount is applied during the year(s) before you reach your full retirement age, and a higher exempt amount is applied during the year you reach your full retirement age in the months before your birthday.

Because there are two different exempt amounts, Social Security also uses two different formulas for reducing your benefits when your earnings exceed the exempt-earnings amount. When the lower exempt amount applies, one dollar in benefits is withheld for every two dollars of earnings in excess of the exempt amount. When the higher exempt amount applies, one dollar in benefits is withheld for every three dollars of earnings in excess of the exempt amount. As soon as you reach full retirement age, the earnings test will no longer apply: you can keep all the income you earn, without having your Social Security benefit reduced.

If you reach your full retirement age in November 2005, your lower exempt-earnings amount is $12,000 and your higher amount is $31,800. If you retired in March 2004, but continued

ANNUAL RETIREMENT-EARNINGS-TEST EXEMPT AMOUNTS FOR PERSONS UNDER THE NORMAL RETIREMENT AGE

Year	Lower amount[1]	Higher amount[2]
2002	$11,280	$30,000
2003	11,520	30,720
2004	11,640	31,080
2005	12,000	31,800
2006	12,480	33,240

[1] Applies in the years before the year in which a person attains normal retirement age.
[2] Applies in the year in which a person attains normal retirement age, for the months prior to the person's birthday.

to work part-time, Social Security would have reduced your benefits by $1 for every $2 you earned above $12,000 in 2004. If you also worked in 2005, your benefits would be reduced $1 for every $3 over $31,800, through October. In November and beyond, the earnings test would no longer apply.

The earnings limit applies only to earned income, defined as gross income from wages or net income from self-employment. Your benefits generally will not be affected by unearned income—money earned from savings, investments, insurance, and the like—though they may be reduced if you receive a federal, state, or local government pension.

The Windfall Elimination Provision and the Government Pension Offset

The Windfall Elimination Provision (WEP) and the Government Pension Offset (GPO) rules reduce the Social Security benefit amount of people who also receive pensions from work that is not covered by Social Security—in other words, work that generates income on which they don't pay Social Security taxes, such as state or local government employment for which Social Security taxes are not withheld. The WEP uses a special formula to reduce a worker's own Social Security benefit, as well as the benefit the worker's spouse would receive based on the worker's account. It does not affect survivor's benefits. The WEP formula varies according to the worker's earnings and to the number of years worked. It can reduce the Social Security monthly benefit amount paid to a worker, but it will not eliminate the benefit entirely.

The Government Pension Offset applies when a spouse or surviving spouse of a worker receives a pension based on his or her own federal, state, or local government employment not covered by Social Security. The GPO reduces the Social Security benefit the spouse of the worker would have received by two-thirds the amount of the government pension. The GPO could eliminate the spouse's or surviving spouse's entire benefit.

AN EXAMPLE ILLUSTRATING THE GOVERNMENT PENSION OFFSET

Suppose Mrs. Jones expects to receive $500 a month in Social Security benefits based on her husband's work history. Mrs. Jones worked for state government and receives $600 a month in state retirement benefits on her own record. The GPO will reduce the $500 in Social Security benefits by $400, which is two-thirds of $600. Thus, Mrs. Jones will receive only $100 in Social Security benefits based upon her husband's account, plus her own government pension of $600, for a total of $700.

Disability Benefits

Social Security protects all workers under age sixty-five against loss of earnings due to disability. In order to collect disability benefits, you must meet requirements relating to the number of years employed, age, and the severity of your disability.

To be eligible for Social Security disability benefits, you must show that:

- you are unable to engage in substantial gainful activity (work);
- your inability to engage in work is the result of a medically determinable physical or mental impairment; and
- the impairment has lasted or can be expected to last for at least twelve months, or can be expected to result in death.

For purposes of disability benefit eligibility, **substantial activity** is defined as productive work involving significant physical or mental activity, or a combination of the two. **Gainful activity** is defined as work that is for pay or profit, work that is generally performed for pay or profit, or work that is intended for pay or profit.

Your disability must be medically documented, and the applicable guidelines are strict. Once you qualify for disability benefits, payments will continue for as long as you remain medically disabled and unable to work. Your health will be reviewed periodically to determine your ability to return to work. If you do return to work, you may be eligible for certain work incentives, including continued benefits and health coverage. When you reach your normal retirement age (see the sidebar above titled "Age at Which a Person May Receive Full Social Security Benefits"), your disability benefits will become retirement benefits, but the amount of the benefits will remain the same.

Information about Social Security disability insurance, including how to qualify for benefits, how to apply, and what information to provide, is available online at *www.ssa.gov/dibplan/index.htm*.

Family Benefits

In addition to the insured worker, certain other people—including the insured worker's spouse, divorced spouse, and dependents—may receive benefits based on the worker's eligibility for retirement or disability benefits. (In describing the benefits available, it is assumed in this section that the worker is still living.)

Note that Social Security limits the total amount of benefits that one family can receive. The maximum benefit is determined based on the year the worker became eligible for benefits and the size of the worker's primary insurance amount.

Spouse Benefits

To be eligible for benefits on a worker's record, the worker's current spouse must:

- have been married to the worker for at least one year at the time the application is filed; or
- be the natural parent, along with the worker, of a child.

  In addition, the current spouse must be:

- sixty-two years of age or older; or
- caring for a child who is eligible for benefits on the worker's account—that is, a minor under the age of sixteen or a disabled child.

Finally, the worker must be eligible for (although not necessarily receiving) retirement or disability benefits.

TALKING TO A LAWYER

Q. *I have a medical condition and can no longer work. Am I eligible for disability benefits?*

A. To qualify for Social Security disability benefits for yourself and your dependents, you must meet two sets of requirements.

First, you must be insured under Social Security. This means that you must have paid Social Security taxes for enough years to be fully insured. In addition, you must have paid into the program recently enough to have achieved disability-insured status. As a general rule of thumb, a worker is fully insured if he or she has one quarter of coverage for every calendar year after the year in which he or she turned twenty-one. As another rule of thumb, a worker has achieved disability-insured status if he or she has twenty quarters of coverage out of the forty calendar quarters before the disability began.

Second, you must have a physical or mental impairment or combination of impairments that will prevent you from performing substantial work. The impairment or combination of impairments must be expected to last at least twelve months. In making this assessment, your treating physician's opinion is very significant. If you can't provide enough medical evidence to SSA, the agency may send you to a consultative examining doctor for evaluation. The decision maker will determine whether or not you can return to your past work and, if not, whether there are other jobs that you could perform. Factors considered in making this determination include your age, education, work experience, and physical and mental limitations.

There is a five-month waiting period before your first disability check arrives. After twenty-four months on the disability rolls, you are eligible for Medicare benefits.

—Answer by Nancy G. Shor, Executive Director, National Organization of Social Security Claimants' Representatives (NOSSCR), Englewood Cliffs, NJ

The spouse benefit amount is based upon a percentage of the worker's benefit. A spouse who has reached full retirement age (see the sidebar above titled "Age at Which a Person May Receive Full Social Security Benefits") collects one-half of what the insured worker is eligible to receive.

Benefits are reduced for a spouse who:

- begins collecting before reaching full retirement age; or
- has extra income under the retirement earnings test (see above); or
- is subject to the Government Pension Offset (see above).

However, a spouse who collects benefits before reaching full retirement age can receive the full spouse's share of benefits if he or she is caring for a dependent child.

Divorced-Spouse Benefits

To be eligible for benefits on a worker's record, a divorced spouse of the worker must not be eligible for an equal or higher benefit on his or her own Social Security record, or on someone else's record. In addition, he or she must meet three conditions. He or she must:

- be at least sixty-two years old;
- have been married to the worker for at least ten years; and
- be unmarried.

In addition, the worker on whose account benefits are being claimed must be eligible for retirement or disability benefits, unless the divorce occurred more than two years before the date of the application. In that case, a divorced spouse who meets the other requirements still may be eligible for benefits as long as the worker is at least age sixty-two and fully insured.

More than one spouse or divorced spouse can collect on the account of the same retired or disabled worker without affecting the amount received by either the other spouse(s) or the worker. A spouse or divorced spouse who is also entitled to benefits on his or her own work record cannot draw both worker and spouse benefits in full, but will receive the higher of the two benefits.

Dependent-Children's Benefits

Social Security distinguishes between a worker's disabled and nondisabled children. Both receive benefits equal to approximately one-half of the worker's benefits while the worker is still living, and 75 percent if the worker is deceased.

To be eligible for benefits, a dependent nondisabled child must be unmarried, and either:

- younger than eighteen years of age; or
- younger than nineteen years of age, if he or she is attending elementary or secondary school full-time.

A dependent, disabled child of any age may receive benefits on a parent's account if the disability began before the child reached age twenty-two and the child is not married. Each qualified child may receive a monthly payment of up to one-half of the insured worker's benefit amount.

Survivors Benefits

When an insured worker dies, the following family members may qualify for survivor's benefits:

- a spouse who is at least sixty years old;
- a disabled spouse who is between fifty and fifty-nine years old;
- a divorced spouse who is sixty or older, or over fifty if disabled, provided the marriage lasted at least ten years (the length-of-marriage rule does not have to be met if the divorced spouse is caring for the spouse's child who is under sixteen years of age or disabled, and if the child is also receiving benefits);
- dependent children who are under eighteen (or under nineteen if attending elementary or high school full-time), or who are disabled;
- a spouse or divorced spouse of any age caring for a child who is under the age of sixteen or disabled (in which case the benefits are known as **mother's** or **father's benefits**); or
- parents who are sixty-two or older and who received at least half of their support from the worker at the time of his or her death.

Death Benefits

When an insured worker dies, Social Security pays a one-time, lump-sum death benefit of $255 to one of the following family members, in the order of priority listed:

- a surviving spouse living with the worker at time of death;
- a surviving spouse not living with the worker, but eligible for survivor's benefits in the month of the worker's death; or
- a surviving child eligible for dependent's benefits in the month of the worker's death.

If a person receiving Social Security benefits dies, the check for the month in which the person dies must be returned to SSA.

Termination of Benefits

Disability benefits may be terminated if you recover from a disability or if you refuse to accept rehabilitation services.

Retirement or survivors benefits may be terminated if:

- you leave the United States for more than six months;
- you are deported;
- you are convicted of certain crimes, such as treason and espionage; or
- you are in prison due to a felony conviction.

In addition, people receiving benefits as a widow or widower, divorced spouse, mother or father of a dependent or disabled child, or parent of a worker may lose their benefits if they remarry. There are many exceptions to this rule. If you are receiving benefits and are considering remarriage, review your circumstances with an SSA claims representative. (See Chapter 1, "Divorce and Remarriage," for more information about the legal implications of remarriage later in life.)

If changes in your circumstances cause a reduction or termination of your benefits, you must receive a letter notifying you of the change. You have the right to appeal. (See the discussion below for more information.)

Taxes on Benefits

Every January, the Social Security Administration sends beneficiaries a Social Security Benefit Statement, which details the benefits received during the previous year. Social Security benefits generally are not taxable. However, people with substantial incomes from sources other than Social Security may have to pay taxes on part of their benefits. See IRS Publication 915, *Social Security and Equivalent Railroad Retirement Benefits*, for more information.

Applying for Benefits

If you are planning to retire, you should file for benefits two or three months before your retirement date. Your first check should arrive soon after you stop working. Do not delay filing for either retirement or survivors benefits, because if you are eligible for retroactive benefits, you will only receive them for the six months prior to the month in which you file your application.

For disability benefits, you should apply as soon as you realize that you can no longer work. Disability applications can take much longer to process than applications for retirement benefits. You can receive up to twelve months' worth of retroactive benefits.

When you apply for retirement benefits, bring the following items with you:
- your Social Security card or proof of the number;
- a birth certificate or other proof of your age;
- W-2 forms from the past year or, if you are self-employed, a copy of your last federal income tax return;
- military discharge papers (if applicable), because you may be able to receive extra credit for active military duty;
- your spouse's birth certificate and Social Security number, if he or she is also applying for benefits on your account;
- your children's birth certificates and Social Security numbers, if they are applying for children's benefits on your account;

- proof of U.S. citizenship or lawful alien status if you (or, if applicable, your spouse or child) were not born in the United States; and
- the name of your bank and your account number, so that your benefits can be directly deposited.

If you are applying for survivors benefits, you should also bring:

- a copy of the deceased worker's death certificate;
- a copy of your marriage certificate (for a spouse);
- a copy of your divorce decree (for a divorced spouse);
- a Social Security number, birth certificate, and evidence of financial dependence (for a dependent child);
- evidence of financial dependence (for dependent parents); and
- the deceased worker's W-2 forms from the past year or, if the worker was self-employed, a copy of his or her last federal income tax return.

If you are applying for disability benefits, you should also bring:

- a list of all your doctors, and a list of the hospitals or institutions where you have been treated, including names, addresses, telephone numbers, and treatment dates;
- medical records from doctors, therapists, hospitals, clinics, and caseworkers;
- any relevant laboratory and test results;
- names and dosages of any medications you are taking;
- a list of all the jobs you have held for the past fifteen years, and the type of work you performed at those jobs;
- information about any other checks you receive on account of your disability; and
- the dates of all of your prior marriages (if you were married before and your spouse is also applying for benefits).

Overpayments

Sometimes, SSA pays benefits incorrectly. If you receive a notice that you have been overpaid, you can file a written request for

BE ORGANIZED!

Whenever you deal with the Social Security Administration, you should try to avoid delays and complications by keeping a full, organized, written account of your communications. Make a note of when you had a conversation on the phone or in person, the name of the person with whom you spoke, and what was said. Your claim will be assigned to a claims representative. Keep this person's name and telephone number handy in case you need to contact SSA. In addition, be sure to keep copies of forms or documents, including everything you send to the Social Security Administration. Since SSA keeps records by Social Security numbers, put your Social Security number on the top of each page you submit.

reconsideration. In your request, you might state that the overpayment did not occur or that the amount of the overpayment was wrongly calculated.

At the same time, you can request that the overpayment be waived. This is important if the overpayment was not your fault, or if it would be a hardship for you to repay the overpaid amount. If you file for a waiver within thirty days, the money will not be taken out of your check until a final decision is reached. You will be asked to fill out an Overpayment Recovery Questionnaire in which you must explain the cause of the overpayment and your ability to repay it.

Your Social Security Check

Social Security will encourage you to have your benefits deposited directly into your bank account. This is safe and convenient, and ensures that your money is in your account even when you are not at home to receive a check. Benefits are paid on a monthly basis. Depending on your birth date, you will either be paid on the second Wednesday of the month (if your birth date is between the first and tenth of the month), the third Wednesday of the month (if your birth date is between the eleventh and twentieth), or the fourth Wednesday of the month (if your birth date is between the twenty-first and the thirty-first). A link to the SSA's Schedule of Social Security Benefit Payments for 2006 can be found on the Internet at *www.ssa.gov/pubs/2006calendar.htm*. The check you receive each month is your benefit for the month that has just ended.

If you are unable to manage your benefits due to disability, Social Security will appoint a representative payee—a friend, relative, or even a staff person or volunteer from a local agency, to receive your checks and pay your bills. Even if a family member has authority to handle your finances under a durable power of attorney, SSA generally will not permit that person to endorse your Social Security checks unless he or she has been appointed your representative payee. A form that will allow you to file for appointment of a representative payee is available from any Social Security office.

SUPPLEMENTAL SECURITY INCOME

Supplemental Security Income (SSI) is a cash assistance program intended to help with basic expenses such as food, clothing, and shelter. The program pays monthly cash benefits to people who:

- are age sixty-five or older, or blind, or disabled; and
- have extremely limited income and personal property; and
- meet certain citizenship or residency requirements.

The Social Security Administration runs the SSI program, but unlike Social Security, you do not need to have a work history to qualify for benefits. To be eligible for SSI, disabled persons must meet the same criteria that must be met in order to qualify for Social Security disability benefits (discussed earlier in this chapter). It is possible to qualify for both Social Security disability and SSI disability concurrently.

To be eligible for SSI, you must have limited assets. Federal law permits a single person to have assets worth up to $2,000, and a married couple to have assets worth up to $3,000. The following assets are exempt and do not count toward SSI eligibility:

- your home and the land on which it is located;
- household goods and personal effects, plus wedding rings;
- one car (if used for transportation);
- life insurance with a combined face value of $1,500 or less;
- trade or business property needed for self-support (e.g., tools and machinery);
- your burial plot; and
- burial funds up to $1,500 (in an account earmarked for burial expenses).

In 2006, SSI paid a maximum monthly benefit of $603 to a single person who had no other income. The maximum monthly benefit for couples was $904. These figures are adjusted each January for cost-of-living increases. SSA's Cost of Living Adjustments fact sheet for 2006 is available online at *www.ssa.gov/cola/colafacts2006.htm*.

Some states supplement SSI benefits in amounts ranging from $15 to more than $150 per month. Some people receive both SSI and Social Security benefits. In most states, if you receive SSI benefits, you will also be eligible for free medical care through Medicaid. (See Chapter 9, "Medicaid and Long-Term-Care Insurance," for more information.)

If you think you may qualify for SSI, check with your local Social Security Administration office. You will need to prove your age, and you will need to provide a great deal of information about your financial situation. If you are applying because of disability or blindness, you will need the same information listed above, in the "Disability Benefits" section of this chapter.

If you are denied SSI, you can appeal. The appeals process is similar to the process for appealing a Social Security claim, outlined below.

WHEN YOU DISAGREE WITH SOCIAL SECURITY'S DECISION

If your claim for Social Security or Supplemental Security Income benefits is denied, you will receive a letter from Social Security listing the reasons for the denial and explaining how to appeal. If an employee of the Social Security Administration tells you over the phone or in person that your claim for benefits is denied, ask for a written denial; you cannot appeal an oral statement.

You have the right to appeal the agency's decisions within sixty days from the date of notification. Since many claim decisions are reversed on appeal, it is usually worth your time and effort to appeal. Also, if you do not appeal, the claim decision becomes final and you give up the chance to appeal later. As early in the appeals process as possible, it is advisable to consult a lawyer who specializes in Social Security issues.

There are several steps in the appeals process, and each step results in a decision. If you receive an unfavorable decision, you have the right to move to the next step, generally within sixty days of receiving written notice of the decision. The Social Security Administration has recently restructured its appeals process. Some levels of appeal have been renamed; others are being gradually eliminated. Here are some general guidelines:

• The first level of appeal will involve a review of your files and the collection of additional information about your claim. This will be handled within the agency and usually will not require that you be present.

• If you disagree with the decision rendered at the first level of appeal, you will have the opportunity for a hearing before an administrative law judge. The judge will consider additional evidence and will hear from you and from other witnesses.

• Under the current system, if you disagree with the administrative law judge's decision, you have the right to have it reviewed by the Appeals Council. The new rules will gradually phase out this level of review for claimants.

• If you disagree with the decision of the Appeals Council (or the administrative law judge, if the Appeals Council where you live has been phased out), you have the right to appeal to federal court. For up-to-date information about the appeals process, visit *www. ssa.gov/pubs/10041.html*.

VETERANS' BENEFITS

The United States Department of Veterans Affairs (DVA) administers a range of service- and non-service-connected benefits programs for veterans, their dependents, and their survivors. Veterans' benefits include cash benefits such as compensation and pensions, health benefits and services, burial and memorial benefits, vocational rehabilitation, education, employment services, and special programs for certain groups such as homeless veterans and women.

Eligibility for DVA programs and services, and the level of those benefits, depends on several issues, including:
• the length and dates of the veteran's military service;
• the way in which the veteran was discharged from the military;
• the date and circumstances of the veteran's death, if applicable;
• the extent of any disability and whether the disability is service-connected;
• the relationship of the applicant to the veteran; and
• the applicant's income and resources.

THE WORLD AT YOUR FINGERTIPS

• Social Security offices are listed in the "United States Government" section of your telephone directory. You can also call the Social Security Administration (SSA) at its nationwide toll-free number, 1-800-772-1213.
• SSA also has a consumer-friendly website at *www.ssa.gov/*

notices/supplemental-security-income/text-understanding-ssi.htm, which features general information about programs and eligibility, forms, and more.

• The National Organization of Social Security Claimants' Representatives (NOSSCR) provides a referral service to help you find attorneys experienced in handling Social Security claims. Contact: NOSSCR, 560 Sylvan Ave, Englewood Cliffs, NJ 07632; 1-800-431-2804; *www.nosscr.org*.

• For more information about veterans' benefits, contact the toll-free information line of the U.S. Department of Veterans Affairs at 1-800-827-1000. Fact sheets, programs, and general information about related issues can also be accessed at *www.va .gov/opa/fact*.

REMEMBER THIS

• Social Security benefits include retirement, disability, dependent, and survivors benefits. To collect Social Security benefits, you must meet two qualifications. First, you or the worker on whose account the benefits are paid must be insured under Social Security. And second, you must meet requirements for the particular benefit—that is, you must be the appropriate age, or be able to prove disability, or be the dependent of an insured worker, or be the survivor of a deceased worker.

• Social Security benefits provide only a floor of retirement security. You will need other sources of income, such as a pension or income from savings, to maintain your style of living during retirement.

• Certain other people *may* receive benefits based on a wage earner's eligibility for retirement or disability benefits. Such people include the spouse, divorced spouse, and dependents of the insured worker.

• If you are planning to retire, you should file for benefits two or three months before your retirement date.

• If you disagree with Social Security's decision regarding your claim for benefits, appeal the decision.

CHAPTER 4

Private Pensions and Income Tax Breaks

Everything You Need to Know About Your Pension

Angela is fifty-two years old and beginning to think about retirement. She wants to better understand the retirement plans offered by her employer and what risks she may face.

Typically, private retirement plans are set up by a company or by an agreement between a labor union and one or more employers. There are several types of retirement plans, including pension plans, (also known as "defined-benefit plans"), profit-sharing plans, 401(k) savings plans (sometimes known as "thrift plans"), and employee stock ownership plans, which are a kind of defined-contribution plan. Less than half the employees working for private companies are covered by private retirement plans.

Private pension plans must meet minimum standards established by federal law. The most important law protecting pension rights is the **Employee Retirement Income Security Act of 1974 (ERISA)**. ERISA covers most company-sponsored and union-sponsored pension plans. But ERISA does not cover plans sponsored by federal, state, or local governments, religious entities, or the military. These plans have their own rules.

This chapter begins with an overview of private pensions, and ends by describing the various income tax breaks available for seniors.

TYPES OF PENSION PLANS

There are two major kinds of retirement plan. Under the traditional **defined-benefit pension plan**, an employer promises you a specific monthly benefit at retirement, based on a formula that generally considers length of service and amount of earnings. Often these plans are the result of bargaining between employers and unions. A common formula is based on your years of service multiplied by a percentage, multiplied by the average of your last three (or maybe five) years' salary. For example, if you received two percentage points for each year of service and worked thirty-three years, you would be entitled to 66 percent of your average salary during your last three years of employment. However, the law does not require the use of any particular formula.

The primary advantage of defined-benefit plans is that employees are guaranteed a set level of benefits, and the employer bears the risk if the pension fund's investments perform poorly. If the plan goes broke, most benefit amounts are insured up to certain limits by the Pension Benefit Guaranty Corporation (PBGC). Currently, there are about 44 million Americans whose retirement incomes are protected by the PBGC.

In a **defined-contribution plan**, such as a profit-sharing plan or a 401(k) plan, no specific benefit amount is promised at retirement. Instead, money is contributed to your individual account, either by you, your employer, or both. In many plans, you contribute funds to the plan and your employer matches your contribution, or contributes a set percentage of your earnings. These contributions are invested, leaving your benefits to vary depending on how well they are invested. Upon retirement, your benefits are based upon the total amount contributed, plus investment earnings, minus investment losses. Your total benefit will depend on how well your invested contributed amounts do. Defined-contribution plans are not insured by the PBGC, which means that you, the employee, bear substantial risks.

A 401(k) plan is a particular kind of "do-it-yourself" defined-contribution retirement plan sponsored by employers. Your retirement savings grow without you paying taxes until you begin taking out your money. You make contributions, which the employer may match up to a certain amount or according to a schedule.

PENSIONS AND SOCIAL SECURITY

Social Security payments may affect your retirement benefits. Under some plans, benefits decrease depending on how much you receive from Social Security. This decrease is known as **integration of benefits**. Check with your plan's administrator to find out whether your plan will be affected. Under federal law, plans that take Social Security payments into account when calculating pension benefits must leave you with at least half your pension. But the law applies only to pension benefits earned after 1988. Under your plan's rules, benefits earned in earlier years could be eliminated entirely after taking into account your Social Security payments.

PARTICIPATION IN A RETIREMENT PLAN

Employers are not required to provide retirement plans. And even if an employer does offer a retirement plan, it need not provide pensions for all its workers. An employer may exclude certain categories of employees—for example, hourly workers or workers in a particular division. Employer pensions are not allowed to cover only the higher-ups in an organization—it is illegal to discriminate in favor of higher-paid workers—but as long as nondiscrimination rules are followed, some employees may be excluded from coverage.

Employers may set some minimum requirements before an employee can participate in a retirement plan. As a new employee, you may be required to complete one year of service, or reach the age of twenty-one, or both, before becoming eligible to participate in a plan. And companies can require employees to work at least one thousand hours per year in order to be part of a plan. This means that if you have always worked part-time, you may never be eligible.

VESTING

Retirement plans usually require you to work a specified number of years before earning the right to receive benefits at retirement age. Once you have worked the required length of time, your employer's contributions to your plan **vest**, meaning that you have a legally enforceable right to collect them, even if you leave the job. Until your benefits vest, you can accrue benefits or receive contributions in each year you are a member of the plan, but you will not be able to collect them. If you also contribute to your pension plan from your own salary, your contributions always vest immediately.

 HOW VESTING WORKS

To understand how vesting works, let's examine the work history of Nancy Smith. Nancy worked from 1976 to 1991 for Acme Department Stores. From 1991 to 1999, she worked for Zenith Food Warehouse. Then she worked for Pinnacle Designs from 2000 to 2004. Under Pinnacle's partial-vesting scheme, after four years of service an employee is entitled to a pension that is equivalent to a percentage of her full pension, which vests after seven years. After leaving Pinnacle in 2004, Nancy worked two days a week for Nadir, Inc. until her retirement in 2005.

Assuming that all these companies had pension plans, Nancy would be entitled to the following retirement benefits: a pension from Acme based on her fifteen years of service; a pension from Zenith based on her eight years of service; and a pension from Pinnacle based on their graduated-vesting schedule. She would not be entitled to a pension from Nadir, because she did not work there at least half-time; her two days a week added up to less than the one thousand hours per year required for vesting. Nancy would start collecting all of these pensions upon her retirement in 2005, once she attains the retirement age specified by the plans.

Once benefits vest, they cannot be taken away—even if you stop working for the employer before retirement age. On the other hand, if you leave your job before your benefits vest, you may lose the benefits provided by your employer.

Under ERISA's vesting rules, retirement benefits may either become 100 percent vested after a certain number of years of service (not more than five), or the plan may employ a **graduated vesting schedule**, which means that part of the benefits vest after you have worked no more than three years, with an increasing portion vesting in years four, five, and six. Under this type of schedule, full vesting must occur by your seventh year of employment. In order to vest in your employer's matching contributions in a 401(k) plan, you need to have three years of vested service.

You may be entitled to collect retirement benefits earned through several employers, as long as you worked in each job long enough for the benefits to vest.

RETIREMENT AGE

Pension plans set a "normal" retirement age at which vested employees become eligible to collect a full pension without any reduction for age. For purposes of collecting pensions, normal retirement age is generally sixty-five. Although most plans allow employees to retire earlier—for example, by age fifty-five or sixty—with reduced benefits or full benefits, depending on the number of years worked, pension plans are not required to offer early retirement.

If you are hired between age 60 and 65 and the normal retirement age is 65, you still have to earn five years of credit to vest in your benefits.

DISTRIBUTION OF BENEFITS UPON RETIREMENT, DEATH, OR DIVORCE

Your retirement plan may provide for several forms of benefits payments. Defined-benefit pension plans ordinarily provide a monthly pension for the rest of your life, but may allow you to choose alternative forms of payment such as a lump sum. However, they are not required to do so.

If you are married, the basic payment from a defined-benefit pension plan is called a **joint and survivor annuity**. Under this type of payout plan, your monthly benefit is reduced; the exact amount of the reduction varies from plan to plan, but the ages of you and your spouse are a factor. When you die, your spouse then receives a reduced benefit for the rest of his or her life. Under federal law, your spouse's pension must usually be equal to at least 50 percent of the pension you were collecting. If you are married, you cannot sign away the right of your spouse to receive a survivor annuity without your spouse's written consent.

The rules are different for profit-sharing plans, 401(k) plans, and other defined-contribution plans. Such plans may only offer a lump-sum benefit. However, you can continue to defer taxes on your benefits by rolling over the distribution into an individual retirement account (IRA) or a new employer's plan, if it permits. Ordinarily your spouse will receive 100 percent of the account balance if you die before benefits are distributed, unless your spouse consents to a different beneficiary. Similarly, if you leave your job you can withdraw the funds in a lump sum without spousal consent.

If you are divorced, you may be entitled to a share of your former spouse's benefits. The benefit rights of divorced spouses are governed by state law and must be awarded by a state court through a qualified domestic relations order (QDRO). You may be able to begin collecting your benefit after your spouse retires, after he or she dies, or, in some cases, before your spouse retires, if the QDRO provides for it.

KNOW YOUR RIGHTS
UNDER YOUR PLAN

ERISA requires your employer to provide you with detailed information about your plan, including a **summary plan** description—a booklet that summarizes the plan rules, explains how benefits are figured, and tells you when you can collect—and a financial summary based on the full annual financial report that the law requires your employer to file regularly with the government. The financial summary helps you analyze whether your pension plan is financially sound and prudently managed. You also have a right to your individual benefit statement, which tells you whether you are vested and the level of benefits you have accrued so far. Many plans give these statements to employees automatically each year. If your company does not, you can make a written request for your individual benefit statement once every twelve months.

Your pension plan administrator should be able to provide

 PLANS IN TROUBLE

A company can terminate a retirement plan at any time. If a pension plan is terminated, and does not contain sufficient funds to pay promised benefits, a worker's defined-benefit pension is likely to be insured by the PBGC. (Remember, however, that defined-contribution plans are not insured.) Some benefits are not covered, such as certain disability pension benefits and some early retirement benefits. So if your plan fails, the safety net has lots of holes in it. Your summary plan description will tell you whether your benefits are covered by the PBGC.

If your employer terminates your pension plan with enough money to pay promised benefits in it, your plan administrator will send you a notice explaining the termination, the amount of pension benefit you have accrued, and your payment options. Plans usually will purchase an annuity for you from an insurance company. The PBGC does not guarantee pensions that are paid off through an annuity after a solvent pension plan is terminated.

these documents. If you request the documents in writing, the plan administrator must respond within thirty days.

The summary plan description and financial reports are also available from the U.S. Department of Labor, Employee Benefits Security Administration. You can request a report by writing to: U.S. Department of Labor, Pension and Welfare Benefits Administration, Public Disclosure Room, 200 Constitution Ave., NW, Room N-1513, Washington, DC 20210. Or telephone their office at (202) 693-8673; their office is open on weekdays from 8:30 A.M. to 4:30 P.M. Be sure to provide the exact name of your plan and your employer's federal ID number (found on your W-2 form).

CLAIMING YOUR PENSION

Each plan establishes its own procedure for submitting benefit claims. Each plan also must have an appeals process that you can use if you are not satisfied with the plan's action on your claim. Your plan summary should inform you of the filing procedure and appeals process. If your claim is denied, the plan must give you written notice of the decision and state specific reasons for the denial. Then you may file a written appeal with the plan administrator. When filing an appeal, be sure to submit all relevant information and documentation—for example, the number of years you have worked for the employer, the hours you worked, and the dates of any breaks in service. You may not get another opportunity to submit evidence. The plan should review your appeal promptly and notify you of the result. If you still believe you have been denied benefits unfairly, you have the right to sue in court. If you decide to sue, you will definitely benefit from representation by an attorney who specializes in this area of law.

If you think you are entitled to a pension from an old job but are unable to get in touch with your former employer, the Pension Benefit Guaranty Corporation may be able to help you, especially if the plan was terminated.

TAXATION OF RETIREMENT PLAN BENEFITS

Tax treatment of distributions from IRAs and retirement plans are complex, and the rules change often. You should consult your tax advisor when taking distributions.

As a general rule, distributions from retirement plans and IRAs are fully taxable as ordinary income. If you were born before 1936, special tax rates may apply to any lump-sum distributions you receive from a retirement plan. Roth IRAs are subject to different rules, and the entire amount of any distribution—not just the contributions—may be tax-free when paid.

A distribution from a retirement plan may be transferred (rolled over) to an IRA or another retirement plan within sixty days of when the funds are withdrawn from the first plan. If the distribution is rolled over, it will not be subject to taxes until it is paid out from the second IRA or retirement plan. A monthly pension or required minimum distributions, described below, cannot be rolled over.

If your benefits are distributed before you reach age 59½ and you do not elect to roll them over, you generally will be subject to a 10 percent additional tax. Distributions made after your death, or payable in annuity form, will not be subject to this additional tax. Distributions also will not be subject to the additional tax if your employment terminates after you reach age fifty-five. Certain other limited exceptions may also apply.

You must begin taking distributions from a retirement plan when you reach age 70½, unless you are still working for the employer that offers the plan, and unless you own less than 5 percent of the company. The minimum amount you must take is determined by the size of your benefits, and by your life expectancy and that of your spouse or beneficiary. If you do not take the required minimum distribution each year, you may be liable for an additional tax equal to 50 percent of the amount that you should have taken.

Benefits paid after your death will be taxable to your beneficiaries or your estate.

INCOME TAX BREAKS FOR OLDER AMERICANS

Age plays a role in eligibility for some tax benefits. The following paragraphs highlight just a few of the special tax breaks that may be available to you or your parents. Talk to a tax advisor to explore how these tax breaks may apply to your particular situation.

More Generous Filing Requirements

Under the current tax laws, older persons are allowed a somewhat higher threshold income than younger persons before they are required to file federal income tax returns. The reason is that additional standard deductions are available for any person who is sixty-five or older (or blind). For the tax year 2004–2005, for example, a single adult under age sixty-five had to file a return if his or her gross income exceeded $8,200. But for a single person sixty-five or older, the threshold income amount was $9,450. The applicable exemptions and standard deductions are adjusted annually for inflation.

Even if you are not *required* to file a tax return, you should still do so if you are entitled to a refund.

Claiming a Parent as a Dependent

An adult taxpayer may claim an older parent or other relative with little taxable income as a dependent, but the following requirements must be met:

• The adult taxpayer must have provided over half of the dependent's support for that calendar year.

• The dependent's gross income must be less than the exemption amount for the year in question (e.g., $3,200 in 2005).

• The dependent must not have filed a joint return with a spouse.

• The dependent must have been an American citizen, resident or national, or a resident of Canada or Mexico, for at least some part of the calendar year.

Usually the claimed dependent is the taxpayer's parent, but dependent status can also be claimed for other relatives, including aunts and uncles, or even nonrelatives who meet the criteria listed above.

Tax Credit for Dependent Care

Employed taxpayers who care for an incapacitated parent, spouse, or other dependent in their homes may claim a tax credit for household or day-care expenses that enable the taxpayer to be employed. The dependent's principal residence must be the taxpayer's household. The taxpayer may not claim a tax credit for food and clothing costs, but he or she may do so for the cost of care provided outside the home, such as in a day-care center, even if food is included in those costs.

Tax Credit for the Elderly or Disabled

People age sixty-five or older, or people with disabilities, may be entitled to a tax credit if their nontaxable benefits or adjusted gross income are below certain levels. You must file Form 1040 to claim the credit. You cannot claim it using form 1040EZ or Form 1040A.

Earned Income Tax Credit

The Earned Income Tax Credit (EITC) or Earned Income Credit (EIC) is a federal income tax credit for low-income workers. The credit reduces taxes and may be obtained as a refund.

The amount of the tax credit depends on your income and family size. To qualify for the credit in 2005, a single taxpayer with no qualifying children needed earned income and adjusted gross income of less than $11,750. The limit was $13,750 for a married

A NOTE ON TAX PLANNING

Tax planning is only one factor in planning for your later years. One transaction—such as the transfer of a home or property that has gained in value over the years—may have very different impacts under income tax rules and gift or estate tax rules. But apart from tax consequences, you should plan your affairs around your likely health- and long-term-care needs, as well as your hopes and desires for living, loving, and growing, even if the end of life is in sight. This is why a holistic approach to lifetime planning—one that takes into account more than just tax and legal technicalities—is especially appropriate for older adults.

couple filing jointly. The limit for a single taxpayer with one qualifying child was $31,030, and the limit for a married couple filing jointly was $33,030. The EITC generally does not affect eligibility for Medicaid, Supplemental Security Income (SSI), food stamps, or low-income housing. Information about the EITC is available on the Internal Revenue Services website at *www.irs.gov*.

Sale of Personal Residence

If you sold your home after May 6, 1997, you may be able to claim an exclusion of up to $250,000 ($500,000 for certain married taxpayers filing a joint return) on any capital gain. To qualify for the exclusion, you must have owned and lived in the property as your principal residence for a period of at least two years out of the five-year period ending on the date of sale. The exclusion may be allowed each time you sell your main home, but usually not more than once every two years.

If you sold your home before May 7, 1997, the old rules may still apply to you. Those rules were stricter, allowed the exclusion only once in a lifetime, excluded only $125,000, and limited the exclusion to persons fifty-five or older.

Medical Expenses

You may deduct the cost of medical care for yourself, your spouse, and your dependents if such costs exceed 7.5 percent of your adjusted gross income. This deduction can be valuable for anyone with significant medical expenses in the family. Tax advisors and the IRS can provide detailed lists of eligible and ineligible expenses.

THE WORLD AT YOUR FINGERTIPS

- The U.S. Department of Labor provides readily accessible consumer information on ERISA and the different categories of pension plans at *www.dol.gov/dol/topic/retirement/erisa.htm*.
- The Pension Benefit Guaranty Corporation publishes various fact sheets and other consumer information about the federal government insurance program. For the publication *Your Guaranteed Pension* and other information, access *www.pbgc.gov*.
- The Internal Revenue Service (IRS) provides answers to many technical questions about pensions and retirement plans at *www.irs.gov*. IRS lawyers and actuaries can also respond to individual inquiries about specific provisions of tax laws affecting company and union pension plans by phone, at 1-800-829-3676.
- The Pension Rights Center is a consumer organization with expertise on all aspects of pension law. The Center's many publications include *The Pension Book: What You Need to Know to Prepare for Retirement*; visit *www.pensionrights.org*.

REMEMBER THIS

- Employers are not required to provide you with a retirement plan. And even if they do offer a retirement plan, they need not provide benefits for all their workers.
- There are two major types of retirement plans: defined-benefit plans and defined-contribution plans. There are several

forms of payment available once you retire, depending on your plan.

• You can accrue benefits in each year you are a member of a retirement plan. However, you will not collect benefits contributed by your employer unless you work long enough to have those benefits vest.

• Social Security payments may affect your retirement benefits. Some plans reduce benefits based on how much you receive from Social Security.

• There are several income tax breaks available for older persons or family members caring for aging parents. A tax advisor will help you explore how these tax breaks may apply to your particular situation.

CHAPTER 5

Estate Planning and Probate

A Crucial Step for You and Your Family

Since her husband died two years ago, Evelyn has lived comfortably alone in her own modest home. She has four wonderful adult children, and she figures that she has little need for any fancy will or estate plan. After all, her son is an accountant and is named jointly on her savings account, and her daughter—who is the closest to her of all the children—is named on her checking account.

But the truth is that Evelyn should write a will. Estate planning will help Evelyn to ensure that all of her property—not just the contents of her savings and checking accounts—is distributed according to her wishes.

Planning your estate is about caring for your loved ones and making sure that your hard-earned property is distributed according to your wishes.

This chapter introduces the basics of estate planning: wills, trusts, and other means of planning for your death. It is drawn from the *ABA Guide to Wills and Estates* (see the end of this chapter for more information), which more fully explains all of these options. The other key component of planning, planning for incapacity, is covered in Chapter 6, "Financial Planning for Incapacity."

TEN THINGS ESTATE PLANNING CAN DO FOR YOU

Estate planning can help you achieve the following ends:

1. Providing for your immediate family. Couples generally want to provide enough money for the surviving spouse, perhaps through life insurance. Couples with children want to ensure their proper education and upbringing. If you are caring for

children or grandchildren under the age of eighteen, both you and your spouse should have wills nominating personal guardians for the kids, in case you both die before they grow up.

2. Providing for disabled adult children, elderly parents, or other relatives. Do you have family members whose lives might become more difficult without you? You can establish a special trust fund for family members who need support in the event that you will not be there to provide it.

3. Getting your property to beneficiaries quickly. After your death, you want your beneficiaries to receive promptly the property you have left to them. Options for achieving this goal include: avoiding or greatly easing **probate** (the process by which a court distributes assets left in a will) by means of joint tenancies, living trusts, insurance paid directly to beneficiaries, or other means; using simplified or expedited probate; and taking advantage of laws in certain states that provide partial payments to beneficiaries while a will is still in probate.

4. Planning for incapacity. During estate planning, you may also plan for the management of your affairs in the event of your mental or physical incapacity due to illness or accident. (For more information on this topic, see Chapter 6, "Financial Planning for Incapacity.")

5. Minimizing expenses. Keeping down the cost of transferring property leaves more money for your beneficiaries. Good estate planning can reduce estate-planning expenses significantly.

6. Choosing executors and/or trustees for your estate. Your **executor** will be responsible for carrying out the directions you express in your will. A **trustee** carries out the directions expressed in a trust. Choosing a competent executor and trustee, and providing each with clear directions, is an essential part of estate planning.

7. Easing the strain on your family after your death. You can alleviate the burden of your grieving survivors by having a good estate plan, including a plan for your funeral arrangements.

8. Helping a favorite cause. Your estate plan can support religious, educational, and other charitable causes, either during your lifetime or upon your death, and may even save you money in taxes.

9. Reducing taxes on your estate. A good estate plan provides as much as possible to your beneficiaries and as little as possible to the government. Tax concerns become especially important as the value of your estate increases, because estates worth more than a certain amount are subject to federal estate tax. For example, if you were to die in 2006, only the first $2 million of your estate would be exempt from taxes. The exempt amount increases yearly until 2009, when it is anticipated to reach $3.5 million. Congress has passed legislation repealing the federal estate tax as of 2010; however, it is important to note that Congress could revive the tax in another form before that time.

10. Making sure your business continues to run smoothly after your death. Through careful estate planning, you can provide for an orderly succession and continuation of your business.

DYING WITHOUT A WILL

If you die **intestate** (without a will), your property still must be distributed. If you do not leave a valid will or trust, and do not transfer your property in some other way (such as through insurance, pension benefits, or joint ownership), then you have in effect allowed the state to decide how your property will be distributed. The state will then make certain assumptions about where you would like your money to go—assumptions with which you may not agree.

 HOW MANY AMERICANS HAVE WILLS?

Percentage of adults **age fifty and older** with wills: 60 percent*
Percentage of **all adults** with wills: 40 percent

*Source: AARP, *Where There is a Will . . . Legal Documents Among the 50+ Population: Findings From an AARP Survey,* released April 2000, available on AARP's website at *http://assets.aarp.org/rgcenter/econ/will.pdf* ; American Bar Foundation, "Survey of the Public's Use of Legal Services" (1989).

Depending on your state, intestacy laws may dictate that a surviving spouse inherits your entire estate, or that the estate is to be split by your spouse and children. If you are not survived by a spouse or children, intestacy laws generally require distribution to your closest kin (however "closest kin" is defined by the applicable statute). If you have no surviving relatives, even remote ones, then your property goes to the state. Only by planning your estate can you exercise control over who benefits from your estate, and how much. Planning also gives you the opportunity to exclude almost anyone you wish from receiving a part of your bounty (though state law gives your surviving spouse the right to a share of your estate).

WILLS

A **will** is a revocable document that provides for the transfer of your property after your death. In your will, you usually designate someone as an **executor** to carry out the will's terms. There is no such thing as a "standard" will; all wills are different. What you include in your will depends on what property you have, to whom you want that property to go, the dynamics of your family, and any other factors you deem relevant.

Although the rules for making a valid will vary from state to state, the following guidelines generally apply:

• You must be of legal age to make a will (eighteen years old in most states).

• You must be of sound mind and memory, which means that you should know you're executing a will, know the general nature and extent of your property, and be able to identify the people who you would like to receive your property—that is, your spouse, descendants, and other relatives who would ordinarily be expected to share in your estate. The law presumes that a **testator** (the person making a will) is of sound mind and memory, and the standard for proving otherwise is very high—proving mere absentmindedness or forgetfulness is not sufficient.

• The document must indicate that you really intend it to be your will—that is, the final word on what happens to your property.

- Although some states do allow oral wills in very limited circumstances, wills generally must be written (printed or typed).
- As the testator, you must voluntarily sign your will—unless illness, accident, or illiteracy prevents you from doing so, in which case you can direct someone else to sign for you. (But do not allow someone else to sign for you unless you have a clear understanding of your state's law on this matter.)

 TYPES OF WILLS

Here is a brief glossary of legal terms that refer to various kinds of wills:

- A **simple will** provides for the outright distribution of assets in an uncomplicated estate.

- A **testamentary-trust will** sets up one or more trusts to which some of your assets will be transferred after you die.

- A **pour-over will** transfers ("pours over") some or all of your assets to a trust that you had already established before you signed the will.

- A **joint will** is a document, which might constitute a contract, that covers both a husband and wife (or any two people). It is not advisable to create a joint will, because such wills are difficult to change and often result in litigation.

- A **holographic will** is an unwitnessed will written in the testator's own handwriting. Holographic wills are valid in about half the states.

- An **oral will** (also called a **nuncupative will**) is a will that is spoken, not written. Few states permit oral wills; typically such wills are permissible only if created during a last illness, and only if they dispose of personal property of small value.

- A **living will** is not really a will at all, since it has force while you are still alive and does not dispose of property. Instead, it informs doctors and hospitals of your wishes regarding end-of-life treatment. (See Chapter 7, "Advance Planning for Health-Care Decisions," for more information on this topic.)

- A formal will must be properly witnessed. In most states, this means that the signing of the will must be witnessed by at least two adults who understand what they are witnessing and who are competent to testify in court. In most states, the witnesses must be disinterested (i.e., not receiving any benefit, such as a transfer of property, from your will).

- A will must be properly executed. This means that it should include a statement (usually at its conclusion) indicating the date and place of signing, attesting that it is your will, and attesting that you have signed the will before witnesses, who then signed the will in the presence of you and in the presence of each other. Most states allow self-proving affidavits, which eliminate the need for witnesses to testify after your death that they witnessed the signing of your will.

If your will does not conform to these guidelines, it could be disallowed by a court. If a court disallows your will, your estate will be distributed in accordance with any previous wills or with your state's intestacy laws.

Legally, you do not have to use a lawyer to write your will. If it meets the legal requirements in your state, a will is valid whether or not you wrote it with a lawyer's help. Nonetheless, studies show that more than 85 percent of Americans who have wills used a lawyer to help prepare them. It is especially advisable to use a lawyer to prepare a will if you own a business, if your estate is substantial, or if you anticipate a challenge to the will from a disgruntled relative or anyone else.

PROBATE

The term **probate** refers to both the legal procedure used by courts to determine the validity of your will, and the process by which your assets are:
- gathered;
- applied to pay debts, taxes, and expenses of administration; and
- distributed to beneficiaries of your will.

Many people think that probate should be avoided, if at all possible. But times have changed, and it is now less common for probate to be the expensive, time-consuming beast it once was. Avoiding probate may be a primary goal of some estate plans, such as those involving substantial property in several states. But for many other estates, it can actually be more troublesome and expensive to avoid probate than to go through it.

There are three types of probate administration:

• **Supervised administration.** This is the most formal and expensive probate method. In supervised administration, the court plays an active role in approving each transaction. Depending on your state, as well as the size of the estate or choice of personal representative, supervised administration may be mandatory or optional. In states where it is optional, supervised administration is generally only used when an estate is contested, when an interested party requests it, or when the executor's ability is questioned.

• **Unsupervised** or **independent administration.** This is a simpler, cheaper method of probate in which the executor's duties are reduced and the court's role is diminished or eliminated.

ESTATE PLANNING IN COMMUNITY PROPERTY STATES

In community property states—Arizona, California, Idaho, Louisiana, Nevada, New Mexico, Texas, and Washington—most property acquired during the marriage by either spouse is held equally by the husband and wife as community property. (The major exception is property acquired by inheritance or gift.) When one spouse dies, only his or her half of the community property passes by will or intestacy; the other half continues to belong to the surviving spouse.

If you receive property before you are married in a community property state, the property still belongs to you, even after you are married. After marriage, if you receive a personal gift or inheritance, you continue to own that property separately.

TALKING TO A LAWYER

Q. I have a small piece of real estate in another state. Do I have to have a separate will for that property?

A. No, you do not need a separate will for real estate property in another state. However, you may need some special provisions concerning that property. Your will may have to go through "ancillary probate" in the state where the real estate is located (in addition to the state where you reside) and the ancillary probate may require the appointment of a different executor to meet the requirements of the second state or some specific powers provided for that executor. Another idea might be to use a revocable living trust rather than a will. During your lifetime you can create the trust and transfer the real estate property to the trust by deed. At your death, the property does not need to go through probate in the state where it is located.

—Answer by Kelly A. Thompson,
Kelly A. Thompson, PLC, Arlington, VA

This method of probate is used for estates that exceed the asset limit for small-estate administration (see below), but that don't require heavy court supervision. Unsupervised administration often requires the consent of all beneficiaries, unless the will specifically requests unsupervised administration.

• **Small-estate administration**. This is the simplest and fastest form of probate, but it's not available in every state. Small estates range in value from $1,000 to $100,000, depending on state law. In this type of administration, property is often transferred by affidavit, and the whole process may take only a few weeks.

The details of probate vary by state. You should talk to a lawyer to determine whether avoiding probate should be one of your principal estate-planning goals.

ESTATE-PLANNING TOOLS
OTHER THAN WILLS

In most cases, a will does not dispose of all of a person's property. For example, it does not govern the transfer of non-probate property. **Non-probate property** is property that passes to someone on your death through statute or contract. Common types of non-probate property include:

- jointly owned property;
- trusts;
- annuities and retirement benefits; and
- life insurance.

Other types of property not controlled by wills include: trust property, insurance policies, individual retirement accounts (IRAs), income savings plans, savings bonds, retirement plans, and property held in joint tenancy with right of survivorship.

Retirement Benefits and Annuities

Typically, a retirement plan will pay benefits to beneficiaries if you die before reaching retirement age. After retirement, you can usually choose to continue payments to a beneficiary after your death. In most cases, the law requires that some portion of these retirement benefits be paid to your spouse. Retirement benefits do not go through probate, but they are generally taxed to your heirs.

Individual retirement accounts (IRAs) provide a ready means of cash when one spouse dies. If your spouse is named as the beneficiary of your IRA, the proceeds will immediately become his or her property when you die. They also pass without having to go through probate.

There are two types of IRAs: the traditional IRA and the Roth IRA. A **traditional IRA** is a personal savings plan that provides you with tax advantages when you set aside money for retirement. Contributions you make to a traditional IRA are deductible, fully or in part, depending on your circumstances.

Generally, the amount in your IRA (including earnings and gains) is not taxed until it is distributed, and minimum distributions are required starting at age 70½. Thus, funds cannot accumulate in the account indefinitely. This deferral of taxes until distribution is an advantage for most people, because they earn less after they retire and are charged less income tax on IRA distributions than they would be charged on ordinary income.

You can open and contribute to a traditional IRA if:

• you or your spouse received taxable compensation during the year; and

• you will not have reached age 70½ by the end of the year.

You can open a traditional IRA whether or not you are covered by any other retirement plan. However, you may not be able to deduct all of your contributions if you or your spouse are covered by an employer retirement plan. If both you and your spouse have received taxable compensation and are under age 70½, each of you can set up an IRA—but you can't have the same IRA. Finally, the law limits how much you can contribute to any IRA.

A **Roth IRA** differs from a traditional IRA in that you cannot deduct contributions to a Roth IRA. If you satisfy the applicable requirements, however, the distributions from a Roth IRA are tax-free, including distributions to heirs. Also, there are no minimum distribution requirements for Roth IRAs during the lifetime of the owner, and contributions can be made to your Roth IRA even after you reach age 70½. Thus, you can accumulate funds in your Roth IRA for as long as you live.

Both traditional and Roth IRAs have specific contribution and eligibility limits based on the owner's income. IRAs are often used by small businesses as a simple way of providing employee retirement plans. In those circumstances, IRAs must meet requirements for Simplified Employee Pensions (SEP-IRAs), SIMPLE IRAs, and related qualified plans.

Life Insurance

Life insurance is often an effective estate-planning tool because you pay relatively little up front for such insurance, but your

TALKING TO A LAWYER

Q. For retirement planning, is it better to use a traditional IRA or a Roth IRA?

A. For most people, adequate financial planning is their primary retirement concern. When it comes to specific questions about which method of financial planning is best, the answer depends on many factors, including one's tax bracket and how far in advance the individual is planning for retirement.

A Roth IRA is usually best for someone who does not expect to be in a much lower tax bracket during retirement than he or she was while working, and does not expect to withdraw funds from his or her IRA for 10 or more years. In such a case, there are long-term benefits associated with a Roth IRA that make it favorable and may outweigh the added tax cost. However, if you have a shorter time frame, the tax bracket issue may be very important, making the traditional IRA a better option.

—Answer by Jason A. Frank, Frank, Frank & Scherr, LLC, and Michael W. Davis, Davis, Agnor, Rapaport & Skalny, LLC

beneficiaries receive a large sum when you die. When you name beneficiaries (other than your estate), the money passes to them directly without going through probate.

Younger families generally find life insurance to be an important means of replacing a deceased spouse's lost income, paying for children's education, or covering major living expenses such as mortgages. Older adults are more likely to need only a modest amount of life insurance (perhaps $5,000 to $10,000) to cover the costs of death, such as hospital, funeral, and burial bills.

An important issue to address when purchasing life insurance is whether the policy may result in taxation of your estate after your death. If the value of your estate—with the life insurance proceeds included—approaches the threshold for federal estate taxation ($2 million for years 2006 through 2008), then both the designation of beneficiaries and the ownership of the policy are important issues. The proceeds of the insurance will be included in your gross estate for estate tax purposes if any of the following three situations exist:

(1) The proceeds are payable to your estate.

(2) You own the policy, or

(3) You transferred ownership of the policy to someone else within three years of your death.

If you avoid these three circumstances, then the proceeds of the policy are not included in your gross estate for tax purposes. You can designate anyone you want as beneficiary of the policy, including one or more named persons, your probate estate, or a trust. You can also purchase a policy on your own life without actually being an owner of it. This means that someone else beside you has all the rights of ownership—for example, the power to name or change beneficiaries, borrow against the policy, cash in the policy, or assign it to another. If you pay for the policy but someone else owns it, or if you transfer a policy you own to someone else, such a transaction is a gift and the cash value of the policy will be potentially subject to gift tax. However, the gift may be small enough as to have little or no tax impact. Everyone's circumstances need to be weighed individually.

LIFE ESTATES

If you sell your home to a buyer but retain the right to live in the home during your lifetime, you have retained a **life estate**, and you have sold a **remainder interest** to the buyer. Life estates, along with other strategies for giving away or selling an interest in real estate while retaining a right to live there (e.g., sale-lease-backs, charitable remainder trusts) are discussed briefly in Chapter 11, "Housing and Long-Term-Care Choices."

JOINT OWNERSHIP

The most common form of joint ownership is **joint tenancy with right of survivorship**. "Right of survivorship" means that when one joint owner dies, the surviving joint owner (or owners) automatically receives full legal ownership of the property, regardless of what is expressed in the will of the deceased owner.

Many states grant the surviving owner instant access to the property. This type of joint ownership can be a useful way to transfer property at death, but it also has drawbacks. Family automobiles, bank accounts, and homes often pass this way. Particularly in old age, people often place bank accounts or stocks in joint tenancy with their spouse, with one or more children, or with friends. The transfer avoids probate, although it does not avoid estate taxes if the estate is large enough to incur such taxes.

Should you put property in joint tenancy as part of your estate plan? The answer depends on your circumstances, but most estate planners urge caution. You may want to *avoid* joint tenancy in the following circumstances:

1. **When you don't want to lose control.** Giving someone co-ownership gives him or her co-control. If you make your son a co-owner of your house, you cannot sell or mortgage the house unless he agrees. If you do sell the house, your son may be entitled to part of the proceeds.

2. **When you cannot be sure of your co-owner.** An untrustworthy co-owner could withdraw all the money from a jointly held bank account, or creditors of the co-owner could put a lien on the co-owned property. Moreover, if the co-owner were to become legally incapacitated, you would not be able to sell or transfer titled property, such as a home, without going through a cumbersome court proceeding.

3. **When you are in a shaky marriage.** In most states, separate property becomes marital property once it is transferred into joint names.

4. **When your intentions may change.** When you transfer property into joint tenancy, you make a gift of one-half of the

TALKING TO A LAWYER

Q. A charity I support said that I could somehow donate property to them now but still keep it until my death. How does that work?

A. If the property is real estate, you can make a gift of the "remainder interest" in the property to the charity, but retain the lifetime rights, called a "life estate." This gift is made by registering a new deed, retitling the property. At the time of the gift/deed, you may take a deduction for the value of the remainder interest to the charity. This is determined based on IRS actuarial tables.

If the property is stocks, bonds, or other securities, then you can create a charitable remainder trust to hold the property. The trust then pays you an income—the income can be a fixed amount per year, or a percentage of the value of the trust each year. Again, you can take a charitable deduction now for the value of what will eventually pass to charity. You can name one or a combination of charities to eventually receive the money on your death. You can even retain the right to change the charity during your lifetime and you can be trustee of the trust.

A third option is a gift annuity. You can transfer a sum of money to the charity in return for their promise to pay you an annual income for life. The rates that the charity pays are governed by a council in which most major charities participate.

—Answer by Kelly A. Thompson,
Kelly A. Thompson, PLC, Arlington, VA

property to the new joint tenant. If you later change your mind, you can't "undo" the gift.

5. When you are using co-ownership to substitute for a will. Joint tenancy is seldom a complete substitute for a will. The reason is that a deceased person almost always has some property that was not jointly owned, so probate may still be necessary. Joint tenancy also does not help if all the joint tenants die at the same time. Each joint owner still needs a will.

DON'T CONFUSE JOINT TENANCIES WITH TENANCIES IN COMMON

Tenancy in common is another common form of ownership. It is only available to married couples, and it differs from joint tenancy. In joint tenancy, you and your co-owner both own the *entire* property. In tenancy in common, you each own a *half share* of the property, and either of you may sell your half share without the other's consent (though not many buyers are interested in purchasing half a house). Another difference between these two forms of ownership relates to the transfer of ownership after death. With tenancy in common, the share of each tenant in common passes as provided in his or her will. It is subject to probate, even if you expressly stated in your will that your spouse should inherit your share of the property. In joint tenancy, each co-owner's share automatically passes to the other co-owner at death.

6. **When co-ownership might cause confusion after your death.** For example, it might be unclear whether a bank account held in joint ownership was created to help a child manage bill payments, or whether the money in the account was intended as a gift. This type of confusion could cause strife among heirs.

Even if none of the above red flags seem to apply to you, you still should exercise caution in using joint accounts; they may result in unexpected tax consequences for either or both owners, and may also affect your eligibility for public benefits such as Medicaid.

Some states have a special form of joint ownership for married couples called **tenancy by the entirety**. Only married couples are entitled to use this form of joint ownership. In some states, only real estate can be held in tenancy by the entirety. Neither spouse can sell or mortgage property owned in this way without the other's approval. When one spouse dies, the other automatically receives title. Despite its different name, tenancy by the entirety is virtually identical to joint ownership.

Inter Vivos Gifts

Federal tax laws now encourage people to transfer property through means other than their wills, often before they die. Trusts are the most common means for accomplishing this goal, but you can also make cash gifts.

Gifts made while you are alive, called **inter vivos gifts**, are an especially good idea if you have a large estate. Such gifts can help to reduce the size of your estate, thus lessening taxes and helping the estate to avoid full-fledged probate.

You can give a gift of any amount to your spouse without tax consequences. But if given to anyone other than your spouse, an inter vivos gift that exceeds a certain amount will be subject to gift taxes. As of 2006, the law permits you to give tax-free up to $12,000 per person per year ($24,000 for a gift made by a couple). You can make gifts to any number of people, and the recipients need not be related to you. If the gifts are made to a charity, you may also benefit from an income tax deduction.

Make clear whether a gift to a beneficiary of your estate is intended to be an advancement. For example, suppose that in the month before you die, you make your son a loan of $12,000 to pay for a year of college. If you then leave him $25,000 in your will without specifying that the $12,000 was an advancement against that amount, the probate court might give him the full $25,000 specified by the will. Your intention in making any loan should be put in writing.

Finally, keep in mind that gift giving could seriously affect your eligibility for public benefits such as Medicaid. (See Chapter 9, "Medicaid and Long-Term Care Insurance," for more information on this topic.)

Trusts

Trusts can serve many functions. They can help you plan for incapacity, avoid probate, and plan for the care of young or disabled children or grandchildren in the event of your death. If you wish to maintain some control over gifts to others, trusts can establish almost any management rules you wish. If your estate is large enough to require tax planning, trusts can play a key role in reducing your taxable estate.

A **trust** is a legal relationship in which a trustee (which can be one person or a qualified trust company, such as a bank) holds property for the benefit of another (the **beneficiary**). The property can be any kind of real or personal property: money, real estate, stocks, bonds, collections, business interests, personal possessions, or other tangible assets. It is often established by one person for the benefit of another. In those cases, it involves at least three people:

• a **grantor** (the person who creates the trust, also known as the **settlor** or **donor**);

• a **trustee** (who holds and manages the property for the benefit of the beneficiaries); and

• one or more **beneficiaries** (who are entitled to the benefits).

You can be the grantor of a trust, and also be its trustee and its beneficiary. This type of setup allows you to keep full control over all the property held in trust. In these circumstances, you would name a successor trustee to transfer the property to other beneficiaries upon your death, or to take care of you if you become incapacitated.

Trusts can be either **revocable** (changeable) or **irrevocable** (unchangeable). As these terms suggest, a revocable trust is more flexible than an irrevocable trust, but the latter type of trust may have more significant tax advantages.

Putting property in trust transfers legal title of the property from you to the trustee. The trustee has legal title to the trust property, but must hold the property "in trust" for its beneficiaries. For most purposes, the law regards trust assets as though they are owned by the trustee. But trustees are not the full owners of the property; they have a legal duty to use the property as provided in the trust agreement and permitted by law. The beneficiaries retain what is known as **equitable title**: the right to benefit from the property as specified in the trust.

If you use your will to establish a trust that will take effect upon your death—a **testamentary trust**—then you retain ownership of the property during your lifetime, and on your death it passes to the trustee to be distributed to your designated beneficiaries.

Just as there is no such thing as a "standard" will, there is no such thing as a "standard" trust. You can include any provision you want in a trust, as long as it does not conflict with state law or public policy. The provisions of a written trust instrument govern how the trustee holds and manages the property. These provisions can vary greatly, depending on why you set up the trust in the first place.

Despite the flexibility of trusts, the truth is that most older persons do not need them. Trusts do have advantages—most notably that they can facilitate avoidance of probate (which can be lengthy, expensive, and invasive of the parties' privacy). But in some cases the costs of creating and managing trusts may outweigh their benefits. A lawyer in your own state who specializes in estate planning should evaluate your particular situation.

Special-Needs Trusts

Trusts can be very helpful in planning for the care of a disabled child or other person with a disability. A trust can enable property to be used and managed properly for the beneficiary. However, trust planning must be handled carefully in cases where the disabled individual may also need to rely on public benefits such as Medicaid or Supplemental Security Income. In such a case, an outright distribution of assets from your estate would likely cause the disabled individual to lose eligibility for such benefits, because eligibility is based in part on financial need.

In these types of cases, it may be possible to establish a **special-needs trust**. This type of trust will allow the beneficiary to receive goods or services paid for by the trust, without jeopardizing his or her eligibility for public benefits. The law imposes strict requirements and limitations on these kinds of trusts. Generally, the trust funds cannot be used for the general maintenance of the individual—e.g., for food, housing, or health care. Instead, the funds may be used only for special medical, educational, or personal needs that are not otherwise provided for the individual. Lawyers drafting these kinds of trusts need expertise not only in trust law but also in Medicaid, Social Security, and public-benefits law.

THE WORLD AT YOUR FINGERTIPS

• The *American Bar Association Guide to Wills and Estates: Everything You Need to Know About Wills, Trusts, Estates, and Taxes (Second Edition, 2004)* is available in bookstores or online at *www.abanet.org/abastore*. It covers in much greater detail the subject matter addressed in this chapter.

• The ABA Section of Real Property, Probate and Trust Law is one of the most active and productive sections within the ABA, and many of its members practice estate planning, estate and trust administration, and disability planning. The Section also offers published information that should help answer some common questions: visit *www.abanet.org/rppt/home.html*.

• AARP's Estate Planning Section provides a wide variety of consumer publications and other valuable information for senior consumers, such as *Final Details: A Guide for Survivors When Death Occurs*. Contact: AARP, Estate Planning Section, 601 E Street, NW, Washington, DC 20049; 1-888-OUR-AARP (1-888-687-2277); *www.aarp.org/estate_planning*.

• The Internal Revenue Service (IRS) also maintains information on estate planning and probate. Publication 555, *Community Property*, is a very useful resource. Contact: 1-800-829-1040; *www.irs.gov*.

REMEMBER THIS

• Estate planning is an important task—not just for elders, but for adults at any stage of life.

• Estate planning gives you control over your property and its ultimate distribution, can save you money in taxes and fees, and can provide a way for you to plan for possible incapacity and for the care of your survivors.

• Everyone should have a will, but there are also many other ways of managing property and passing it on: joint tenancy, trusts, retirement accounts, and life insurance, to name just a few. Each of these methods has its own advantages and disadvantages.

• Joint bank accounts and other forms of joint ownership are the most common will substitutes, but they almost never serve as complete substitutes, and there are a number of risks inherent in naming a joint owner.

• Trusts aren't for everyone, but they can be quite valuable for larger estates and for managing property in the event that you or your survivors are unable to manage your own affairs.

CHAPTER 6

Financial Planning
for Incapacity

Powers of Attorney and Trusts

Martin and Mary are in their late fifties. They are both still
working, but are thinking about retiring. They were in relatively good health until a few months ago, when Martin suffered a mild heart attack. He underwent bypass surgery and
has been recovering very well, but the scare made both him
and Mary concerned that they might not be prepared to deal
with unexpected health problems in the future. If something
happens, how can Martin and Mary be confident that their affairs will be handled by the right person or persons, and in the
way that they both want?

Financial planning for incapacity ensures that you will be
able to maintain control over important decisions to the
greatest extent possible. Planning requires you to think clearly
about whom you would want to manage your property and finances if you were seriously ill—even temporarily—and how
you would want them to do so.

Several legal tools can help ensure that the people you
trust to call the shots will have the authority to do so. You can
also take steps to help them to make the decisions you would
want. This chapter covers financial-planning tools, and the
next chapter covers legal tools for health-care decision making.
Think of these legal planning tools in the same way you think
of life or health insurance: You would be happy never to have to
use them, but they are essential to your financial and personal
security. And by using them, you will lessen the anxiety of your
family and friends, who otherwise would not know your wishes
if you could not speak for yourself.

WHAT IS INCAPACITY?

The legal tools discussed in this chapter are most important when you lose mental capacity or competency. (We will use the terms "mental capacity" and "competency" interchangeably in this chapter.) Interestingly, there is no universal legal test for incapacity, and laws vary from state to state. However, some general principles apply.

First, incapacity is always measured in connection with specific tasks: The question is always, "Incapacity to do what?" Different legal standards of capacity may apply to different tasks, such as executing a will, driving, making medical decisions, or managing financial affairs.

Second, just because you can no longer perform certain mental or physical tasks does not mean that you are *legally* incapacitated. A finding of legal incapacity requires a court proceeding in connection with a guardianship or conservatorship petition. In a typical court proceeding, most states use some variation of a two-part test to determine incapacity. The first part

---

 PLANNING FOR MANAGEMENT OF YOUR FINANCES

The primary legal tools for managing the financial affairs of an incapacitated person are:

- joint ownership (particularly joint bank accounts);
- durable powers of attorney (DPAs);
- trusts; and
- money management services.

Guardianship and conservatorship can also be important means of managing an incapacitated person's financial affairs, but only as a last resort.

---

of the test requires proof of some type of disabling condition or cognitive impairment—for example, mental illness, mental retardation, and/or Alzheimer's disease. The second part of the test requires a finding that the disability prevents you from performing activities essential to managing your personal needs or property. Most courts will also insist that all feasible alternatives to guardianship or conservatorship have been explored before appointing someone to manage your affairs.

Most planning for incapacity is aimed at *avoiding* the need for guardianship or other judicial intervention. The goal is to set up personalized, voluntary arrangements for managing your estate or personal affairs if you become incapacitated.

JOINT OWNERSHIP

You will be familiar with joint ownership if you have ever had a joint bank account or owned a house or other property jointly. This is perhaps the simplest and most common form of sharing ownership.

Joint tenancy with right of survivorship is the most typical form of joint ownership. The "right of survivorship" means that when one joint owner dies, the surviving joint owner or owners automatically receive full legal ownership of the property. Property passes to the joint owner regardless of what it says in the deceased person's will. Joint tenancy with right of survivorship is a common form of joint ownership for:

- homes;
- stocks and bonds;
- cars; and
- bank accounts.

The key feature of a typical joint bank account is that either party has the legal right to deposit or withdraw any or all funds. Usually, these accounts will be held by the parties as joint tenants with right of survivorship. Do not confuse a joint checking account with an **agency account** or **convenience account**. In those accounts, the second party whose name is on the account is your agent, who has authority to make deposits or withdrawals on your behalf. The agent is not an owner of the account. Such accounts really just constitute a specialized form of power of attorney.

Joint ownership of a bank account is a simple and very common form of ownership, and is a convenient way to manage the income of an incapacitated person, especially when combined with direct deposit of the person's checks. Moreover, if there is a right of survivorship, joint property automatically passes to the surviving joint owner(s) on the death of the other joint owner. Thus, it is a simple and quick way to transfer money at death.

However, joint accounts also pose plenty of potential risks including unexpected tax consequences and vulnerability to creditors. Therefore, it is best not to rely on them as your primary planning strategy. Instead, you should use a durable power of attorney, and make use of an agency or convenience account for your major bank accounts.

POWERS OF ATTORNEY

A **power of attorney** is a written authorization for a person you name to act on your behalf for a specific purpose that you have spelled out in writing. When discussing powers of attorney, two terms are important:

- The person creating the power of attorney is called the **principal**.
- The person appointed by the principal is called the **agent** or **attorney-in-fact**. Do not confuse an attorney-in-fact with an attorney-at-law. The agent does not have to be a lawyer.

Durable Powers of Attorney

A **durable power of attorney** (DPA) is a power of attorney that continues to operate and be legally valid even after the disability or incapacity of the principal. Historically, a power of attorney

automatically terminated upon the incompetency of the principal. But this result is precisely the opposite of what most of us
would want—after all, it is when we become incompetent that
we need the power of attorney most. Fortunately, every state now
has passed legislation providing for powers of attorney that sur-
vive the incapacity of the principal. In most states, the DPA document must state that it continues to be valid even after
incapacity. Otherwise, it will terminate when the principal becomes incapacitated.

A standard DPA is normally effective at the time it is signed.
The agent can act for the principal immediately, although the
agent must always follow the principal's directions. Another
form of DPA, recognized in most states, is the springing power of

 TALKING TO A LAWYER

*Q. What is better in most cases, a springing power of attorney or one
that becomes effective immediately?*

A. A springing power of attorney does not become effective until the
trigger event occurs—such as a doctor's certification of your incapacity. While you may initially like the idea that your agent will not be able
to step in until absolutely necessary, a springing power can create
some problems for your agent. For example, your agent may have to
continually prove to third parties that the trigger event has occurred.
While each individual has a unique situation, most of my clients
choose to sign a power of attorney that is immediately effective, especially if the agent is a trusted spouse or child. Ask your lawyer about
ways to limit the potential for exploitation by your agent—for example, by limiting the agent's power to make gifts, naming co-agents, or
requiring reporting by the agent to a third party.

—Answer by Jeffrey Marshall, The Elder Law Firm
of Marshall, Parker & Associates, LLC, Williamsport, PA

attorney. A **springing power of attorney** is a power that does not become operative unless and until the principal becomes incapacitated. If the principal does not need it, it simply remains dormant. If the principal become incompetent, it "springs" to life. The creation of a springing power requires careful drafting: it must identify who is responsible for determining that you are incompetent, and what criteria they must use to make their determination. One approach is to direct your agent and attending physician to make a joint determination of incapacity. Historically there was concern that third parties, such as banks, would be reluctant to recognize springing powers because of uncertainty as to when the powers had truly sprung into effect. This has become less of an obstacle as springing powers have become more widely used.

How Much Power Does An Agent Have?

A general DPA grants the agent very broad powers. However, a few state laws restrict what an agent can do, especially with respect to real estate transactions.

A **special** or **limited power of attorney** grants the agent only specific powers designated in the document. For example, a special power of attorney might state:

- "I authorize my agent to sell my property, located at 352 Smith Street"; or
- "I authorize my agent to endorse checks on my bank account, No. 12345, at First National Bank."

It is important to be as specific as possible in describing the powers delegated in any power of attorney. Courts tend to interpret powers of attorney quite narrowly, so it is best to clearly spell out the extent of the agent's power, if any, to:

- make gifts;
- give loans or support to others;
- sign IRS forms and tax returns;
- open safe-deposit boxes;
- create, modify, or revoke a trust;

YOU REMAIN LEGALLY IN CONTROL!

No matter what power you delegate in a durable power of attorney, you do not forfeit any control while still mentally competent. You can still make or direct any decision you choose, and your agent cannot legally override or act against your wishes. You can also revoke a power of attorney at any time while still mentally capable.

- change beneficiaries under a pension or life insurance policy;
- compensate himself or herself as agent;
- delegate the agent's authority to someone else; and
- make health-care decisions. (But note that health-care decisions are usually handled in a separate health-care advance-directive document. See Chapter 7, "Advance Planning For Health-Care Decisions," for more information.)

How to Choose Your Agent

In most states, you can name any person or institution you wish as your agent. This choice is the single most important decision you will make when executing your durable power of attorney. If you become incapacitated, your agent will have tremendous power over your property and affairs. If there is really no one whom you trust to act as your agent, then a DPA may not be right for you.

Most states allow you to name multiple agents. Your DPA may specify that your agents must exercise all the powers jointly (i.e., all must agree, or the majority must agree), or that they may exercise powers separately (i.e., any one may act alone). The disadvantage of a joint exercise of power is that any disagreement among agents will cripple the usefulness of the DPA. Even in the most loving and well-intentioned families, disagreements happen, especially under the stress of family illness. An alternative to using multiple agents is to require approval by a second agent only for major transactions, such as the sale of your home or other real estate. This provides the safeguard of a second person's oversight in major transactions.

The most common method of choosing an agent is to name one agent and a successor agent or agents in case the prior agent cannot or will not act for any reason. In selecting an agent, it is important to name someone whom you know is trustworthy, is responsible in financial matters, and will act solely in your best interests.

Writing Your DPA

Do not run to your local stationery store looking to buy a standard power-of-attorney form; there is no such thing as a "standard" DPA. Each must be tailored to the user's individual situation. It is advisable, although not required, to have a lawyer draft your DPA for property management. (See Chapter 15, "Finding Legal Help," for more information.) A lawyer can ensure that your document meets your state's requirements and that the powers you give your agent are spelled out in language that will be legally effective.

Many states have enacted statutory short-form powers of attorney to simplify the process. These forms list the various powers typically granted to agents. In completing the form, you simply check off or initial the powers you wish to grant to your agent, and strike through those powers that you do not wish to grant. Short forms greatly simplify the process of completing a power of attorney, but they are by no means foolproof. It is still best to seek advice from a lawyer about the level of authority you want to give to your agent and how best to meet your unique needs.

Signing a power of attorney is fairly simple; however, you must comply exactly with your state's law. Timing is important, because you must be mentally competent in order to execute a power of attorney. Of course, your signature as principal is always required, and many states also require the document to be

TALKING TO A LAWYER

Q. My father has recently been diagnosed with Alzheimer's disease. Can he still sign a valid durable power of attorney?

A. Despite the fact that your father has some mental limitations he may still be legally competent to sign a power of attorney. Your father should meet with a lawyer who is experienced in dealing with incapacity issues. Try to set the meeting at the time of day when your father is most alert.

The lawyer will evaluate whether your father has sufficient understanding of what he is doing to consent to the power of attorney. The level of understanding required may vary depending upon the type of authorization being granted to the agent. Capacity has been compared to a light with a dimmer switch instead of an on-off switch. More light may be needed for some purposes than for others. For example, a higher level of capacity may be required to authorize gifting by the agent.

—Answer by Jeffrey Marshall, The Elder Law Firm
of Marshall, Parker & Associates, LLC, Williamsport, PA

witnessed and/or notarized. Even if notarizing is not required by state law, it is standard practice. If the document is to be used for real estate transactions, you must normally sign and record it in the same manner as deeds to property. Finally, although the signature of your agent is not required on the document in most states, it is a good idea for your agent to sign, since a signature will help to verify his or her identity.

Using Your DPA

After completing a DPA, you should either give your agent a signed original copy, or store it in a safe place that your agent knows about and to which he or she will have access. Your agent will need to show the document to any third party with whom he

SIGNING DOCUMENTS

Your agent should always sign documents in a way that clearly communicates that he or she is signing as your agent:

Correct Forms of Signing	**Incorrect Form of Signing**
Mary Doe, as agent for John Doe	Mary Doe
John Doe, by his agent Mary Doe	John Doe by Mary Doe

If Mary intends to sign a document as John Doe's agent but signs incorrectly, she may unintentionally make herself personally financially responsible for the principal's legal obligations, such as a hospital bill. But if she signs correctly, no personal liability is created. Instead, she obligates only the estate of John Doe.

---

or she does business. Third parties, such as banks or hospitals, may also want to keep a copy. Occasionally, a third party may insist on an original document; as a result, you may wish to sign more than one original. Another option is to have the local court clerk provide you with certified copies of the original. These will contain the seal of the court or its clerk and a certification as to their authenticity.

Terminating Your DPA

A DPA can terminate in four ways:

• Your death terminates all powers of attorney, either automatically or after your agent learns of your death.

• The document itself can spell out a termination date or event (e.g., "This power shall terminate on June 30, 2010," or "This power shall terminate upon completion of the sale of my house.")

• You can revoke a power of attorney at any time simply by notifying the agent. Naturally, it is safer to do this in writing, and some states *require* that you notify the agent in writing when

EXAMPLE OF REVOCATION

The following is an example of a valid revocation of a power of attorney: "I, John Doe, of 352 Smith Street, hereby revoke the power of attorney granted to Mary Doe on January 15, 1997." A statement of revocation should be signed, dated, and acknowledged by a notary public, especially if the power of attorney has been recorded. The principal should destroy the old power-of-attorney document, or boldly mark each page as "VOID."

at all possible. Third parties with whom the agent transacted business should also be notified in writing of the revocation.

• If your agent is no longer available due to death, incapacity, or some other reason, AND there is no successor agent appointed, the power of attorney terminates. In some states, divorce or the filing of divorce will automatically terminate the former spouse's authority as agent.

Also, remember that if a power of attorney is NOT durable, it will terminate if and when the principal is rendered incompetent.

Will Everyone Accept a DPA?

Third parties occasionally are reluctant to honor powers of attorney. Third parties can be banks, businesses, individuals, or anyone else with whom your agent transacts business on your behalf. A few states require third parties to accept DPAs made in accordance with state law, but problems may still arise.

To minimize problems, you should avoid adding conditions or unusual features to your power of attorney that may raise doubts about the agent's authority. This may mean that it makes sense to avoid using springing powers or multiple agents if they are not commonly used in your state. Fortunately, springing powers are becoming more and more common.

Banks, insurance companies, and brokers sometimes have their own power-of-attorney forms and insist that they be used. Check with the institutions with whom you do business, and obtain their forms while you are still competent. If it is too late to do this, your lawyer will probably be able to convince these institutions to recognize your DPA.

Normally a durable power of attorney is effective across state lines, but you may need to have separate DPAs executed in different states if you have property or other affairs in more than one state.

Staleness becomes a potential problem if a long period of time has elapsed since you created your DPA. Even though there is normally no legal time limit on the efficacy of DPAs, third parties are sometimes reluctant to accept a DPA that was signed a number of years ago. Review your DPA and other legal documents every few years, update them, and re-execute them if circumstances have changed.

Preventing Misuse of the DPA

An agent stands in a **fiduciary** relationship to the principal, and must live up to standards imposed by state law. This means that the agent must act in good faith with respect to the DPA—that is, in a trustworthy, confidential, and honest manner. However, the law does not provide for automatic oversight of the agent's actions. This means that if you become incompetent or frail, there is no person who will automatically complain or take legal action against your agent for abusing his or her authority. Besides, agents are usually family members or friends of the principal, with little understanding of what it means to serve as a fiduciary, and abuse often occurs through ignorance of fiduciary duties. For example, a son acting as an agent for his father may assume that it is perfectly acceptable to combine the bank accounts of the principal (his father) with his own, but fiduciary standards require that such accounts be kept separate. To avoid abuses of power, unintentional or otherwise, agents should be educated about their duties under

TALKING TO A LAWYER

Q. *What is the difference between a durable power of attorney and a guardianship or conservatorship?*

A. If you are ever unable to manage your property and finances, someone else will have to act on your behalf. Powers of attorney and guardianships are two distinct legal tools that are used to authorize a substitute to act for you. The power of attorney is a voluntary tool that you create in advance of your incapacity. You decide who will act on your behalf, when they may act, and what actions will be permitted. Guardianship is an involuntary legal tool that is created by court order when consensual tools like power of attorney are non-existent or inadequate to meet the needs of an incapacitated person. The court decides who will act for you and what types of decisions they can make. Because power of attorney is voluntary, you can terminate it at any time. Guardianship must be terminated by the court.

—Answer by Jeffrey Marshall, The Elder Law Firm of Marshall, Parker & Associates, LLC, Williamsport, PA

the law. (Informational material may be available from your attorney or local courts.)

Another way to prevent abuse of an agent's power is to include additional safeguards in the DPA, such as:

- clear instructions or guidelines for your agent;
- a requirement that the agent provides an annual financial accounting to you or, if you are incapacitated, to some other named person; and
- a requirement that someone else you name co-signs documents if the transaction involves more than a specified amount of money.

The primary safeguard against abuse is to choose only those persons in whom you have the greatest amount of trust, and to make sure they understand their responsibilities. If there is no person or institution you trust, do not use a DPA.

TRUSTS

A **trust** is a legal arrangement under which a person or institution (the **trustee**) holds title to property for the benefit of another person or persons (the **beneficiaries**). The person who creates the trust is called the **grantor** or **settlor**. Trusts can be useful planning tools for incapacity, because the grantor can be a trustee and a beneficiary at the same time. This means that if the grantor/trustee loses capacity, a successor can step in to manage the trust and the grantor can benefit from the trust he or she established—for example, by receiving a monthly income. The trust can operate for the benefit of the grantor as long as needed, but with successor or concurrent beneficiaries also named. Unlike durable powers of attorney, a trust may continue in operation after your death—for example, if you have minor or disabled children who need someone to manage their finances.

Establishing a Trust

There is no special form necessary to establish a trust. But trust language usually is complex, technical, and lengthy. The tax consequences of your trust should also be considered, as well as its effect on any future public benefits such as Medicaid. Trust drafting really ought to be done by an attorney who specializes in estate planning.

Advantages and Disadvantages of Trusts

There are several advantages to trusts. They can provide for management of funds in case you become incapacitated. Trusts are accepted in the business and financial community, and seldom run into problems of acceptance, as powers of attorney sometimes do. They can also serve as will substitutes, and can be structured to continue operating after the death of the grantor. Unlike wills, they offer the additional advantage of avoiding

SOME VARIATIONS ON THE TRUST

- An **inter vivos trust** is a trust set up and made operative during the grantor's lifetime. It is also referred to as a **living trust**.

- If a trust is set up in a will, it is called a **testamentary trust**.

- A **standby trust** is a particular type of inter vivos trust. When it is established, a standby trust need not include any actual property, or it may include only a nominal amount of property or a nominal sum. The grantor then signs a durable power of attorney that gives the agent authority to transfer funds to the trust if the grantor becomes incapacitated.

- Trusts may be **revocable** or **irrevocable**. You can change or terminate a revocable trust at any time while you are still competent. In planning for incapacity, you should normally use a revocable trust. As the name suggests, you cannot change or terminate an irrevocable trust. If you have many assets, tax considerations may be a factor in deciding whether to make the trust revocable or irrevocable.

some of the troubles of probate administration, so they may have multiple uses in one's estate plan. (Chapter 5 deals with this aspect of trusts.)

The main disadvantage of a trust is cost, including the legal expense of creating the trust, the cost of transferring property to the trust, and management fees. When a bank or trust company serves as a trustee, it typically charges a minimum fee and an annual percentage fee. And it may have little interest in managing your trust unless substantial assets are involved—often as much as $400,000 or $500,000. A family member or other individual can be named trustee, but the required paperwork, completion of tax returns, and property management duties can be demanding.

Trusts may also have a negative effect on your future eligibility for public benefits, such as Medicaid, which many people count on to pay for nursing-home care. Medicaid frowns on most trusts, and its trust rules are quite complicated. Good legal advice is essential.

One other disadvantage of trusts is that a trustee's authority is limited to the assets that have been transferred to the trust. In comparison, an agent's authority under a general durable power of attorney can extend to all the principal's assets. A common mistake in using trusts is not funding them adequately. Funding requires actual transfers of property to the trust. But even under the most fully funded trust, other property (such as personal effects) is likely to be outside the trust. Thus, other estate-planning tools such as a will and power of attorney are still needed to complement the trust.

MONEY MANAGEMENT SERVICES

Money management programs, also known as **daily money management** or **voluntary money management**, help people who need assistance managing their financial affairs. The services provided by such programs may include check depositing, check writing, checkbook balancing, bill paying, Medicare and insurance claim preparation and filing, tax preparation and counseling, investment counseling, and public-benefit applications and counseling.

This type of assistance may be provided by an individual or an organization on a for-profit or not-for-profit basis. Services may be free, offered on a sliding fee scale according to income, or at a flat rate.

Because these kinds of services are not standardized or regulated by the government, you need to take great care in evaluating the quality of a potential money management provider. If you are considering such a service, make sure it has a system of cash controls to prevent, or at least lessen, the risk of mismanaging your funds. It should also be bonded and insured. Check with your area agency on aging to find reputable money management services; do not simply flip through the Yellow Pages.

TALKING TO A LAWYER

Q. Will a living trust enable me to avoid the long delays that usually occur when an estate goes through probate?

A. Probate is the process by which property is transferred from a decedent to the inheritor when there is no other mechanism for doing so. Some living trusts can result in probate being avoided, but it is not the existence of a trust that enables probate to be avoided. It is the fact that the assets have been transferred to the trust's ownership during the decedent's lifetime, and that the trust gives those same assets to third persons, not your estate, at your death. Since the assets are not owned by the person who has died, these assets do not go through probate.

There are other, less expensive, ways for probate to be avoided for some assets without transferring them to a living trust. The following assets will also avoid probate:

- Assets for which there is a beneficiary form, including retirement funds and life insurance.

- Assets held by the decedent and others in joint ownership with the right of survivorship. This can include both real estate and personal property.

- POD Accounts. These accounts designate third persons who should receive the account's balance at the death of the owner. These are usually bank and other financial accounts, including brokerage accounts.

Whether any of the various arrangements, including trusts, are appropriate in your circumstances should be discussed with an attorney. Their misuse can be very costly to your heirs.

You should also discuss with the attorney whether probate avoidance is even necessary or desirable. In many states probate is not expensive or time consuming. States have truncated procedures or informal proceedings that simplify the entire process. In addition, probate can offer oversight that will ensure that a decedent's wishes will be carried out. Probate procedures can also give the heirs protection against creditors who show up after the estate has been distributed.

—Answer by Helen Cohn-Needham,
Needham, Mitnick & Pollack, PLC, Falls Church, VA

A money management program may help you to avoid a future need for guardianship. But such programs work on a voluntary basis, so you must be able to request help or accept an offer of help from the program (although some money management organizations will also serve as court-appointed guardians when needed). Money management services may be particularly useful if you have no one trustworthy to act as your agent or trustee.

THE WORLD AT YOUR FINGERTIPS

• For information about AARP's Money Management Program, visit *www.aarpmmp.org*. Contact: AARP, 601 E Street NW, Washington, DC 20049; 1-888-OUR-AARP (1-888-687-2277).
• Nolo Press provides a great deal of practical information about powers of attorney, trusts, bank accounts, and a host of other legal matters on its website at *www.nolo.com*.

REMEMBER THIS

• Every adult needs a financial durable power of attorney to plan adequately for the risk of incapacity. Simply having one's property in joint ownership is usually not a secure plan.
• While some states have statutory short-form powers of attorney that can serve as simple starting documents, all powers of attorney need to be customized. Use of standard forms is risky without professional advice.

• Trusts provide a way of professionally managing assets while you are still competent, and can continue beyond disability and even death. However, they can be quite costly and complicated to manage, so they are usually not feasible for people with cash assets under $400,000 or $500,000.

• Money management services are not uniformly available everywhere. But where available, they can provide a practical strategy for managing day-to-day bill paying and other simple financial matters.

CHAPTER 7

Advance Planning for Health-Care Decisions

Your Guide to Health-Care Advance Directives

Ninety-one-year-old Grandma Ellie watched some of the TV news stories about Terri Schiavo, the young woman in a persistent vegetative state whose family battled for years in the courts over whether to stop her tube feeding. At a family gathering, Grandma commented to her daughter, Gail, and son-in-law, Tom, that she would never want to be kept alive that way. Tom said that he felt the same way. But Gail disagreed. She felt that if all she needed was food and fluids, she would not want those treatments stopped. Gail and Tom's twenty-one-year old daughter, Lisa, expressed mixed views, and said she wasn't sure what she would want. She said only that she would want to rely on her partner, Diane, to make the right decision.

The one thing that everyone in this extended family has in common is that no one has completed an advance directive for health-care decision making. As a result, none of them can be confident that their particular wishes will be known if the need arises, or that the required decisions will be made by the desired people.

Whether you're twenty-one or ninety-one, health-care advance planning is an ongoing task that is an essential part of planning for your future. Planning for your health ensures that you will be able to maintain control over important decisions to the greatest extent possible.

Planning requires you to think clearly about questions such as: Whom would I trust to make health-care decisions for me? How and where would I want to live the end of my life if I were terminally ill, or if I were so impaired that I could no longer care for myself? How would I want to be treated?

As you get older, an infinite number of medical scenarios

may arise. You don't have to think about them all, but you do need to think about what would be important to you, at least generally, if you were too ill to speak for yourself. This chapter explains some of the legal tools you can use in planning your health care.

HEALTH-CARE ADVANCE DIRECTIVES

A **health-care advance directive** is a legal tool that enables the person or persons of your choosing to make health-care decisions on your behalf when you cannot speak for yourself. The term is used generally to refer to any written statement concerning your future health-care wishes that you make while you are competent. Living wills and health-care powers of attorney (defined below) are types of health-care advance directive. These legal tools evolved separately, but today may be drafted as separate documents or merged in a single, comprehensive document. All fifty states and the District of Columbia have passed laws recognizing advance-directive use.

When planning for future health-care decisions, you should understand that merely completing an advance-directive form will do very little good if you skip the most important part of the process: reflecting on what you want, and discussing what you want with your family. In order to be effective, the planning process requires that you share your wishes, fears, and priorities with your physician, family, and whomever else you will choose to speak for you when you cannot. Think of the process as a continuing conversation that you will likely need to have more than once. After all, your views may change as you age, and they may change dramatically in the event of serious illness. For example, your thinking about end-of-life options would probably be different if you were a healthy thirty-five-year-old than if you were a chronically ill eighty-five-year-old. Completing an advance-directive form should be the end product of an ongoing conversation that is resumed at various turning points in our lives.

Every state recognizes some kind of advance directive.

directive is the preferred legal tool for planning these types of decisions. Many states have comprehensive advance-directive statutes with simple suggested forms. However, be careful: State your instructions carefully, and be clear about whether you want them strictly followed, or whether you intend them only as guidelines for your agent to consider (in conjunction with any other knowledge he or she may acquire about your wishes over time). In some jurisdictions, lawyers advise clients not to combine living wills and health-care powers of attorney. Instead, they advise clients to rely solely or primarily on the health-care power of attorney. The concern is that any written instructions will be construed as absolute and inflexible, rather than as general guidelines for the decision maker. Whether this concern is truly warranted will depend more on local practice and custom than on the provisions of your state's statute.

Can't I Just Tell My Doctor What I Want?

Telling your doctor and others what you want is essential, but is usually not sufficient in today's complex and fragmented health-care system. Effective planning requires recurring conversations between doctors, patients, and loved ones. If you do not complete a written directive, conversations can indeed provide important evidence of your wishes, especially if your doctor

 TALKING TO A LAWYER

Q. Which is more powerful: a living will or a health-care power of attorney?

A. A health-care power of attorney will allow an agent to make health-care decisions on your behalf for general health-care. A living will is much more narrow, as the agent has authority only when your life is at an end.

—Answer by Doris E. Hawks, Los Altos, CA

However, confusion persists over the applicable terminology, over the different types of advance directives. To clear up confusion, let's compare the traditional living will and health care power of attorney with a comprehensive health-care advance directive.

A **living will** (also known as a **medical directive** or **declaration** or **directive to physicians**) is a type of advance directive. It is simply a written instruction spelling out any wishes you have about your treatment or care in the event that you are unable to speak for yourself. Many states limit the application of living wills to situations involving terminal illness, permanent unconsciousness, or other advanced progressive illness. A living will says, in effect, "Whoever is deciding, please follow these instructions!" On its own, a living will is very limited—it usually applies only to end-of-life decisions, and standard instructions tend to be general. Unless you happen to have a magic crystal ball, it is impossible to anticipate every future medical scenario in which you might find yourself.

A **health-care power of attorney** (also known as a **health-care proxy** or **medical power of attorney**) is a document that appoints someone of your choosing to be your authorized agent (or **attorney-in-fact** or **proxy**). In a health-care power of attorney, you can give your agent as much or as little authority as you wish to make health-care decisions; the decisions are not limited to end-of-life decisions. Appointing someone as your agent provides that person with the authority to weigh all the medical facts and circumstances and interpret your wishes accordingly. A health-care power of attorney is broader and more flexible than a living will, and is thus the more important element of any advance directive.

A **comprehensive health-care advance directive** combines the living will and the health-care power of attorney into one document. The document may also include any other directions you wish, including your choices about whether to donate or receive organs, and where and how you prefer to be cared for. Because it is more comprehensive and flexible than the other available planning tools, a comprehensive health-care advance records your wishes in your medical record. In a few states, oral instructions, if properly recorded by the doctor, can have the same legal standing as a written advance directive. However, both legally and practically, it is far better to talk to your doctor *and* make a written advance directive. The written advance directive will carry more weight and is more likely to be followed.

Will Doctors And Hospitals Recognize My Advance Directive?

Most doctors and health-care facilities want to respect your wishes. However, some may refuse to honor certain wishes expressed in an advance directive, perhaps because of religious beliefs. For example, a desire to withhold tube feeding or hydration can conflict with the policies of some religiously based hospitals. If a facility has such a policy, it should inform you at the time of admission. Doctors generally do not have the same obligation to inform you of such policies ahead of time, so it is up to you to find out your doctor's views. If a health-care provider refuses to honor the wishes you express in an advance directive, the law in

---

 TALKING TO A LAWYER

Q. Is there any way to enforce my health-care advance directive if health-care providers won't go along with it?

A. There are several avenues by which to approach a non-compliant health-care provider. The less formal, less costly, and usually faster method, is to involve an institutional "patient representative" or an ethics committee. If informal methods fail, a health-care agent or other party can go to court to obtain an order requiring the provider to comply. In the alternative, the agent or other party can try to remove the patient to another facility which will comply with his or her wishes.

—Answer by Natalie J. Kaplan,
Law Offices of Natalie J. Kaplan, New York, NY

most states requires that the provider make all reasonable efforts to transfer you to another provider who will comply with your wishes.

Can you demand treatment that a hospital or other facility does not consider medically appropriate? For example, can you demand surgery for a cancerous tumor that the physician determines is medically inoperable? In general, the answer is "no." But the effectiveness or appropriateness of many treatments is

 THE PATIENT SELF-DETERMINATION ACT

Most hospitals, nursing homes, home health agencies, and HMOs routinely provide information on advance directives at the time of a patient's admission. They are required to do so under a federal law called the **Patient Self-Determination Act (PSDA)**.

The PSDA is essentially an information-and-education statute. It does not change your underlying legal rights under state law or tell the states what laws they must pass. It simply requires that most health-care institutions do the following:

- provide you, at the time of admission, with a written summary of your health-care decision-making rights;

- make available to you information about their policies regarding recognition of advance directives;

- ask whether you have an advance directive and, if you do, document that fact in your medical record (though it is up to you to provide a copy of the directive);

- educate their staff and the local community about state law governing advance directives; and

- never discriminate against a patient based on whether he or she has an advance directive. (This means that it is against the law for health-care institutions to require patients to have or not have advance directives.)

not always clear. So by all means, state in your advance directive any particular type of care you are certain that you want.

Writing Your Advance Directive

There are many kinds of advance-directive forms available—both official forms created by the states, and unofficial forms created by state medical and bar associations, national organizations, and others. No form is perfect for everyone. Keep in mind that the purpose of such a form is to aid, and not take the place of, communication. The form is a tool for planning, not the final outcome of planning. Thus, any form you use should be personalized to reflect your own values after thoughtful discussion with health-care providers, family, and advisors. And after the form is properly signed, discussion should not cease. After all, your views are likely to evolve over your lifetime.

The instructions you set forth in an advance directive may address the following types of health-care issues:

• conditions or levels of functioning (e.g., permanent unconsciousness or severe dementia) in which you would or would not want life-sustaining treatment;

• the types of life-sustaining treatment you may or may not want;

• the use of artificial nutrition and hydration;

• instructions about any other specific medical procedures that may be expected in light of your personal and family medical history;

• your wishes regarding organ donation;

• your preferences regarding pain control and comfort care;

• your preferences regarding other aspects of end-of-life care, such as the place of care, environmental wishes, and hospice care; and

• your preferences regarding participation in medical research. Your agent may not have authority to consent to your participation in medical research—especially research that will not help your condition, but which may help future generations—unless you clearly grant him or her that authority.

Selecting An Agent

In appointing an agent, you will need to consider not only who your agent and alternative agents will be, but also the scope of their authority. A broadly drafted advance directive usually gives an agent authority to:

• consent to or refuse any medical treatment or diagnostic procedure relating to your physical or mental health, including artificial nutrition and hydration;

• hire or discharge medical providers, and authorize admission to medical and long-term-care facilities;

• consent to measures for comfort care and pain relief;

• have access to all medical records; and

• take whatever measures are necessary to carry out your wishes, including granting releases or waivers to medical facilities and seeking judicial remedies if problems arise.

Remember, you can limit the authority of your agent in any manner you wish. Be clear about how much discretion you want your agent to have. Most people want their agents to have broad flexibility in deciding how to interpret or apply their written instructions, but you also have the option of insisting that your written instructions be strictly followed.

Selecting your agent is the most important part of the health-care planning process, because your agent will have great power if you become incapacitated. There is normally no formal oversight of an agent's decisions, and the role of an agent is not one with which most people have typically had any experience. Therefore, keep in mind that the persons best suited to serving as your health-care agent will:

• meet the legal criteria in your state for acting as an agent, proxy, or representative (each state has different rules, but most prohibit your doctor and other health-care providers from serving as your agent, unless they are related to you);

• be willing to speak on your behalf;

• be able to act on your wishes and separate their own feelings from yours;

- live nearby, or be able to travel to be at your side if needed;
- know you well and understand what's important to you;
- be someone you trust with your life;
- talk with you now about sensitive issues, and listen to your wishes;
- be available well into the future;
- be able to handle conflicting opinions between family members, friends, and medical personnel; and
- be a strong advocate in the face of an unresponsive doctor or institution.

Though an ideal agent would meet each of these qualifications, no single person is likely to meet them all. Speak to the person you wish to name as your agent before you complete your health-care directive, and explain your intentions. Confirm the agent's willingness to act and understand your wishes. This will mean talking honestly and openly about death and dying.

Avoid naming coagents, which can create potential for disagreement and logistical complications. If you really want coagents, you should have a plan that addresses what happens if they disagree about a decision. And although coagents are not generally a good idea, it is often wise to name a successor agent or agents in case your primary agent becomes unavailable.

If you trust no one to be your agent, do not name one. Instead, write a living will. You might also consider limiting the authority of your agent, by giving the agent authority over some but not all treatment decisions, or by requiring concurrence between your agent and physician.

You can also identify persons whom you do *not* want to make decisions about you, and who will have *no* authority to challenge a decision of your agent.

Formalities of Signing an Advance Directive

All states require certain formalities in the signing of an advance directive. Most states require two witnesses to your signature. A few require notarization, or offer it as an alternative to witnessing.

Find out the witness restrictions in your state and strictly follow them. In most states, you will comply with the witnessing requirements if you avoid using witnesses who:

- are related to you by blood or marriage;
- are heirs or potential claimants to your estate;
- serve as your physician or other medical provider;
- are employed by a health-care facility that is treating you; or
- are responsible for your health-care costs.

For individuals in nursing homes or other institutions, some states also require a state nursing-home ombudsman, a patient advocate, or another designated individual to witness the signing.

Changing or Terminating Your Advance Directive

You can change or revoke your advance directive at any time while you still have the mental capacity to do so. Moreover, provided that you are mentally competent, no one can make a health-care decision for you over your own objection. You can revoke your directive orally or in writing by just about any means, though it is preferable to do so by writing to your agent, physician, and anyone else who has a copy of your directive.

If you want to change your advance directive, it is best to execute a new one, since an amendment will require the same signature formalities of a new document anyway.

What to Do With the Advance Directive

Your work is not over when you sign an advance directive. Keep the original in a safe place where it can easily be found. Give a copy to:

- your doctor, asking that it be made part of your medical record;
- your agent, making sure he or she knows where to find the original;

CROSSING STATE LINES: IS MY ADVANCE DIRECTIVE STILL GOOD?

Health-care providers normally try to respect your wishes, regardless of the form you use to indicate those wishes or the state in which you executed the form. Only if you spend significant amounts of time in more than one state do you seriously need to consider executing an advance directive for each state. In such cases, you should find out whether one document will meet the formal requirements of each state. As a practical matter, you may want to name different agents if one agent is not easily available in all locations. Generally speaking, your agent should be physically close to your place of care.

• any successor agent or family member who is likely to be involved in decisions regarding your health care;

• any health-care facility that you know will be treating you in the future; and

• your lawyer, if you have one who advises you on estate- or personal-planning matters.

Consider carrying a wallet card that indicates you have an advance directive and provides information about how to contact your agent. State and national groups distribute such cards, but anyone can create a homemade version. In addition, a few national and state registries of advance directives can make your directive available electronically to health-care providers.

Talk to your doctor and agent to make sure they understand your directive and have an opportunity to ask you questions. The more they understand your wishes, the better they will be able to carry them out.

Reviewing Your Advance Directive

Priorities and goals change as your life circumstances change, so review your health-care advance directive periodically. Such review is particularly important when you experience any of so-called **Five Ds**:

1. Decade—when you start a new decade of your life;
2. Death—when you experience the death of a loved one;
3. Divorce—when you experience a divorce or other major family change;
4. Diagnosis—when you are diagnosed with a serious health condition; or
5. Decline—when you experience a significant decline or deterioration of an existing health condition, especially when it diminishes your ability to live independently.

FAMILY CONSENT (OR DEFAULT SURROGATE CONSENT)

Most people assume that their spouse or an adult child will automatically have the authority to make health-care decisions for them. And doctors and health facilities rely on family consent quite frequently. But whether family members actually have the legal authority to make health-care decisions, and the scope of that authority, depends on the law of your particular state. As a practical matter, informal family consent may work fine, as long as family members have some idea of what you want and your family and physician agree on the course of your care. However, these are two big "ifs"; it is not always easy to get everyone on the same page. If family members disagree with each other, or with the treating doctors, then your family's authority to make decisions may be called into question. If the wishes of an incompetent patient are unclear, family members may have to go to court to obtain the authority to direct certain medical actions, such as terminating life support. That can be unpleasant, costly, and disruptive.

Currently, more than half the states have statutes governing **default surrogate decision making** (i.e., decision making by persons not formally granted decision-making power by the patient). While we refer to these decision makers as **default**

surrogates, your state may use another term or no particular term at all. Such laws usually lay down ground rules concerning such issues as:

• **Order of Priority**. Most family consent laws provide for an order of priority in which family members are authorized to act—usually starting with a person's spouse, then shifting to his or her adult children, and continuing another step or two based on the surrogate's degree of kinship.

• **Scope of Authority**. The surrogates may be permitted by statute to make all health-care decisions, or only limited decisions for the patient.

• **Handling of Disagreements**. In situations involving surrogates at different decision-making "priority" levels, some laws require the unanimous consent of all members who occupy the same level—for example, all of a person's adult children. Some statutes require the consent of just one surrogate, some require the consent of a majority of surrogates, and some statutes do not specify the type or degree of consent required at all. Most permit a judicial procedure by which an interested party can challenge the authority of the presumed decision maker.

• **Lack of Available Family**. Increasingly, applicable laws classify close friends as permissible surrogates, usually at a lower priority level than family members. For health-care decision-making purposes, close friends are individuals who have an established close relationship to the patient, know the patient's values, and are willing to take on the responsibilities of a surrogate.

When it comes to advance planning for health-care decisions, the take-home message is this: *Do not rely only on family consent.* It is far better to spell out your wishes and appoint an agent through an advance directive. This is especially true if you are in a committed relationship but are not married, because your partner either will have no authority to make decisions, or will occupy a low priority level under the law if he or she attempts to make those decisions as an authorized surrogate. Spelling out your wishes and appointing an agent also helps spare family members the agony of having to make painful decisions without knowing what you would really want.

GUIDANCE FOR PROXIES OR SURROGATES

The task of acting as someone's health-care proxy or surrogate is new to most of us and requires a profound personal commitment to the patient, whose life may hang in the balance. The following guidelines apply whether you are an appointed proxy or a family member or friend recognized under the law as the authorized surrogate.

Your Authority

In general, you will have authority to make any and all decisions that a patient would otherwise make. This authority includes the right to:

- receive the same medical information the patient would receive;
- confer with the medical team;
- review the patient's medical chart;
- ask questions and receive explanations;
- discuss treatment options;
- request consultations and second opinions;
- consent to or refuse medical tests or treatments, including life-sustaining treatment; and
- authorize the patient's transfer to another physician or institution, including another type of facility (such as a hospital or skilled nursing home).

Steps to Follow in Making Health-Care Decisions

When you need to make a decision on behalf of another person, it may be helpful to take the following steps:

1. **Find out the medical facts.** This requires talking to the patient's doctors and getting a complete picture of his or her situation. It may help to ask the following questions:

- What is the patient's medical condition?

- If you don't know exactly what's wrong, what are the possibilities for diagnosing and treating the patient?
- Are tests needed in order for the doctors to know more? Will the results of further testing make any difference in the planned course of treatment? (And if not, is further testing truly necessary?)
- What is the purpose of each test? Does the testing involve risks?
- Is the information to be gathered worthwhile or necessary, given the risks involved with performing the proposed tests?
- What are the current effects of the condition on the patient? How do you explain the patient's symptoms?
- In terms of physical symptoms and effects, what usually happens to patients with this condition?
- What do you think will be the likely course of this disease or condition?
- How severe or advanced is the condition?

2. **Find out the options.** Make sure the physician describes the risks and benefits of each treatment option. You may want to ask:

- How will this treatment option improve the patient's condition or make the patient feel better?
- Statistically, what is the success rate of this treatment option?
- Can this procedure be performed on a trial basis and then reevaluated? What is an appropriate length for a trial? Are you willing to stop the treatment option after an agreed-upon trial period?
- What constitutes success in the context of this treatment option? (And would you and the patient define "success" in the same way?)
- How will this treatment option change the patient's quality of life?
- If death is inevitable, how might this treatment option affect the circumstances of the patient's death? (For

example, will it likely require hospitalization instead of home care?)

• What are the possible side effects of this treatment option?

• What treatment option do you recommend, and why?

When making health-care decisions for another person, make those decisions as though you were in the patient's shoes. There are three ways to accomplish this:

• If you know the patient's preferences, adhere to them.

• If you do not know the patient's wishes regarding the decision at hand, but you have evidence of what he or she might want, try to figure out what he or she would decide. This is called **substituted judgment**, and it requires you to imagine yourself in the patient's position. Consider his or her values, religious beliefs, past decisions, and past statements. The aim is to choose as the patient would, even if the outcome is not what you would choose for yourself.

• If you have very little or no knowledge of what the patient would want, then you and the doctors will have to make a decision based on what a reasonable person in the same situation would decide. In other words, your goal is to make decisions in the patient's **best interest**. Evaluate the benefits and burdens of the proposed treatment. For example, will the treatment cause the patient pain or suffering? Is it likely to make him or her better?

What If There Are Disagreements?

If feelings run high and opinions differ sharply, you may need help in resolving conflict. Consider calling upon the following resources:

• **Hospital patient representatives**. Many hospitals have representatives to help patients exercise their rights and to serve as advocates for patients in the health-care system. These representatives will try to ensure that the voice of the patient—or the proxy—will be heard.

- **Ombudsmen.** Under federal law, all the states and many local areas offer long-term-care ombudsman programs. Pursuant to these programs, **ombudsmen** (independent staff members or volunteers in hospitals, nursing homes, or assisted-living facilities) serve as advocates for patients and residents. Ombudsmen can be very helpful in resolving complaints, mediating problems, or helping a patient and his or her proxy stand up to a medical team or institution.
- **Facility social workers.** Nursing homes and assisted-living facilities may have in-house social workers to help residents and families meet their needs.
- **Members of the clergy** or **spiritual advisors.**
- **Institutional ethics committees** or **ethics consultants.** Most hospitals and some nursing homes have an ethics committee or ethics consultation team. Such committees help to educate the facility's staff and to sort out difficult problems. They usually

 TALKING TO A LAWYER

Q. My sister had a terminal condition but lived at home until her death. On the day her heart stopped, a family member called 911 and the ambulance team that showed up insisted on trying to resuscitate her, even though we showed them her living will that said, "I don't want CPR." Why did that happen and how can it be prevented?

A. That happened because the family member called 911, which is a call for emergency help. The ambulance team is not empowered to determine whether a living will is effective. Such a response can be prevented by not calling 911. If someone makes that error, only a doctor's "Out of Hospital Do Not Resuscitate Order," in the possession of the patient—or someone with the patient—at the time an ambulance team arrives, can authorize the withholding of CPR.

—Answer by Natalie J. Kaplan,
Law Offices of Natalie J. Kaplan, New York, NY

don't make decisions; instead, they act as advisors. They may help families or medical staff to better understand each other's views and explore their options, and they may help to mediate solutions.

THE WORLD AT YOUR FINGERTIPS

• Most hospitals and agencies on aging have information and forms on advance directives that are legally recognized in your area, as do many state bar associations and medical societies. State-approved forms and state-specific information are also available from the National Hospice and Palliative Care Organization's Caring Connections program at *www.caringinfo.org.*

• For useful guides to help you reflect on, talk about, and define your values and wishes, try the following resources:

  • "Consumer's Tool Kit for Health Care Advance Planning," by the American Bar Association (ABA) Commission on Law and Aging, available at *www.abanet.org/aging/toolkit.*

  • "Five Wishes Advance Directive," published by Aging with Dignity. This nationally used and very popular advance directive focuses on ways of talking about health-care wishes and needs. It can be purchased and downloaded at *www.agingwithdignity.org/5wishes.html.*

• For a more comprehensive guide on dealing with chronic and eventually fatal conditions, try the *Handbook for Mortals: Guidance for People Facing Serious Illness,* by Joanne Lynn, M.D., and Joan Harrold, M.D. (New York: Oxford University Press, 1999), available through the website of Americans for Better Care of the Dying at *www.abcd-caring.org.*

REMEMBER THIS

• Health-care advance planning, if done right, accomplishes four things:

  • It helps ensure that the person you want to speak for you has the legal authority to do so.

- It helps ensure that your wishes about your health care are known and respected.

- It avoids unnecessary, intrusive, and costly medical treatment after the point at which you no longer want it.

- It reduces the suffering experienced by your loved ones, because they will have your guidance in making decisions regarding your care. Making serious medical decisions on a loved one's behalf without his or her guidance is an agonizing experience.

- Advance planning requires two basic things: *talking and writing*. The **talking** you need to do is with the person whom you appoint to speak for you, with your loved ones, and with your doctor. Those discussions provide the crucial background that people need to understand your wishes. The **writing** part is the easier part, because you can use advance-directive forms that are widely available. Remember, the document is only as useful as the discussion it is based on.

- If you are a health-care proxy or surrogate, the most important rule of thumb is to know your obligations and the limits of your authority, and to follow the steps for making decisions outlined in this chapter: Find out the medical facts; determine the patient's medical options; apply the patient's values and wishes to determine what choice the patient would make; if conflict arises, don't let it tear everyone apart. There are resources available to help you, including ombudsmen, social workers, clergy, and ethics consultants or committees.

CHAPTER 8

Medicare and Private Health Benefits

Alphabet Soup

Joan is about to become eligible for Medicare Parts A, B, and D. She understands that she doesn't have to do anything in order to sign up for Medicare Parts A or B. But she does want to learn more about what these parts cover, how much she will have to pay for services, and whether Medigap insurance will cover some of her costs.

Joan is also concerned about Part D. According to Joan's doctor, Part D may not cover the cost of the drug that she has been taking to control her epilepsy for the last five years. In addition, she must take certain steps to enroll in Part D, and pay a monthly premium. If she doesn't enroll when she becomes eligible, then she may be penalized. Should she consider joining? How does she sign up? And where can she find more information?

Provided by the federal government, **Medicare** is a program of basic health-care insurance for older and disabled persons. Practically everyone sixty-five and older is eligible.

Do not confuse Medicare with **Medicaid**, which provides medical benefits for qualified people with low incomes. Medicare and Medicaid are not the same, though some older people qualify for both. Medicaid coverage rules vary from state to state, but the coverage requirements for Medicare are generally the same all over the United States.

This chapter examines Medicare, private Medigap insurance, and employer group coverage used to supplement Medicare coverage. Medicaid is discussed in the next chapter.

Medicare has been revised many times, and more revisions are likely. The most current information is usually available from the Centers for Medicare and Medicaid Services (CMS), your local Social Security Administration (SSA) office, as well as from other organizations (see "The World at Your Fingertips" section at the end of this chapter for contact information).

MEDICARE

Medicare consists of three main parts. The hospital insurance part, **Part A**, covers medically necessary care in hospitals and other facilities—for example, care at skilled nursing facilities and psychiatric hospitals, home health care, and hospice care.

Part B, the medical-insurance part of Medicare, covers medically necessary physician's services and a variety of other services and supplies not covered by Part A. Coverage under Part B is also known as **Supplementary Medical Insurance**.

Part D, the Medicare prescription drug benefit, covers outpatient generic and brand-name medications. The drug benefit is provided only through private entities, such as health insurance or managed-care plans.

 TALKING TO A LAWYER

Q. I currently have Medicare Parts A and B as well as retiree health insurance with drug benefits. Do I have to enroll for drug benefits under Medicare, too?

A. You will need to find out if your retiree coverage offers drug benefits that are at least as good as the basic Medicare drug benefit. You should get notice from your former employer providing you with this information. Such notice might be provided in a letter from your company, in a newsletter, or, if you receive other company notices electronically, in an e-mail.

—Answer by Hilary Dalin,
Health Assistance Partnership, Washington, DC

MANAGED-CARE ORGANIZATIONS

Managed-care organizations provide or arrange for all Medicare-covered services under Parts A and B, and generally charge a fixed monthly premium and small co-payment (or no co-payment) for services. They may also offer Medicare drug benefits or benefits not covered by Medicare, such as some preventive care. However, managed-care plans often restrict your choice of providers, your access to specialists, and your treatment options. Original Medicare, in contrast, pays a fee for service to any qualified provider who renders medically necessary care. (More information about managed-care plans is available in the section commencing on page 140.)

Medicare beneficiaries can get Medicare coverage through traditional fee-for-service Medicare or through Medicare managed-care programs (described in the "Managed-Care Organizations" sidebar above). In the past, most Medicare coverage was provided on a fee-for-service basis—that is, Medicare paid a fee for each service in which a qualified provider provided medical care to a beneficiary. However, in 2003, Congress changed its Medicare Advantage (formerly Medicare + Choice) program to allow more private health insurance companies to offer health coverage to Medicare beneficiaries. Under Medicare Advantage, Medicare beneficiaries have the option of joining a preferred provider organization (PPO), a health maintenance organization (HMO), or another managed-care organization that participates in Medicare, or of obtaining care on a private fee-for-service basis.

Enrolling in Medicare Parts A and B is easy. Everyone who is turning sixty-five and applying for Social Security or railroad retirement benefits is automatically enrolled in Medicare Parts A and B. However, you must opt to enroll in Part D (enrollment is discussed in more detail in the "Signing Up for Medicare" section later in this chapter). You are eligible for Medicare even if you continue to work beyond age sixty-five. Younger persons who have received Social Security disability benefits for more than twenty-four months are also eligible, as are persons receiving continuing dialysis for permanent kidney failure or who have had kidney transplants. The Centers for Medicare and Medicaid Services (CMS) is the federal agency responsible for administering Medicare. The specific coverage rules and limitations for Medicare are complex. The actual coverage decisions and payments for care are handled by a variety of private insurance companies under contract with CMS.

Hospitals, doctors, and other health-care providers can choose to participate in Medicare. Those that do so are called **participating providers**. Most hospitals, nursing homes, and home health agencies participate, meet federal standards, and are certified as Medicare participating providers. Doctors have more flexibility than hospitals, with the option of accepting or rejecting Medicare patients on a case-by-case basis. Even if doctors do not participate in Medicare, the government limits the fees they can charge Medicare patients.

What Does Medicare Part A Cover?

Medicare Part A helps pay for medically necessary hospital care, skilled nursing care, home health care, and hospice care.

 BENEFIT PERIOD

Under Part A, benefit limits and beneficiary out-of-pocket costs are based upon a **benefit period**. A benefit period begins the first day you receive inpatient hospital care. It ends when you have been out of a hospital and have not received skilled-care services for sixty days in a row. A subsequent hospitalization begins a new benefit period. At the beginning of each benefit period, a new cycle of benefits, deductibles, and coinsurance starts.

Hospitalization

Under Medicare Part A, a benefit period begins when you are hospitalized. In 2006, you will have to pay an initial deductible of $952. Deductible amounts change each year. Medicare then pays for all covered hospital care through day sixty of the benefit period. For the sixty-first through ninetieth days, you will have to pay $238 per day in 2006. After ninety days, you can choose to pay a coinsurance amount of $476 per day in 2006 for up to sixty life-time reserve days, or else pay the full charges yourself. **Lifetime reserve days** (i.e., days for which you may receive coverage after paying the required co-insurance amount) are days that you get to use only once in your lifetime. Unlike other hospital benefits that are renewed at the beginning of each benefit period, lifetime re-serve days are not renewed with a new benefit period. Your benefit period ends sixty days after discharge from the hospital, or sixty days after you stop receiving skilled care in a nursing home facil-ity. If another hospital admission occurs after that, you will have to pay another deductible, as well as the other cost-sharing amounts.

Medicare coverage of inpatient hospitalization includes:

• a semiprivate room (i.e., a room with two to four beds) and board;

• meals, including accommodation for special diets;

• general nursing;

• treatment by special-care units, such as intensive-care or coronary-care units;

• drugs furnished by the hospital during your stay;

• blood transfusions;

• lab tests, X-rays, and other radiology services such as radia-tion therapy;

• medical supplies and equipment, such as casts, dressings, and wheelchairs;

• operating room and recovery room costs;

• rehabilitation services, such as physical therapy, occupa-tional therapy, and speech therapy; and

• hospitalization in a participating psychiatric hospital (up to a lifetime maximum of 190 days, though in most cases psychi-atric care in a general hospital is not subject to this limit).

Medicare does *not* cover the following:
- personal convenience items, such as a telephone or television;
- private-duty nurses; and
- private rooms, unless such a room is medically necessary.

Skilled Nursing Home Care

Medicare covers *skilled* nursing facility inpatient care following a hospitalization of at least three days. Your condition must require, on a daily basis, skilled nursing or skilled rehabilitation services that, as a practical matter, can only be provided in a skilled nursing facility. You must be admitted within a short time (usually but not always within thirty days) after you leave the hospital, and the daily skilled care you receive must be based on a doctor's order. If you qualify, you pay nothing for the first twenty days, except for any charges that Medicare does not allow. For the next eighty days, you pay charges of up to $119 per day, and Medicare pays all remaining allowable charges. No benefits are available after one hundred days of care in a given benefit period.

Most nursing home residents do not require nursing services that are considered "skilled" for purposes of Medicare coverage. Not every nursing home participates in Medicare or qualifies as a skilled nursing facility. If you are unsure of a facility's status, ask members of its staff.

If the requirements for skilled-care coverage are met, Medicare covers:
- a semiprivate room (i.e., a room with two to four beds);
- meals, including medically necessary special diets;
- general nursing services;
- physical, occupational, and speech therapy;
- prescription drugs (including over-the-counter drugs) furnished during your stay;
- medical supplies and equipment such as oxygen, casts, splints, and wheelchairs; and
- routine personal hygiene items and services such as basic personal laundry services, hair and nail hygiene care, combs, soap, specialized cleansing agents, lotions, toothbrushes and tooth-

SKILLED CARE OR CUSTODIAL CARE?

Medicare helps pay only for "skilled" nursing home care, not "custodial" care. However, the distinction between these two types of care is often fuzzy, and many Medicare denials based on a finding of custodial care can be successfully appealed. Generally, **custodial care** is care aimed primarily at helping the resident with daily living needs, such as eating, bathing, walking, getting in and out of bed, and taking medicine. Skilled nursing and skilled rehabilitation services require the skills of technical or professional personnel such as registered nurses, licensed practical nurses, or therapists. Examples of skilled nursing care include administration of intravenous injections and tube feedings, or the changing of sterile dressings. Such care may also include observation of a changing condition, evaluation of that condition, and patient education.

---

paste, denture supplies, deodorant, sanitary napkins, and incontinence care and supplies.

Home Health Care

Medicare Part A covers part-time or intermittent skilled nursing; physical, occupational, and speech therapy services; medical social services; part-time personal care provided by a home health aide; and medical equipment for use in the home. It does not cover medications for patients living at home, nor does it cover general household services or services that are primarily custodial.

To be eligible, you must meet four conditions. First, you must be under the care of a physician who determines your need for home health care and sets up a plan of care. Second, you must be **homebound**, meaning that you leave the home infrequently and with difficulty, or you need somebody to help you when you leave the home. You need not be bedridden. Any absences from home for medical care, to attend adult day care or religious services, or for infrequent or short periods of time, do not disqualify you from classification as homebound for purposes of Medicare coverage. Third, the primary care you need must include part-time or intermittent skilled nursing, physical therapy, or speech therapy, although other services may be provided if you meet these four qualifying conditions. Fourth, your care must be provided by a home health-care agency participating in Medicare. You are *not* required to have a hospital stay before home health services are covered. If you are in need of home health care, contact a home health agency. Hospital discharge planners can also make home health-care referrals. There is no cost to you for Medicare home health care.

Hospice Care

The Medicare hospice benefit is different from other Medicare benefits in that it covers care that is not directed towards your recovery or the regaining of functional abilities. Rather, hospice care provides pain relief, palliative care, symptom management, and supportive services to people with terminal illnesses. Hospice services may include physician or visiting-nurse services, psychological support for you, your family, and close friends, inpatient care when needed, home health aide services, drugs (including outpatient drugs for pain relief), and respite care. **Respite care** is short-term (up to five consecutive days) inpatient care in a facility aimed at providing family caregivers with temporary relief. Respite care is not available on a regular basis.

For a patient to be eligible for hospice care, a doctor must certify that the patient is **terminally ill** (meaning that he or she has a life expectancy of six months or less); the patient must choose to receive hospice care instead of standard Medicare benefits for the terminal illness; and the hospice must be a Medicare-participating program. Even while the patient receives hospice care, regular Medicare still helps pay for treatments not related to the terminal illness. For example, if you break your leg, you will receive treatment to repair the fracture since it is not related to your terminal condition.

Medicare pays the hospice directly. You are responsible only

FOREIGN TRAVEL

Medicare generally does not pay for hospital or medical services provided outside the United States. (Puerto Rico, the U.S. Virgin Islands, Guam, American Samoa, and the Northern Mariana Islands are U.S. territories and are thus considered part of the United States for purposes of Medicare coverage.) However, Medicare will pay for care provided in certain emergency situations in Canada and Mexico. When in doubt, ask your Medicare contractor.

for 5 percent of the Medicare-approved amount for inpatient respite care, and up to a maximum of $5 per outpatient prescription. The charges for respite care may change every year, and may be different in different parts of the country.

What Does Medicare Part B Cover?

Medicare Part B covers a wide range of outpatient and physician expenses, regardless of where they are provided—at home, in a hospital or nursing home, or in a private office. Covered services include:

• doctors' services, including some limited services by chiropractors, dentists, podiatrists, and optometrists;

• outpatient hospital services, such as emergency room services or outpatient clinic care, radiology services, and ambulatory surgical services;

• diagnostic tests, including X rays and other laboratory services, as well as some pap smear screenings;

• durable medical equipment, such as oxygen equipment, wheelchairs, and other medically necessary equipment that your doctor prescribes for use in your home;

• outpatient rehabilitation therapy, including physical, occupational and speed-language therapies;

• kidney dialysis;

- ambulance services to or from a hospital or skilled nursing facility, or ambulance transport necessitated by an individual's medical condition;
- certain services of other practitioners, such as clinical psychologists or social workers;
- diabetes self-management services, blood glucose monitoring, and blood-testing strips; and
- many other health services, supplies, and prosthetic devices not covered by Medicare Part A.

Medicare Part B also has begun covering certain preventive services, such as vaccinations for flu, pneumonia, and hepatitis B, prostate cancer screenings, pap smears, pelvic examinations, mammograms, and bone mass measurements.

Part B does not cover:

- routine physical examinations;
- most routine foot care and dental care;
- examinations for the purpose of prescribing or fitting eyeglasses or hearing aids (though some exceptions are made if the beneficiary has had cataract surgery);
- most cosmetic surgery;
- personal comfort items and services; and
- any service not considered "reasonable and necessary."

Call the Medicare carrier that handles your medical claim to get answers to questions about specific cases. You can find your carrier by calling 1-800-MEDICARE, consulting the *Medicare & You* handbook, or visiting *www.medicare.gov*.

What Does Medicare Part D Cover?

On January 1, 2006, Medicare began to cover outpatient drugs for its beneficiaries. Unlike other Medicare benefits, the drug benefit is provided only through private entities, such as health insurance or managed-care plans. Although there is a standard benefit, each plan has significant flexibility (within certain guidelines established by the government) to decide what drugs to cover and to set its own premiums, deductibles, coinsurances, and co-payments. Each plan may limit coverage to a specific list of drugs (called a **formulary**), and the list can change during the year upon sixty days' notice to you and your treating doctor.

If you are covered by both Medicare and Medicaid, you can no longer get prescriptions through Medicaid as of January 1, 2006; instead, Medicare now covers prescriptions through Medicare drug plan. If you previously enjoyed prescription drug coverage under Medicaid, the government will have automatically enolled you in a Medicare drug plan to ensure that you experienced no loss of drug coverage. However, you can change to a different plan at any time. After you change plans, the new plan will become effective at the beginning of the following month.

The following four options are available to Medicare beneficiaries:

1. Stay with original fee-for service Medicare and enroll in a stand-alone prescription drug plan (called a **PDP**).

2. Join or remain in a Medicare Advantage plan (such as an HMO or PPO) and get all Medicare and prescription drug benefits through the plan.

3. Retain your current coverage from another source. If you receive drug coverage from another source, such as an employer, a union, the Veterans Administration, TRICARE, or a Medigap policy, you will be notified by your current plan if its current drug coverage is at least as comprehensive as Medicare drug coverage. You will need to find out how the current drug plan works with Medicare before making the decision whether to enroll in a Medicare drug plan.

4. Decide not to enroll in a Medicare plan at this time, and go without prescription coverage altogether. If your current drug coverage is not at least as comprehensive as Medicare drug coverage, and if you wait until a later time to enroll in a Medicare plan, then you will have to pay 1 percent more per month on your premium for every month you wait to enroll in a Medicare plan. You will have to pay this higher premium for as long as you receive Medicare drug coverage. You cannot enroll in a Medicare drug plan at any

EXTRA HELP

Medicare beneficiaries with limited incomes and resources may be able to get extra help paying for prescription drugs. Beneficiaries that qualify for this extra help will pay no or reduced premiums, deductibles, and co-payments for prescription drugs. Generally, if an individual or couple has income totaling less than 150 percent of the poverty level, and has limited assets ($10,000 for an individual and $20,000 for a couple), the individual or couple should apply for extra help. An application can be made by calling or visiting the Social Security Administration or the local Medicaid office. Applications can also be made online at *www.ssa.gov*.

time; you can only enroll during an annual enrollment period or, in certain circumstances, during special enrollment periods.

There are many Medicare drug plans, and every Medicare beneficiary has a wide range of stand-alone PDPs and Medicare Advantage Plans from which to choose. **State Health Insurance Assistance Programs** (also called **SHIPs**) can help you to identify the most important factors to consider in making your selection. Such factors may include the annual cost of a plan (i.e., the cost of premiums, deductibles, and co-payments), whether the drugs you need are included in the plan formulary, and whether your local pharmacy is included in the plan network.

The Cost of Medicare

Part A coverage is provided to you at no cost if you are sixty-five or older and eligible for Social Security, or have been receiving Social Security disability benefits for twenty-four months. Part A is funded by payroll deductions from every wage earner's paycheck. If you are not eligible for Social Security benefits, you may still enroll in Part A after you turn sixty-five, but you will have to pay a sizable monthly premium.

Part B is available to all Part A enrollees for a monthly premium that changes yearly.

There are three types of costs that you will incur for Medicare coverage:

1. **premiums** (the regular monthly purchase price for coverage under Medicare Parts B and D);

2. **deductibles** (payments made by you before Medicare begins paying for a service or supplies); and

3. **coinsurance** (payments equal to a percentage of the total cost of a service). In some cases, a beneficiary must pay a fixed amount for a service instead of a percentage of the service's total cost, in which case the payments are called **co-payments**. Under both Parts A and B, beneficiaries must pay certain deductibles and coinsurance payments, depending on the type of service.

Your premiums, deductibles, and coinsurance amounts will change regularly, some of them according to an annual inflation formula. Not surprisingly, costs always go up—never down.

Medigap insurance (a type of private insurance that supplements Medicare coverage) may cover all or part of these deductibles and co-payments. Also, certain low-income beneficiaries may have these costs covered by Medicaid.

Under Part A, your costs are based on benefit periods. A benefit period begins on the first day you receive inpatient hospital care. It ends when you have been out of a hospital and have not received skilled nursing facility services for sixty days in a row. A subsequent hospitalization begins a new benefit period. Under Part B, benefits are based on a simple calendar year cycle, meaning that a certain deductible must be paid during each calendar year. In the calendar year 2006, you are responsible for paying a $124 deductible for Part B benefits before Medicare will pay for any portion of those benefits.

Costs under Part D are significantly different from those under Parts A and B, because Part D benefits are provided solely by private entities. As previously explained, each entity or plan can set its own premium, deductibles, coinsurances, and benefits, subject to some government restrictions.

HELP FOR LOW-INCOME MEDICARE BENEFICIARIES!

If you are eligible for both Medicare and Medicaid, your state's Medicaid program will cover your share of Medicare costs and pay for many expenses not covered by Medicare. If your income is limited but you are not eligible for Medicaid, you may still qualify for help from Medicaid in paying your share of Medicare costs through a Medicare Savings Program (MSP). There are three slightly different Medicare Savings Programs: the **Qualified Medicare Beneficiary (QMB) Program**, the **Specified Low-Income Medicare Beneficiary (SLMB) Program**, and the **Qualifying Individual (QI) Program**.

The QMB Program will pay your Medicare monthly premiums and all Medicare deductibles and coinsurance. To qualify for a QMB Program, your financial assets (excluding your home, car, and certain other items) cannot exceed $4,000 for one person or $6,000 for a couple. However, some states have loosened these criteria, allowing more people to qualify. And your income (with certain deductions) must be at or below the national poverty line, which is adjusted yearly. The 2005 poverty line for monthly income is:

	Individual	Couple
Continental U.S.	$ 817	$1,100
Alaska	$1,021	$1,375
Hawaii	$ 939	$1,265

For individuals whose income is within 100 to 120 percent of the poverty line, less extensive assistance is available under the SLMB program. This program pays only the monthly Part B Medicare premium.

Individuals whose income is within 120 to 135 percent of the poverty line may be eligible for a QI Program that also pays the monthly Part B Medicare premium.

You can find more information about MSPs in Chapter 9.

MEDICARE BENEFIT AND COST SUMMARY FOR 2006

Coverage Per Benefit Period* Under Parts A and B:

MEDICARE SERVICE		MEDICARE PAYS	YOU OR MEDIGAP
PART A	**Hospital Inpatient**		
No monthly premium for most beneficiaries	Days 1–60	All costs after a deductible of $952	$952
	Days 61–90	All costs after co-payment	$238/day co-payment
	Days 91–150 (once per lifetime)	All costs after co-payment	$476/day co-payment
	Days 151 and beyond	Nothing	All costs
	Skilled Nursing Home Care	(If patient meets skilled-care conditions)	
	Days 1–20	All costs	Nothing for first 20 days
	Days 21–100	All costs after co-payment	$119/day co-payment
	Days 101 and higher	Nothing	All costs
	Home Health Care Skilled Visits**	100 percent of approved amount if patient meets conditions	Nothing for home health-care services; 20 percent of the Medicare-approved amount for durable medical equipment

MEDICARE SERVICE	MEDICARE PAYS	YOU OR MEDIGAP
Hospice		
210 days	All costs for hospice care; most costs for outpatient prescription drugs and respite care	Nothing for hospice care; small co-payment ($5) and 5 percent of the Medicare-approved amount for inpatient respite care
Blood		Pay for the first 3 pints of blood, unless you or someone else donates blood to replace what you used
PART B Monthly premium of $88.50	**Physician/ Medical Expenses**	80 percent of approved amount after $124 deductible	20 percent of approved amount and charges above the approved amount
	Clinical Lab Services	100 percent of approved amount	Nothing
	Outpatient Hospital Treatment	80 percent of approved amount	20 percent of approved amount

MEDICARE SERVICE	MEDICARE PAYS	YOU OR MEDIGAP
Blood		Pay for the first 3 pints, then 20 percent of the Medicare-approved amount for additional pints of blood, unless the used blood is replaced by donations

Coverage Under Part D:

AMOUNT OF DRUG COSTS	WHO PAYS WHAT?
$250 or less	Plan pays zero. Beneficiary pays initial deductible of $250.
$251–$2,250	Plan pays 75 percent. Beneficiary pays 25 percent of drug costs.
$2,251–$5,100	Plan pays nothing. Beneficiary pays 100 percent of drug costs.
$5,100 and over	Plan pays 95 percent. Beneficiary pays up to 5 percent of drug costs.

*For **Part A,** a benefit period begins on the first day you receive services as an inpatient in a hospital. It ends after you have been out of the hospital or a skilled nursing facility for sixty days in a row, or if you remain in a skilled nursing care facility but do not receive care there for sixty days in a row. For **Part B,** a new benefit period begins each January 1.

**Home health care is also covered under Part B to the same extent.

Physician Bills

The amount of your liability for the costs of medical care depends on whether your doctor accepts **assignment**. If your physician accepts assignment, it means that he or she agrees to accept the Medicare-approved amount as payment in full for Part B services and supplies. Going to a doctor who accepts assignment will help you avoid excess charges. Doctors and suppliers who agree to accept assignment under Medicare on all claims are called **participating** doctors and suppliers. Nonparticipating providers may still choose to accept assignment on a case-by-case basis. You can get a directory of Medicare-participating doctors from your Medicare carrier or through the CMS website at *www.medicare.gov*. The directory is also available for your use in SSA offices, state and area agencies on aging, and most hospitals.

 PHYSICIAN BILLS: AN EXAMPLE

Here is an example that demonstrates the significance of a provider accepting assignment. Mrs. Jones sees Dr. Welby on June 1 for medical care. Dr. Welby normally charges $250 for such a visit. The Medicare-approved amount for such services is $200. Let us assume that Mrs. Jones has already met her $110 calendar-year deductible for Medicare Part B.

- *If Dr. Welby accepts assignment:*

  - Mrs. Jones pays a $40 co-payment (in other words, 20 percent of the $200 approved amount); and

  - Dr. Welby submits the bill to Medicare and receives reimbursement for $160.

- *If Dr. Welby does* not *accept assignment,* he may require Mrs. Jones to pay the full bill up front, but he can charge no more than 15 percent over the Medicare-approved amount. Since the Medicare-approved amount is $200, the maximum he can charge is $230. Furthermore, *the doctor must submit the claim to the Medicare carrier on behalf of Mrs. Jones.* Mrs. Jones will receive a check from Medicare in the amount of $160 (which is 80 percent of the $200 approved charge). Thus, Mrs. Jones' total out-of-pocket cost in this example should be no more than $70 (the $40 coinsurance charge plus the $30 excess charge). Mrs. Jones will receive a Medicare Summary Notice form explaining her obligations and rights.

The Medicare-approved amount is based on a fee schedule created by Medicare for every possible service or procedure. Your liability is limited to a coinsurance payment of 20 percent of the Medicare-approved amount. So if the Medicare-approved amount was $100 for a procedure, you would owe only $20 to a physician who accepts assignment.

A nonparticipating provider can charge you for the entire cost of the services he or she provides, including amounts over the Medicare-approved amount, but cannot charge more than 15 percent over the Medicare-approved amount. Doctors cannot get around this limit. If they attempt to do so, they may be fined by the government.

At least eight states have laws that further limit what your doctor can charge you. These states include Connecticut, Massachusetts, Minnesota, New York, Ohio, Pennsylvania, Rhode Island, and Vermont. If you live in one of these states, call the State Health Insurance Assistance Program (SHIP) in your state for more information. You can find your state's SHIP phone number through the national Medicare hotline at 1-800-MEDICARE (1-800-633-4227). TTY users should call 1-877-486-2048.

The amount your doctor charges you should appear on the Medicare Summary Notice sent to you by Medicare. If there is any discrepancy, notify the Medicare carrier whose name appears on that form. If you think a doctor has charged you too much, ask for a reduction or refund or contact your Medicare carrier or SHIP for help in getting your charge corrected.

Opting for Medicare Managed Care

Managed-care plans are called **Medicare Advantage Plans** and have several advantages and disadvantages. On the positive side, they provide all the covered Medicare benefits and usually more, and there is little or no paperwork to handle or submit. Some plans charge a fixed monthly premium in addition to your Medicare Part B premiums and/or a small co-payment each time you use a service. You do not pay any Medicare deductibles or coinsurance. This arrangement makes your health expenses more predictable and usually eliminates the need for a Medigap policy. (Caution: Read the "Medigap Insurance" section of this chapter before considering dropping any Medigap policy you have.) Moreover, certain types of Medicare Advantage Plans, such as preferred provider organizations (PPOs) and health maintenance organizations (HMOs), often provide extra benefits such as routine physicals, eye and hearing exams, and inoculations, though additional services and costs vary substantially.

On the negative side, a managed-care plan generally requires that you use its network of doctors and facilities. Usually, you may choose a primary-care doctor to oversee your care and serve as the gatekeeper for referrals to specialists and admissions to hospitals (except in emergencies or urgent-care situations). Whether you can get services out-of-plan—that is, from a doctor or other provider who is not a member of the plan—depends on your type of plan. Most Medicare Advantage Plans handle out-of-plan services in one of three ways:

• Through **lock-in requirements** that restrict you to receiving *all* covered care through the plan or through referral by the plan. If you receive services out-of-plan, neither the managed-care organization nor Medicare will cover the service, unless it constitutes emergency or urgent care.

• Through a **point-of-service option**, under which you can receive certain services outside the provider's network. However, you will pay more of the cost for the services than you would if you had gone to a provider within your plan.

• In the case of private **fee-for-service plans**, by paying for Medicare services so long as the applicable provider accepts the plan's payment terms. The plan, rather than Medicare, decides how much the provider will be paid and how much you will pay.

You can find out about available plans in your area by contacting your local SHIP, by calling the 1-800-MEDICARE number, or by using the Medicare Personal Plan Finder at *www .medicare.gov*. It can be quite confusing to compare plan benefits, costs, services, and quality, so seek help in evaluating your options. All plans available under Medicare have an Annual Coordinated Election Period from November 15 to December 31 of

EMERGENCY CARE OUTSIDE YOUR MEDICARE ADVANTAGE PLAN

Your Medicare Advantage Plan must pay for emergency care and for unforeseen, urgently needed, out-of-area care you get from non-plan health-care providers, including necessary follow-up care.

Emergencies are situations in which you need medical care immediately because of sudden or suddenly worsening illness or injury, and in which the time needed to reach your plan doctor or hospital appears to you to risk permanent damage to your health.

Urgent-care situations are situations in which you experience an unexpected illness or injury while you are temporarily outside your plan's service area. Your plan must cover the care if you are temporarily away from the plan service area, and your illness or injury is unexpected and requires medical care that cannot be delayed until you return home.

In either case, if coverage is declined, you should consider appealing that decision.

---

each year. You can also change your Medicare health plan during an Open Enrollment Period from January through March each year. Plans cannot reject Medicare beneficiaries because of poor health.

Once you join a managed-care plan, you can stay in the plan as long as it remains approved by Medicare, or you can leave to join another plan or return to the original Medicare fee-for-service program during the Annual Coordinated Enrollment Period or the Open Enrollment Period. To change from one Medicare Advantage Plan to another, you must enroll in the new plan. You will be automatically disenrolled from the first plan. To disenroll and return to the Original Medicare fee-for-service arrangement, send a signed request to the plan or to your local Social Security office. If you make your change during the Annual Coordinated Election Period, the new coverage begins on January

1. If you make the change during the Open Enrollment Period, your new coverage will be effective the first day of the month after the month in which the plan receives a completed enrollment form. If you drop out of a Medicare Advantage Plan to go back to regular Medicare, be sure you have or can get an adequate Medigap policy. If you have any preexisting medical conditions, many insurance companies will not sell you a Medigap policy or will impose a waiting period for coverage with respect to those conditions. (Note: If you joined a Medicare Advantage Plan when you first qualified for Medicare, or if you dropped a Medigap policy to join a Medicare Advantage Plan, then there are certain protections that guarantee you will be issued a Medigap plan.)

Signing Up for Medicare

Enrolling in Medicare Parts A and B is easy. Everyone who is turning sixty-five and applying for Social Security or railroad retirement benefits is automatically enrolled in Medicare Parts A and B. If you do not want Part B coverage (perhaps because you have company retiree health benefits), you must notify the Social Security Administration (SSA). If you are one of the few people not eligible for Medicare, you can purchase the coverage, but the premium for Part A is fairly costly. If you are receiving Social Security retirement or railroad retirement benefits before age sixty-five, you should automatically receive a Medicare card prior to the month in which you turn sixty-five. Medicare benefits normally begin on the first day of the month in which you turn sixty-five. If you are under sixty-five and receiving Social Security disability benefits, your enrollment in Medicare will begin automatically as soon as you have been receiving disability benefits for twenty-four months. Once your benefits start, your Part B premium will be deducted from your monthly Social Security check.

Enrollment in Part D is different. It is not automatic, and you usually must pay a separate monthly premium directly to the plan. When you become eligible for Medicare, you need to take the affirmative step of enrolling in a Part D plan that is available in your community. If you do not enroll in a Part D plan when you are first eligible, and you do not have drug coverage from another source that is at least as comprehensive as the coverage provided by the Medicare drug plan, then you will have to pay an additional 1 percent per month for every month you wait to enroll in Part D. You will have to pay this higher premium for as long as you have Medicare drug coverage.

If you have not applied for Social Security or railroad retirement benefits because you are planning to work beyond age sixty-five, or for any other reason, you must file a written Medicare application through your local SSA office when you decide to enroll. You must apply during one of three enrollment periods. Your **Initial Enrollment Period** begins three calendar months before the month of your sixty-fifth birthday, and extends three months beyond the month of your sixty-fifth birthday. You can enroll at any time during this seven-month period. If you delay enrollment beyond this initial period because you are in a group health plan, you may enroll during a **Special Enrollment Period** beginning on the first day of the month in which you are no longer in a group health plan. The Special Enrollment Period lasts for seven months after you are no longer enrolled in the group plan. If you do not enroll in Medicare during either of these periods, you can enroll during **General Enrollment Periods**, which run from January 1 to March 31 of each year. If you enroll during a General Enrollment Period, your Medicare coverage will become effective on July 1 of the year in which you enroll. However, you will pay a higher monthly premium if you delay enrollment beyond your Initial or Special Enrollment Period. Each year you delay results in a further increase in your premium.

Many people on Medicare continue to be covered by an employer's health insurance program, because either they or their spouses are still employed or otherwise eligible for employer coverage. In these cases, Medicare is the secondary payor of covered medical expenses *after* the other insurance pays out its benefits. To make sure you receive maximum coverage, talk to your employer's benefits office or your local SSA office.

The Claims Process: How Are Original Fee-for-Service Medicare Claims Filed and Paid?

For Part A benefits, providers submit claims directly to Medicare's **fiscal intermediary** (a private insurance company under contract for your geographic area). The provider will charge you for any deductible or coinsurance payment you owe.

For Part B claims, doctors, suppliers, and other providers are required to submit your Medicare claims to the Medicare **carrier** (an insurance company that may be the same or different than the fiscal intermediary to which Part A claims are submitted). Your doctor cannot legally ask you to sign any agreement waiving this filing obligation. A participating provider can charge you directly for any deductible or coinsurance. A nonparticipating provider can charge you for the entire bill, including amounts over the Medicare-approved amount, as long as the excess charge does not exceed the limit set by Medicare, as explained earlier in this chapter.

After your doctor or other Part B provider or supplier sends in a claim to Medicare, you will receive in the mail a **Medicare Summary Notice** telling you what Medicare is covering on the claim. This is an important notice, because it tells you:

- the name of the provider, type of service, date, and cost;
- the amount Medicare is paying;
- the amount for which you are responsible, including information about your annual deductible;
- whether your physician or other provider has accepted assignment; and
- how to appeal any aspect of the Medicare determination with which you disagree (the appeals process is explained on the back of the form).

For Part D, the claims process may vary depending on the type of prescription drug plan in which you enroll, whether you receive the prescription from a local network pharmacy or by mail order, and whether the medication is on the plan's formulary. However, you will probably have to pay the required deductible or co-payment at the pharmacy, and the pharmacy will then be paid by the plan.

If you belong to a Medicare-participating health maintenance organization (HMO), you usually will not have to file any claim forms, nor will you generally have to pay a deductible or co-payment for any covered services.

Potential Trouble Areas Under Medicare

This section describes a number of situations in which problems with Medicare coverage often arise. If you find yourself in one of these situations, and are unhappy with the coverage you receive, you should consider appealing Medicare's determination.

Early Discharge from the Hospital

You should never be discharged from a hospital because your hospital coverage under Medicare is running out. If you have a medical need for hospitalization, your coverage should continue, although your co-payment responsibilities will kick in after sixty days. If your stay is longer than normal or your treatment is especially complicated, the hospital may lose money on your particular stay. But in all cases, the decision to discharge should be based only on medical necessity and not on Medicare payment rules. Discuss any problems regarding your medical care with your doctor.

Discharge Before a Skilled Nursing Bed in the Area is Found

Medicare law provides for continued hospital care of a patient when no bed is available for that patient in an appropriate skilled nursing facility in the area. The main burden of locating a skilled nursing facility falls upon hospital discharge planners.

Denial of Skilled Nursing Facility Coverage

Most such denials are based on a determination by a nursing home that daily skilled care is not medically necessary. Sometimes, nursing homes interpret the term "skilled" too narrowly in classifying the services they provide. They may ignore Medicare rules that require your overall condition to be considered.

Early Terminations of Home Health Care

Often patients are told that there is a time limit on home health-care coverage. However, Medicare imposes no absolute time limit on such coverage. Instead, Medicare provides for home health-care coverage in cases where an eligible person needs skilled nursing or rehabilitation on a part-time basis (generally up to eight hours per day) or on an intermittent basis (generally less than seven days per week or, even if care is needed seven days a week, for a time-limited period).

The requirement that a patient be "homebound" in order to be eligible for home health-care coverage often creates coverage disputes. Note that you can still be considered "homebound" for purposes of Medicare coverage if you leave home, with assistance, for medical appointments or for other occasional purposes.

"No-Improvement" Denials

Physical, occupational, and speech therapy are sometimes improperly terminated when further medical improvement for a patient is no longer possible. But if skilled therapy is needed to prevent or delay further deterioration or to preserve current capabilities, the service should be covered.

 ## DEALS YOU CAN'T REFUSE: OFFERS OF "FREE" SERVICES OR EQUIPMENT

Be suspicious of anyone offering free screenings, testing, or medical equipment in exchange for your Medicare number, or anyone who promises that you will not have to pay the normal 20 percent coinsurance charge for Medicare coverage. These types of offers and promises may be signs of fraudulent operations. If you suspect fraud, call your Medicare carrier or intermediary (whose name and number will be on any Medicare Summary Notice form), or the Medicare hotline at 1-800-MEDICARE (1-800-633-4227).

DENIALS OF BENEFITS

As a Medicare beneficiary, you should closely observe the First Commandment of Medicare: *Never accept a denial of benefits without further questioning.* Unfair denials of Medicare benefits occur with surprising frequency. Medicare beneficiaries who appeal unfair denials have a substantial likelihood of success on appeal.

If You Disagree With Medicare . . . Appeal!

Remember, you have the right to appeal all decisions regarding coverage, services, or the amount Medicare will pay on a claim. Consider appealing even partial denials, especially if the basis of a denial is unclear. A substantial percentage of claims are successful on appeal. Even if an appeal is unsuccessful, the appeal may still help to clarify the reason you were denied benefits.

The starting point for any appeal is an initial determination from Medicare. *Never accept an oral notice of denial or termination of services.* You are not obliged to pay a bill until you receive proper written notice; ask your provider to furnish you with an official Medicare determination. If you request such a determination, the provider must file a claim with Medicare on your behalf. If you disagree with the determination, then you may appeal, provided the required minimum amounts of money are in dispute. (The process is somewhat different if you are enrolled with a Medicare managed-care organization.)

Unfortunately, if you need to appeal beyond the first stage of the appeals process, it may take many months to resolve your case. If you receive an unfavorable decision at any stage in the process, you have the option of appealing the decision, and thus advancing to the next stage of the process, within a specified time limit. If you wait too long to appeal, you may lose your rights. In 2005, the applicable regulations were changed to make the appeals process for Parts A and B more consistent. For most steps in the appeals process, you have sixty days from the date of receiving a notice to submit your appeal request. Always put your appeal request in writing. To ask for Part B reviews and hearings by the carrier (i.e., the insurance company, not the Social Security Administration), you have 120 days. Hospital decisions should be appealed immediately if you want to remain in the hospital, since time is of the essence.

Pursuing an appeal takes some patience and persistence, but it often pays off. Many people handle Medicare appeals on their own. Getting the provider to submit additional information often results in approval of a claim. However, each step in the appeals process gets more complicated. You will be in a stronger position if you have representation by or help from an attorney, trained paralegal, SHIP counselor, benefits specialist, or trained outreach worker. See Chapter 15, "Finding Legal Help," for suggestions on finding legal assistance. Appeal forms can be obtained and downloaded from the CMS website at *www.medicare .gov/Basics/forms/default.asp*.

Appeals of Hospital Denials Based on Issues of Medical Necessity or Appropriateness

Decisions regarding hospital coverage are normally made by **Quality Improvement Organizations (QIOs)**, organizations that employ doctors and other health-care professionals to review care given to Medicare patients. QIOs are obligated to review complaints about the quality of care given by inpatient hospitals, hospital outpatient departments, hospital emergency rooms, skilled nursing facilities, home health agencies, Medicare Private Fee-for-Service Plans, and ambulatory surgical centers.

When you are admitted to the hospital, you should receive a notice entitled *An Important Message From Medicare: Your Rights While You Are A Medicare Hospital Patient*, which explains the role of QIOs and describes your appeal rights. When hospital coverage is being terminated, you should ask for a written **notice of noncoverage** if you disagree with the decision to terminate coverage. This notice will explain how to appeal.

If you wish to appeal a hospital's denial of care, take the following steps:

1. Immediately request a review of the decision by calling the appropriate QIO. A toll-free number should be listed on the notice of noncoverage, or call 1-800-MEDICARE for the QIO's telephone number. If you request a review by noon of the day after you received the notice of discharge, then you will normally receive a decision by the close of business on the following day. If you appeal within this time limit, the hospital cannot charge you for any inpatient services rendered before noon of the day after you receive the QIO's decision.

2. To appeal an adverse decision by the QIO, you must request a reconsideration by the QIO.

3. To appeal an adverse QIO reconsideration decision, in cases where at least $200 in benefits is in dispute, you must request a hearing. Hearings are conducted by independent Administrative Law Judges (ALJs) through the Department of Health and Human Services (DHHS).

4. To appeal an adverse ALJ decision, you must request a review by the Medicare Appeals Council (MAC) of the DHHS.

5. To appeal a MAC decision, you must file for judicial review in a U.S. district court. (The amount in dispute must be at least $2,000.)

Appeals of Decisions Terminating Nursing Home, Home Health Agency, and Hospice Care

Before terminating your care, a provider must give you a written notice of noncoverage explaining why he or she believes that Medicare will no longer cover the desired service as of a certain date. This is not an official Medicare determination. If you would like to challenge the termination and to continue receiving care, you need to request a review by the appropriate QIO no later than noon of the day before the service will end. (You cannot appeal the termination if you discontinue services.) The provider must then provide to the beneficiary and the QIO a detailed notice indicating why it thinks Medicare will no longer cover the service. The QIO should make its decision within 72 hours of your request for QIO review. If the QIO decision is adverse, you can be billed for services rendered after the challenged termination or discharge date.

If you want to appeal, take the following steps:

1. Request a redetermination to be filed with, reviewed, and decided by the Medicare contractor (fiscal intermediary). No minimum claim amount is required. The request must be filed within 120 days of receipt of the initial determination.

2. To appeal an adverse reconsideration decision, request a reconsideration determination to be filed with and reviewed by a Qualified Independent Contractor (QIC). No minimum claim amount is required. The request must be filed within 180 days of your receipt of the redetermination notice.

3. To appeal an adverse QIC decision, request a hearing within sixty days. As of 2006, the amount in dispute must be at least $110. (The required minimum amount will increase annually.) Hearings are conducted by independent Administrative Law Judges (ALJs).

4. To appeal an adverse ALJ decision, request a review by the Medicare Appeals Council (MAC) of the DHHS within sixty days. No minimum claim amount is required.

5. To appeal an adverse MAC decision, file for judicial review in a U.S. district court within sixty days. The amount in dispute must be at least $1,090 as of 2006. (The required minimum amount will increase annually.)

Appeals of Decisions Regarding Physician Services or Other Part B Services and Supplies

Part B providers must file claim forms for you. After the provider files a claim, you will receive a Medicare Summary Notice in the mail from the carrier (i.e., the insurance company handling the claim for Medicare). The form will explain what Medicare is covering, the amount of coverage, and your appeal rights.

If you want to appeal decisions regarding physician services or other Part B services and supplies, you need to take the following steps:

1. Request a redetermination by the Medicare contractor within 120 days.

2. To appeal an adverse redetermination decision, request a reconsideration by a Qualified Independent Contractor (QIC) within 180 days.

3. To appeal an adverse QIC decision, request a hearing by an independent Administrative Law Judge (ALJ) through the DHHS within sixty days. As of 2006, the amount in dispute must be at least $110. This amount will increase yearly.

4. To appeal an adverse ALJ decision, request a review by the Medicare Appeals Council (MAC) of the DHHS within sixty days.

5. To appeal an adverse MAC decision, file for judicial review in a U.S. district court within sixty days. As of 2006, the amount in dispute must be at least $1,090 in benefits. This amount will increase annually.

Appeals of Decisions Made by Managed-Care Organizations

If you have Medicare coverage through a Medicare Advantage Plan, such as a health maintenance organization (HMO) or other managed-care organization, your health plan will usually make all decisions about services and coverage. If your doctor states that a decision is one that jeopardizes your health or ability to regain maximum function, the appeals process must be expedited, generally within seventy-two hours.

If you want to appeal decisions made by a Medicare Advantage Plan (MA plan), you need to take the following steps:

1. Request a reconsideration by the MA plan.

2. If the MA plan does not fully rule in your favor, it must submit your reconsideration request to a review contractor with the Center for Medicare & Medicaid Services (CMS). The contractor, an independent entity, must review the case and provide you with written notice of its decision.

3. To appeal an adverse contractor decision, request a hearing before an independent Administrative Law Judge (ALJ) through the DHHS within sixty days. As of 2006, the amount of benefits in dispute must be at least $110. This amount will increase annually.

4. To appeal an adverse ALJ decision, request a review by the Medicare Appeals Council (MAC) within sixty days.

5. To appeal an adverse MAC decision, file for judicial review in a U.S. district court within sixty days. As of 2006, the amount of benefits in dispute must be at least $1,090. This amount will increase annually.

Appeals of Part D Decisions Made by Prescription Drug Plans

If you have Medicare drug coverage through a prescription drug plan (PDP), your PDP will make decisions about which drugs are on its formulary and what it will cover. Each plan must have a special process for handling an **exception request**—that is, a request to cover a non-formulary drug or to reduce a beneficiary's costs. In addition, each plan must have an appeals process in place if it denies payment for a prescribed drug.

If you want to file an exception request or appeal a denial of drug coverage, take the following steps:

1. Contact your plan to make the request. You will need an oral or written statement from your doctor attesting to your need for the particular drug. The PDP must respond to your request within seventy-two hours. You can request that the decision be expedited if your life, health, or ability to regain maximum function is in jeopardy. If your request for an expedited appeal is granted, the PDP will generally make its decision within twenty-four hours.

2. If the plan denies your exception request, you can request a redetermination of the decision within sixty days. The PDP must issue its decision within seven days, or within seventy-two hours if you request and are granted an expedited appeal.

3. If the plan denies coverage of the drug after a redetermination, you can request a review by an independent contractor, called the Independent Review Entity (IRE), within sixty days. The IRE must make its decision with seven days, or within seventy-two hours if you request and are granted an expedited appeal.

4. To appeal an adverse decision from the IRE, you can request a hearing before an independent Administrative Law

Judge (ALJ) through the DHHS within sixty days. As of 2005, the amount in dispute must be at least $100 in benefits. This amount will increase annually.

5. To appeal an adverse decision from the ALJ, you can request a review by the Medicare Appeals Council (MAC) of the DHHS within sixty days.

6. If you disagree with the MAC's decision, you can file for judicial review in a U.S. district court. As of 2005, the amount in dispute must be at least $1050 in benefits. This amount will increase annually.

RETIREE GROUP HEALTH BENEFITS

Your employee benefit package may include a promise to provide health benefits to you after you retire. These benefits can be particularly important to you if you retire before age sixty-five, because until you turn sixty-five you will not be eligible for Medicare. Even if you are over sixty-five, an employer-provided benefit package might save you a lot on health-care costs by supplementing your Medicare coverage.

Unfortunately, many employers have reduced or even eliminated the provision of health benefits to employees who have retired, or they have increased the retirees' share of the cost of such benefits. Employers have the right to make these cutbacks if their health plans give them authority to change or discontinue benefits. Health benefits do not vest as pension benefits do; this means that unless your employer has made an unqualified contract with its employees, you may lose your benefits.

Health Benefits When You Lose Your Job

If you are laid off, terminated, or are leaving your job, but are not retiring, you and your dependents may be eligible to continue your group plan benefits under a federal law called the Consolidated Omnibus Budget Reconciliation Act, usually known as **COBRA**. These benefits are available for a limited period of time (usually eighteen months, but up to twenty-nine months for a person determined to be disabled under the Social Security Act), and you—not the employer—must pay the premiums. The cost of coverage under COBRA will be the same as the cost of coverage under your group plan, which is usually much lower than the cost of individual health insurance. COBRA provisions are complex; be sure to get information from your employer or your health plan, or from an attorney who is knowledgeable about the law in this area.

If you leave your job and then obtain a new one, you may benefit from a federal law designed to make benefits more portable. In the past, insurers could delay providing coverage for **preexisting conditions**—that is, conditions for which medical advice was sought or treatment was recommended during the six months before your enrollment date. These delays in coverage acted as a disincentive to changing jobs and insurance plans. However, the law now requires that, if you have a preexisting condition, the waiting period for coverage can be no longer than twelve months. Moreover, this exclusion period must be reduced by the amount of time for which you had coverage under another health plan, as long as there has been no gap in employer or COBRA coverage of sixty-three days or longer. Thus, for many job changes, your prior coverage may totally eliminate any waiting periods.

MEDIGAP INSURANCE

Medicare provides basic health-care coverage, but leaves gaps in coverage for many beneficiaries. Most older persons need to purchase a supplemental (or **Medigap**) insurance policy to cover some of the costs not covered by Medicare. These policies do *not* cover long-term care. Long-term-care insurance is discussed in the next chapter. Except in Massachusetts, Minnesota, and Wisconsin, a Medigap policy must be one of twelve standardized policies that can easily be compared. Medigap policies must also comply with federal and state laws. For instance, the front of a Medigap policy must clearly identify the policy as "Medicare Supplement Insurance."

While most people need Medigap coverage, you may already have enough coverage without Medigap if you fall into one of four categories:

1. If you are already covered by Medicaid, you do not need a Medigap policy. Medicaid covers the gaps in Medicare and more.

2. If you are not eligible for Medicaid, but your income is low and you have limited resources, you may be eligible for help in paying Medicare costs under the Medicare Savings Programs (MSP). Under MSP, the state may pay your Medicare Part B premiums and could provide supplemental coverage equivalent to a Medigap policy if your income and assets fall below a qualification amount. You must qualify for or buy into Medicare Part A in order to take part in these programs. To apply, contact the local office of your state Medicaid program.

3. If you have retiree health coverage through a former employer or union, you may not need Medigap insurance; often such coverage is comprehensive and has a provision detailing how it coordinates with Medicare. But this coverage may not provide the same benefits as Medigap insurance, and may not have to meet the federal and state rules that apply to Medigap. Examine the benefits, costs, and stability of your coverage to determine whether it is a better option than Medigap.

4. If you belong to a managed-care organization, like an HMO or PPO, you probably do not need a Medigap policy, since HMO and PPO coverage is normally comprehensive. But do not be too quick to give up your Medigap coverage if you are new to a Medicare Advantage Plan (such as an HMO or PPO). If you can afford it, keep your Medigap policy long enough to be sure you are satisfied with the Medicare Advantage Plan. If you become dissatisfied with the plan, you have the right to disenroll from it at any time. But if you have already given up your Medigap coverage, you may not be able to resume coverage—at least not at the same price. Special rules may guarantee your right to the same Medigap policy you previously had under certain

circumstances. Contact a local SHIP counselor for more information about coverage in your state.

Shop for a Good Medigap Policy

Medigap insurers may only sell standardized Medigap benefit plans. There are twelve possible standardized plans, identified as Plans A through L. Plan A is a core package and is available in all states. The other eleven plans have different combinations of benefits. Check with your state department of insurance for additional information. Many states and local SHIPs can provide buyers' guides with more information.

You are only allowed to have one Medigap policy at any time. Multiple policies would generally provide overlapping coverage for which you would pay twice but from which you would benefit only once. In evaluating policies, you should decide which features would best meet your health needs and financial situation. When you compare policies of the same type (i.e., Plans A through L), remember that benefits are identical for plans of the same type. For example, all type-G plans provide essentially the same benefits. However, the premiums and potential for premium increases may differ greatly.

Companies commonly use one of three methods for setting Medigap premiums. Many set the premium based on your **issue age**—that is, your age on the date on which you buy the policy. For example, if you buy the policy at age sixty-five, you will always pay the premium that a sixty-five-year-old pays. However, if the rate for all sixty-five-year-olds increases, your own premium rate will also increase. Other companies set premiums according to your **attained age**, meaning your current age. These premiums increase automatically each year. These policies may appear cheaper initially, but they could cost much more later on. Finally, a few companies charge one standard premium for all policyholders, regardless of age. These policies might be a better deal if you apply for Medigap at an older age. The best way to compare premium costs is to project the likely cost of the policy over several years.

When to Acquire Medigap Coverage

Unless you qualify for Medicare Savings Programs, it is in your best interest to buy a Medigap policy at or near the time your Medicare coverage begins. The reason is that, during the first six months that you are sixty-five or older *and* enrolled in Medicare Part B, insurance companies must sell you any Medigap policy you select, regardless of any health conditions you have. Moreover, they cannot charge you more than they charge others of the same age, or place any conditions on your policy. After this one-time period elapses, you may be forced to pay much higher premiums for the same policy due to your health status. During this open enrollment period, companies may still exclude preexisting conditions during the first six months of coverage under the policy.

Different enrollment rules apply to persons under sixty-five who are eligible for Medicare because of disability.

Beware Of Illegal Sales Practices

Both federal and state laws govern the sale of Medigap insurance. These laws prohibit high-pressure sales tactics, fraudulent or misleading statements about coverage or cost, sale of a policy that is not one of the approved standard policies, or imposition of new waiting periods for replacement policies. If a sales agent offers you a policy that duplicates coverage of your existing pol-

 WHAT IF I HAVE AN "OLD" MEDIGAP POLICY?

If you have a Medigap policy that predates the standardized plans (i.e., a pre-1992 policy), you may not need to switch policies, especially if you are satisfied with your existing policy. Some states have special regulations allowing beneficiaries to convert older policies to a standard Medigap plan. Check with your state insurance department or health insurance counseling service for details.

icy, the duplication must be disclosed to you in writing. If you feel you have been misled or pressured to buy a policy, contact your state insurance department, your State Health Insurance Assistance Program (SHIP), or the federal Medicare hotline at 1-800-MEDICARE (1-800-633-4227); TTY users should call 1-877-486-2048.

THE WORLD AT YOUR FINGERTIPS

• Any Social Security Administration (SSA) office can answer most questions about Medicare enrollment, coverage, and premiums, or help you replace a lost Medicare card. Social Security offices also carry informational publications produced by the Centers for Medicare & Medicaid Services (CMS).

• CMS can also provide a great deal of information about the Medicare and Medicaid programs. You can access the website at *www.cms.hhs.gov.*

• *Making Medicare Choices, Your Medicare Rights,* and *Selecting Medicare Supplemental Insurance* are informational documents available through AARP's Educated Health Care Choices website at *www.aarp.org/hcchoices.*

• Every state, plus Puerto Rico, the Virgin Islands, and the District of Columbia, has a health insurance assistance program that can provide you with free information about and assistance with Medicare, Medicaid, Medigap, and other health insurance benefits. To find the program in your state, visit *www.medicare .gov,* or call 1-800-MEDICARE, your local agency on aging, your state insurance division, or your Social Security office.

REMEMBER THIS

• Medicare primarily consists of three main parts. The hospital insurance part, or Part A, covers medically necessary care in hospitals and other facilities—such as care at a skilled nursing facility or psychiatric hospital, home health care, or hospice care.

Part B, the medical-insurance part, covers medically necessary physician's services and a variety of other services and supplies not covered by Part A. Part D, the prescription drug benefit, covers outpatient generic and brand-name medications.

• Everyone who is turning sixty-five and applying for Social Security or railroad retirement benefits is automatically enrolled in Medicare Parts A and B.

• Enrollment in Part D is different from enrollment in Parts A and B. It is not automatic—you must enroll. In addition, you must pay a separate monthly premium directly to the plan.

• If you disagree with a Medicare decision, appeal. Many appeals are successful.

CHAPTER 9

Medicaid and Long-Term-Care Insurance

Everything You Need to Know About Eligibility, Coverage, and Appeals

Hilary and Don lived fairly comfortably in rural Connecticut on their retirement income, which consisted of income from Social Security, Don's union pension, and some investments. But when Don suffered a debilitating stroke and needed long-term nursing home care, the monthly cost of the nursing home (more than $6,000) threatened to ruin them financially. Their son Ron insisted that they look into getting help from Medicaid, but Hilary thought that Medicaid was only for people on welfare. They discovered that Medicaid could be a lifesaver for them, but that it is a very complicated program.

Medicaid is a medical-assistance program for a broad population of Americans, including older or disabled persons, pregnant women, children, and parents with income below their states' welfare eligibility levels. More than 52 million Americans received Medicaid services in 2005. Unlike Medicare, which offers the same benefits to all enrollees regardless of income, Medicaid is jointly funded by both the federal and state governments, but is managed by individual states. This means that the benefits and eligibility rules vary from state to state.

Medicaid benefits many middle-income individuals, like Hilary and Don in the example above, who are faced with the devastating costs of long-term care. However, the rules for eligibility and coverage are complex, varying from state to state, and the operation of the program is often bureaucratic and frustrating.

This chapter provides a general overview of Medicaid as it applies to older persons, including its special rules of coverage for nursing home care. It then explains the option of purchasing private insurance to pay for long-term care.

MEDICAID: GOOD NEWS AND BAD NEWS

No other program pays for as broad a range of benefits as Medicaid. And once you are eligible, Medicaid requires no premiums or deductibles like Medicare (although a nominal co-payment can be required for some benefits). Moreover, doctors or other providers cannot charge you additional fees beyond the Medicaid reimbursement amount. The nursing home benefit is especially valuable, because Medicaid is the only program that covers significant amounts of nursing home care. Private long-term-care insurance is also emerging as an important resource for older Americans, but compared with Medicaid, it is still a small player in the system.

Despite its many benefits, however, Medicaid also has tremendous disadvantages. For one thing, you must be virtually impoverished before you can qualify for Medicaid. Those who become eligible after "spending down" their income or assets may discover that little is left over. And once you are eligible,

 TALKING TO A LAWYER

Q. If Medicaid is paying for my health care, do I have to pay any deductibles, co-payments, or additional fees?

A. Generally, Medicaid requires no deductibles, co-payments, or additional fees, nor does it impose dollar caps or limits on the amount of coverage. Exceptions apply in the case of certain waiver programs, such as assisted living.

—Answer by Thomas D. Begley, Jr.,
Begley & Bookbinder, PC, Moorestown, NJ

THE MEDICARE-MEDICAID CONNECTION

You may receive both Medicare and Medicaid coverage. And even if you do not qualify for Medicaid, if your income and assets are still fairly low, the Medicaid program may still help you pay for all or part of your Medicare expenses (specifically the premiums, deductibles, and co-payments) if you meet the more-liberal income and resource tests under the Medicare Savings Programs. There are three slightly different versions of this program: the **Qualified Medicare Beneficiary (QMB) Program**, the **Specified Low-Income Medicare Beneficiary (SLMB) Program**, and the **Qualifying Individual (QI) Program**. Chapter 8 contains more information about these programs. More information is also available at *www.cms.gov*.

finding a doctor who participates in Medicaid may not be easy. Finding a nursing home bed for a Medicaid patient may also be tough. Medicaid beneficiaries may have fewer choices and less flexibility in meeting their health-care needs than do persons with private insurance. Finally, since late 1993, Congress has required states to seek reimbursement of Medicaid payments for nursing home costs from the estates of deceased Medicaid beneficiaries.

Applying for Medicaid

Before applying for Medicaid, consult with someone who has expertise in Medicaid-related issues. Then contact your state or local Medicaid agency. The name of the applicable agency will vary from place to place; it may be called the Department of Social Services, Public Aid, Public Welfare, Human Services, or something similar. You can also call your local agency on aging or senior center for more information.

When you apply for Medicaid, you will need to document your financial circumstances in detail, as well as your residency.

SEEK THE ADVICE OF SOMEONE EXPERIENCED WITH MEDICAID

Medicaid rules in general, and especially those that apply to long-term-care coverage, are as complicated as the tax code. Before applying for benefits, or as soon as possible after you apply, seek advice from someone with expertise in Medicaid—such as a private attorney experienced in handling Medicaid issues, a legal-services lawyer, or a benefits counselor at a senior center or health insurance counseling office. Such experts can help steer you through some of the rocks and shoals of the planning and application process.

The application form can be complex, but your local Medicaid agency can help you complete it. If you are homebound, a Medicaid worker can come to your home to help you apply for benefits, but you may have to be patient and persistent to procure this type of help. If you are in a hospital or other institution, a staff social worker can help you apply. Since the start of benefits is linked to your date of application, you should apply and establish an application date as soon as you believe that you qualify for Medicaid assistance. (In certain instances, coverage may be retroactive for up to three months before your month of application.) Almost any written request with your signature is enough to establish your application date, even if you have not yet completed the full application form.

What Medicaid Covers

Federal law mandates that Medicaid provide certain benefits, including coverage for:
- inpatient and outpatient hospital services;
- doctors' and nurse practitioners' services;
- nursing home care;
- rural health clinic services;

- home health-care services;
- laboratory and X-ray charges; and
- transportation to and from health-care providers.

Other services and benefits for which states *may* provide coverage include: private-duty nursing; services from podiatrists, optometrists, and chiropractors; mental-health services; personal care provided in the home; dental care; physical therapy and other rehabilitation; dentures; eyeglasses; and more. At one time, most states also covered prescription drugs, but beginning in January 2006, major changes to the Medicare program transferred most prescription drug coverage for Medicaid beneficiaries to the new Medicare Part D program. (See Chapter 8, "Medicare and Private Health Benefits," for more information.) You may receive covered services only from Medicaid-participating providers, who are generally private health-care providers or facilities that choose to participate in the Medicaid program, or who are part of a managed-care system that contracts with the state to provide Medicaid services.

Most states also have more than one type of **waiver program** that provides narrowly defined populations with specific

 HOW MEDICAID PAYS

Most commonly, Medicaid providers bill Medicaid directly. The state Medicaid program then reimburses providers. Alternatively, some states pay managed-care organizations a negotiated, fixed rate to cover all Medicaid patients. In either case, providers cannot charge you additional amounts for covered services unless the state program requires a nominal co-payment for the services. Medicaid will not reimburse you for charges you paid, but if you happen to be in a situation where Medicaid covers an expense after you already paid out-of-pocket, the provider of services should repay you.

services that would not normally be covered by Medicaid. These services may include home support services, care coordination, or other home- and community-based services.

WHO IS ELIGIBLE FOR MEDICAID?

Medicaid programs in each state have different eligibility standards. All states require that, in order to be eligible, adults without dependent children must:

- be at least sixty-five, or blind, or disabled; AND
- meet income and asset tests.

Because of the variability and complexity of Medicaid, it is important to be aware that one can be eligible for Medicaid in one state and not in another.

Income Test

For purposes of determining Medicaid eligibility, income limits for older persons or persons with a disability are linked to the federal Supplemental Security Income (SSI) program. In most states, persons eligible for SSI are automatically covered by Medicaid. These persons are referred to as **categorically needy individuals**. Most states also cover some people whose income falls below a certain level after they "spend down" a portion of their income on medical bills. These persons are referred to as **medically needy individuals**. Finally, some states set the income cap for eligibility for certain benefits—specifically nursing home care—at three times the maximum SSI benefit for a single individual. This cap changes yearly, since the SSI maximum benefit is adjusted yearly for inflation. (For example, the SSI maximum payment for 2006 is $603 per month. Thus, in 2006 the income cap was $1,809 in these states.) An individual who is even one dollar over the income cap is ineligible, no matter how high his or her medical bills. However, eligibility in these states can be achieved through the use of a very specific type of Medicaid-

SPEND-DOWN

Spend-down is a term used in the context of Medicaid to refer to the amount by which an individual's income or assets exceeds special Medicaid eligibility levels set by the state. When the excess income or assets are not sufficient to cover the individual's medical expenses, the individual may become eligible for benefits by making use of Medicaid's spend-down provision.

Here is how spend-down works: To be eligible for Medicaid each month, a person's medical expenses in that month must equal his spend-down. Once medical expenses equal spend-down, then Medicaid coverage is available to that person for the remainder of the month. For example, if a person's medical expenses equal his spend-down on the tenth day of the month, then from the tenth day of the month forward, he or she will receive Medicaid coverage.

When Medicaid coverage is approved, the individual will receive a notice indicating his or her spend-down amount. This amount is determined through a formula set by Medicaid. The formula subtracts the person's income and/or assets from the maximum amount of income and assets allowed under the law.

Source: *A Guide to Medicaid and Medicaid Waivers*, by the Arc of Indiana, available online at *www.arcind.org/guide_to_medicaid_and_medicaid_w.htm*.

approved trust—sometimes called a **Miller trust**—that is discussed later in this chapter.

Resource Test

Medicaid also imposes an asset (or resource) test to determine eligibility for benefits. In most states, you are only eligible for Medicaid if you have less than $2,000 in assets; a married

THE INCOME CAP STATES

The twenty states listed below are income cap states, meaning that only individuals with gross incomes below a certain maximum amount (or cap) are eligible for nursing home coverage in these states. As of 2006, the income cap was $1,809 per month. (States may set their own caps, but most use this figure.) All other states recognize medically needy eligibility, in which an individual's actual medical costs are deducted from his or her income when calculating eligibility.

Alabama	Mississippi
Alaska	Nevada
Arizona*	New Jersey**
Arkansas*	New Mexico
Colorado	Oklahoma*
Delaware	Oregon*
Florida*	South Carolina
Idaho	South Dakota
Iowa*	Texas*
Louisiana*	Wyoming

*Technically these eight states are not income cap states, but functionally they operate that way with respect to nursing home coverage of the elderly.
**New Jersey employs the principle of medically needy eligibility with respect to nursing home coverage, but utilizes an income cap to determine eligibility for assisted-living and certain home care programs.

couple is only eligible if they have less than $3,000 in total assets. These amounts may be slightly higher in some states. As with SSI, not all resources are counted under the resource test. The resources *not* counted include:

• your home, as long as you live in it, or expect to return to it, or as long as your spouse lives in it. However, as of 2006, a limit to this exemption began—only $500,000 of one's home equity can be exempt (up to $750,000 at the state's option). Equity in

excess of the limit is counted as a resource. But, if a spouse, minor or disabled child lives in the home, the equity cap does not apply.

- most household goods and personal effects, including your wedding ring;
- an automobile;
- the cash value of life insurance, *if* the face value of all the policies you own is $1,500 or less (if the face value is higher, the cash value is counted as an asset);
- trade or business property needed for self-support (e.g., tools and machinery);
- the value of burial plots for you or your immediate family;
- up to $1,500 per person in a burial expense fund for you and your spouse (i.e., any account earmarked for burial expenses); and
- money or property you have set aside under a plan to become self-supporting, if you are disabled or blind.

Special income and asset rules apply to persons who need help paying nursing home bills. These rules are described briefly below in the sections covering long-term care.

 IMMIGRANT RESTRICTIONS

Federal laws passed in 1996 barred almost all current and future immigrants who had not become citizens from receiving most federal- and some state-funded services and benefits designed to assist low-income persons (including Supplemental Security Income, Medicaid, State Children's Health Insurance Programs, and food stamps). In 1997, Congress reinstated eligibility for SSI and Medicaid for most legal immigrants residing in the United States as of August 22, 1996. Legal immigrants arriving after August 22, 1996, are barred from receiving benefits unless they meet very strict guidelines. The immigrant restrictions are complex, vary according to a person's immigration category and the benefits or services in question, and are subject to change.

If you Disagree with Medicaid . . . Appeal!

You have the right to appeal all decisions that affect your Medicaid eligibility or services. You should receive prompt written notice of any decision about your Medicaid coverage. Any such notice will include an explanation of how you can appeal. The appeals process differs slightly from state to state, but always includes the right to a fair hearing before a hearing officer. You do not need legal representation in order to appeal, but it is a good idea to get help from a public-benefits specialist or a lawyer experienced in Medicaid law.

MEDICAID COVERAGE OF LONG-TERM CARE

Medicaid pays almost half of the nation's nursing home expenses, but only for those who are virtually broke. Because the average cost of a private room in a nursing home now tops $70,000 a year, or $192 a day (according to a 2004 MetLife Market Survey), it is easy to become penniless fast. Medicaid will cover nursing home expenses if your condition requires nursing home care,

---

 ## LIFETIME CHANCES OF BEING IN A NURSING HOME (IF YOU ARE NOW 65 YEARS OLD)

Length of Stay	Men	Women
Never Enter	67%	48%
Less than 12 months	19%	21%
1 to 5 years	10%	18%
More than 5 years	4%	13%

Source: *New England Journal of Medicine*, article by P. Kemper and C. Murtaugh, February 1991.

AN EXAMPLE OF THE HIGH COST OF NURSING HOME CARE

Mrs. Smith, a widow, enters a nursing home. She has an income of $1,500 per month and $50,000 in savings. The nursing home private-pay rate in this facility is $5,000 per month. To cover this cost, Mrs. Smith will spend all her monthly income ($1,500), plus an additional $3,500 per month from her savings. At this rate, her $50,000 in savings will be depleted down to the Medicaid asset level ($2,000) in just over a year. It will happen even faster if she has other monthly expenses—as is very likely—for clothing, personal care needs, and so forth. Many persons who are not eligible for Medicaid become eligible, like Mrs. Smith, after spending some period of time in a nursing home.

the home is certified by the state Medicaid agency, and you meet income and resource eligibility requirements.

Other federal programs pay very little for nursing home care. Medicare coverage is narrowly defined and limited to twenty days of full coverage and a maximum of eighty additional days with a large daily co-payment. The Department of Veterans Affairs (VA) pays for some nursing home care for veterans, but the benefit is limited to available resources and facilities. Priority is given to veterans with medical problems related to their military service (service-connected disabilities), very old veterans of wartime service, and very poor veterans. Contact your local VA office for more information.

HOME AND COMMUNITY-BASED SERVICES

Medicaid in your state may cover a variety of home and community-based services, including home health, home-maker, home health aide, and personal-care services. (**Personal-care services** are services that assist individuals with normal activities of daily living, such as dressing, bathing, toileting, eating, and walking.)

Many states also have instituted Medicaid **waiver programs** that allow the states to use Medicaid dollars for home and community-based services that normally would not be covered under Medicaid. These programs usually target persons who might otherwise have to live in nursing homes. Covered services may include personal care, adult day care, housekeeping services, care management, chore and companion services, and respite care that provides caregivers with a break from their responsibilities. Because these waiver programs have limited funding and limited enrollment, many of them can be joined only through waiting lists. Check with your local office on aging or department of human services about the options available in your state.

SPECIAL LONG-TERM-CARE RULES FOR SPOUSES

If your spouse resides in or will be entering a nursing home, Medicaid has special rules that allow the **community spouse** (the spouse remaining outside the nursing home) to keep more income and assets than would be permitted under regular Medicaid eligibility rules. The specifics vary from state to state, but this section sets forth the general structure of these rules.

Income Rules

The community spouse can keep all income that belongs exclusively to him or her, no matter how large the amount. However, joint income is treated differently. The state will require part, and possibly all, of the couple's joint income to help pay nursing home expenses.

Most of the income of the nursing home spouse is considered available to pay for nursing home care. However, part of the nursing home spouse's income may be paid to the community spouse as an allowance for minimum monthly maintenance needs, if the community spouse's income is below the maintenance amount set by the state. Just enough monthly income—or sometimes assets—is taken from the nursing home spouse to increase the income of the community spouse to an amount set by the individual state. The amount must be equal to at least 150 percent of the poverty level for a two-person household, but no higher than a cap set by federal law. (In 2006, the *minimum* spousal allowance was $1,603.75 per month, with the *maximum* set at $2,488.50. The amounts are higher in Alaska and Hawaii.) If the amount of the state's allowance is less than the federal maximum, it may be increased to cover shelter costs (rent, mortgage, taxes, insurance, and utilities) that exceed a specified amount set by the federal government. Additional allowances are made for dependent children.

Resource Rules

Resources are treated quite differently from income. The state applies a two-step rule. First, it takes an inventory of all resources owned individually by *either* spouse or owned jointly. At the option of the couple, this inventory of resources takes place either when you enter a nursing home or when you apply for Medicaid. This inventory will not include the list of excluded resources (e.g., your home, household goods, and so forth, as listed earlier in this chapter).

From the total countable resources inventoried by the state, Medicaid permits the community spouse to keep a resource allowance. The amount of the allowance varies by state, but must be within a range set by the federal government and adjusted annually. In 2006, states could set the spousal resource allowance as high as $99,540. If the amount of the state allowance is less than the maximum amount allowed by federal law, then the spouse is normally entitled to keep one-half the couple's total countable resources, up to a maximum of $99,540 but not less than $19,908 (for 2006). States and the courts have the authority to increase the spousal allowance in individual cases if the spouse's financial circumstances require.

AN EXAMPLE OF SPOUSAL INCOME RULES FOR NURSING HOME CARE

John and Mary are married. John enters a nursing home. The couple own their house and have savings totaling $120,000. John's income is $1,500 per month. Mary's is $1,000 per month. The house does not affect Medicaid eligibility, since Mary lives in it.

Resource allowance: If the state uses the maximum permissible resource allowance of $99,540, then Mary's resource allowance will be $99,540. But suppose the state opted to use a lower resource allowance—for example, $50,000. In that case, Mary would be permitted to keep one-half of the couple's assets, or $60,000 (half of their $120,000 savings), since this amount is greater than the amount of the state allowance.

Monthly income allowance: Suppose the state's monthly spousal allowance is the minimum permitted under federal law ($1,603.75 in 2006). This means that Mary will be entitled to $603.75 per month of John's income, which is the amount required to increase her $1,000 monthly income to the amount of the minimum monthly allowance. Depending on her housing costs, Mary might be entitled to some additional allowance from John for excess shelter expenses. If the state's monthly spousal allowance were the maximum permitted under federal law ($2,488.50 in 2006), then Mary would be entitled to $1,488.50 to supplement her $1,000 monthly income. John and Mary would benefit from legal help to preserve more of their assets for the benefit of Mary.

THE ROLE OF CHILDREN

Children have no legal obligation to pay for their parents' care, though they often feel a moral or personal obligation to help pay for nursing home expenses. In some states, a shortage of Medicaid-eligible nursing home beds puts additional pressure on children to assist parents financially in entering a nursing home. Many nursing homes give admission preference to **private-pay patients** over Medicaid patients, because private-pay rates are usually much higher than the rates paid by Medicaid. Giving priority to private-pay patients is permissible in some states, but illegal in others.

In all states, federal law prohibits nursing homes from *requiring* private payments from families of a resident, or requiring a period of private payment prior to applying for Medicaid coverage. This includes a prohibition on asking for deposits from beneficiaries who have applied for Medicaid but are not yet receiving it at the time of admission. Nursing homes cannot obligate an adult child or other third party to guarantee to pay the nursing home's charges. The child's obligation extends only as far as his or her authority over the parents' assets. For example, a child who is an agent under a parent's durable power of attorney may be obligated *as agent* to pay the nursing home bill out of the parent's assets, but not out of his or her own personal assets. Federal law also prohibits nursing homes from requiring patients to waive or even delay their right to apply for Medicare and/or Medicaid.

MEDICAID ESTATE RECOVERY: PAYING BACK THE COST OF CARE

After a Medicaid beneficiary dies, federal law requires states to seek recovery of some medical costs from his or her estate. Specifically, states are required to seek recovery of the costs of nursing facility care, home and community-based services, and related hospital and prescription drug services provided to individuals who were fifty-five or over when they received Medicaid. Home and community-based services include homemaker services, home health aide services, personal-care services, adult day care, respite care, and case management. In addition to seeking recovery for these services, states have the option of recovering the cost of any other Medicaid benefits received by a person fifty-five or older. The estates of persons under age fifty-five who are permanent residents of nursing homes may also be subject to recovery under Medicaid.

No recovery can occur from the estate of a Medicaid beneficiary until after his or her death and the death of his or her spouse. Moreover, no recovery can occur from the deceased's estate if he or she has a child under the age of twenty-one, or a child who is blind, or a child who is permanently and totally disabled.

For purposes of Medicaid recovery, what constitutes an estate? At a minimum, the term **estate** refers to your probate estate—that is, the property that passes to others under your will or under the laws of succession in the absence of a will. Property that passes by joint ownership, insurance contract, life estate, or trust usually stands outside your probate estate. However, states are permitted to adopt an expanded definition of "estate" to include this non-probate property and any other property in which you have any legal title or interest.

Every state must establish a procedure for providing adequate information about estate recovery to all applicants for Medicaid. In addition, each state must establish an appeals process and criteria for waiving recovery in cases of hardship.

MEDICAID LIENS

One way of ensuring recovery against an estate is to place a **lien** on the property of the Medicaid beneficiary. A **lien** is the legal right or interest of a creditor in another party's property. The lien exists to secure a debt or duty, and lasts until the debt or duty is satisfied. In the context of Medicaid, a creditor will typically place a lien on the beneficiary's home. The lien creates a barrier to the selling or refinancing of the home, and could lead to a foreclosure action by the creditor if the creditor decides to take the debtor to court.

While you are alive, federal law sets strict limits on the use of liens against your home. Liens may be used only to recover the cost of caring for persons who permanently reside in a nursing home or other medical institution. More importantly, the state cannot impose a lien on your home if you have a spouse, or a child under age twenty-one, or a blind or disabled child living in the home. In certain cases, the same applies if your brother or sister co-owns the house and lives there.

The rules change somewhat upon your death. In the probate process, the state's claim for recovery of Medicaid benefits may be converted to a lien against your property, including the home, even when one of the above persons still lives there. However, the state may not seek to *enforce* the lien (i.e., collect the money due) while the surviving spouse is alive or while a child under age twenty-one (or a blind or disabled child) is living, regardless of whether they are actually living in the house. In addition, the state cannot enforce the lien under limited circumstances if your brother or sister lives there, or if an adult child lives there who was your caregiver for at least two years under conditions defined by Medicaid.

One way married couples sometimes reduce the impact of lien and estate recovery provisions is to transfer title of their house to the spouse who remains in the community. Transfers between spouses are permissible under Medicaid. This has the effect of reducing the probate estate of the spouse in the nursing home. However, you should only take this step after seeking the advice of a qualified lawyer, as there might be pitfalls under tax, trust, and estate law.

MEDICAID ESTATE PLANNING

Nursing home costs can be devastating to a family, but planning ahead can make a big difference. Competent Medicaid planning can help an individual who has difficulty paying for long-term care to properly meet the Medicaid financial eligibility requirements. Planning may also slow the depletion of your estate or preserve some of it for your spouse or dependents or your own future needs.

Medicaid planning usually focuses on families who realistically have no other choice but to rely on Medicaid. Few people opt for Medicaid if other choices are available, because of the disadvantages—including less provider choice, limitations in available care, occasional discrimination against Medicaid recipients, and intrusive involvement of the state in your finances and health care. Medicaid planning uses legally permitted options under Medicaid to preserve assets and to provide survivors with some financial security.

Unfortunately, most self-help advice regarding Medicaid planning is fraught with danger. Even with competent advice tailored to your needs, Medicaid planning is not easy. Moreover, the federal and state governments change the rules from time to time. The goal here is to introduce you to the types of planning strategies available—not to provide a do-it-yourself cookbook. If you think Medicaid planning could help you, you should consult with a lawyer.

SPENDING DOWN OR CONVERTING ASSETS

One of the most elementary Medicaid planning steps is to spend down assets on current or recurring debts, such as the balance of a mortgage, home equity loan, car loan, or credit card bills. Other debts that can be anticipated may also be paid down, such as medical bills, legal fees, real estate taxes, or any service or item paid for on a subscription basis. These kinds of spend-downs are beneficial to individuals or couples in the face of crushing long-term-care expenses, because they help to prevent both future default on debts and the loss of needed services.

Converting countable assets into exempt assets can also help you to anticipate future needs that may become financially beyond your reach in light of long-term-care costs. For example, if your home is in need of substantial improvement (e.g., the roof needs replacement), then spending down your savings account to complete the home improvement will effectively convert a countable asset (your savings account) into an exempt asset (your home). This expenditure will either enhance or preserve the financial value of your home.

Another strategy is to spend your savings on home modifications to accommodate your disability. Not only will such an expenditure convert a countable asset (the savings account) into an exempt asset (the home), but it also may delay the point at which institutional care is needed. Alternatively, if you do not own a home, your assets could be used to create a disability-friendly apartment in a child's home for your use.

Similarly, if your automobile is a few years old, and thus at an age when its maintenance costs are likely to increase, purchasing a new car may be a wise strategy. This will lighten the cost of maintenance for the next few years, as well as ensuring you reliable transportation. Prepayment of funeral and burial expenses is also permissible and sensible from a planning point of view. (For more information on prepaid funerals, see Chapter 14, "Consumer Protection.")

 TALKING TO A LAWYER

Q. If my assets must be spent down to the Medicaid eligibility level, are there any restrictions on how I spend my money, other than restrictions on giving assets away?

A. Yes. Unless a Medicaid hearing permits the community spouse to retain more than the community spouse allowance, any amount of the couple's resources that exceeds this allowance and the allowance for the institutionalized spouse may be spent only for the benefit of either spouse. Thus, you may spend down excess resources on a mortgage, home equity loan, car loan, credit card or medical bills, legal fees, real estate taxes, or home repairs and improvement. Other examples of allowable expenditures include the modification of your own or somebody else's home to accommodate your disability, the trading in of your current vehicle and purchase of a new one, and prepayment of funeral and burial expenses.

—Answer by Gregory S. French,
Attorney-at-Law, Cincinnati, OH

Transfers of Assets

Transfers of property for less than full consideration (i.e., giving away property in whole or in part), except for transfers between spouses, can result in a period of ineligibility for Medicaid benefits. On February 8, 2006, the federal Deficit Reduction Act of 2006 changed the transfer of assets rules significantly. The actual implementation date will differ from state to state but will typically be February 8 or later in 2006. Transfers of property that took place *before* the effective date are treated under the old rule; so both the old and the new rules are described here:

Old Transfer Rule

Applies to applications made before the effective date of the Deficit Reduction Act of 2006: When you apply for Medicaid, you must disclose any gifts made within the **last thirty-six months** (sixty months for transfers involving trusts). Such transfers usually trigger a period of ineligibility that *begins on the date of transfer.*

New Transfer Rule

Applies to applications made after the effective date of the Deficit Reduction Act of 2006: When you apply for Medicaid, you must disclose any gifts made within the **last sixty months** (i.e., 5 years). Gift transfers made *after* the effective date will trigger a period of ineligibility, but the period of ineligibility *does not begin until you apply for Medicaid and are otherwise eligible for Medicaid but for the transfer.*

Example:

Mr. Jones lives in an area where the average monthly cost of nursing home care is $5,000 per month. If he gives away $90,000 on January 1, 2006, then he is disqualified from receiving Medicaid until July 1, 2007 (i.e., for eighteen months). This time period is calculated by

Example:

Suppose our same Mr. Jones gives away the same $90,000 but this time on June 1, 2006, *after* the effective date of the new rule. The length of the period of ineligibility is calculated the same way as under the older rule and is therefore eighteen months. But unlike the old dividing the amount of the transfer ($90,000) by a divisor that represents the average monthly private-pay cost of nursing home care ($5,000 in this example). Since $90,000 divided by $5,000 is 18, the length of Mr. Jones' disqualification is eighteen months, measured from the date of transfer. Thus, in order to avoid a penalty, Mr. Jones must wait at least eighteen months from the date of the transfer to apply for Medicaid. Each state determines its own divisor, which may be a statewide figure or a figure that differs by region.

rule, his disqualification does not begin until he actually applies for Medicaid and is otherwise eligible except for the transfer. So even if Mr. Jones waits eighteen months (i.e., until January 1, 2008) before he applies, he will be disqualified for eighteen months *beginning* January 1, 2008, the date of application. The eighteen month penalty will expire on July 1, 2009. Until then, Medicaid will not cover his long-term care. As under the old rule, each state determines its own divisor, which may be a statewide figure or a figure that differs by region.

If you face a disqualification penalty for making gift transfers under either the old or new rule, there are two possible grounds for seeking an exception or waiver from the penalty. One requires proof that you made the transfer solely for a purpose other than to qualify for Medicaid. For example, if you gave $10,000 to a favorite charity at a time when you had no indication that you would need long-term care, this exception may apply. The other ground requires a showing of hardship if the penalty is applied. Hardship should be found if the penalty would deprive you of medical care such that your health or life would be endangered, or deprive you of food, clothing, shelter, or other necessities of life. Unfortunately, the burden falls on your shoulders to show that you meet either or both of these grounds.

Use of Trusts

Irrevocable trusts are another planning tool to help manage the cost of long-term care. Trusts that can be revoked by the creator of the trust are always considered countable assets by Medicaid and do not help establish Medicaid eligibility. However, irrevocable trusts, if created at least *sixty months* prior to applying for Medicaid (this is known as the **look-back period**), may help establish Medicaid eligibility while slowing down the depletion of your estate. Note, however, that the discretion of the trustee to distribute income and principal must be sharply limited. The penalty for transfers within the look-back period is calculated in the same manner as the penalty for transfers to individuals. Therefore, in a state where the average monthly cost of nursing home care is $5,000, if $90,000 is transferred to a trust, the period of ineligibility for Medicaid would be eighteen months (the same as in the transfer-of-asset penalty example above). Federal law also recognizes certain trusts created for the benefit of persons under sixty-five with disabilities. Generally, parents who are planning for the long-term care of an adult disabled child may want to consider this type of trust.

Named after a famous legal case, an irrevocable **Miller trust** is an important tool for persons living in income cap states (discussed in the "Income Cap States" sidebar earlier in this chapter). The problem faced by some persons in these states is that their income may be just over the Medicaid income cap, but less than the amount needed to pay privately for a nursing home bed. To remedy this hardship, federal law requires these states to exempt (for purposes of Medicaid eligibility) trusts created for an individual's benefit if the trust is composed only of a pension, Social Security, or other income, and if at the individual's death the state is reimbursed by the trust for all Medicaid assistance paid on behalf of the individual. These trusts work by paying out a monthly income just under the Medicaid cap and retaining the rest of the individual's income in the trust. The result is that most of the individual's income, supplemented by Medicaid, goes toward payment of nursing home costs. The remainder of the individual's income remains in the trust until his or her death. The accumulated residue is then paid to Medicaid.

Other limited trust arrangements may be helpful in some cases, but they all require careful assessment and advice and a good dose of caution. Remember that Congress periodically changes the rules, so your planning may have to change accordingly.

PRIVATE LONG-TERM-CARE INSURANCE

Long-term-care insurance helps pay for extended periods (usually two or more years) of nursing home care, assisted living, home care, adult day care, and respite care. It is still a relatively new and evolving insurance product, so its typical features continue to change yearly. A medical screening is typically required, so the existence of certain health conditions may exclude you from coverage or make coverage prohibitively expensive. Long-term-care insurance is best for those with income and assets to protect. One rule of thumb is to consider long-term-care insurance if you are at least fifty-five years old and your assets exceed $200,000. Of course, the decision is never quite that simple, since you are also likely to take into account your overall debt load, retirement funding, payment for your children's education, and so on.

Most long-term-care policies pay a preset amount (or percentage of the cost of care) for each day of covered nursing home care or home health care. Sometimes a policy will pay a per-visit amount for home care. Other policies offer insurance in the form of a so-called **bucket of money** that can be utilized as needed for care at any level.

Examine specific provisions carefully before purchasing a policy, since the conditions and limitations on coverage can be extensive and complex. The best policies cover all levels of nursing home care plus care at assisted-living facilities. **Assisted-living facilities** provide a level of support that is less than nursing home care, and may be a better alternative for many people who can no longer live at home. Better long-term-care policies will also cover **home care**, which is broadly defined to include not only skilled home health services, but also nonmedical support services such as homemaker services, home health aide services, and personal-care services. Newer policies even offer coverage options such as adult day care for the individual or respite care for your family.

Costs

The cost of long-term-care insurance depends on your age at the time of purchase, the extent of coverage, and your health history. Age is clearly the single greatest factor. The policy premium can easily run to $1,500 a year for a fifty-five-year-old, $3,000 for a sixty-five-year-old, and $6,000 or more if purchased at age seventy-five. Once you buy a policy, your individual premium is generally locked in. However, a significant exception arises if and when the insurance company seeks an increase of premiums across the board for all holders of the policy. Similarly, if the insurance company runs into financial trouble and is purchased by another company, premiums for all policyholders may face upward adjustments.

Evaluating a Long-Term-Care Policy

In evaluating long-term-care policies, compare several policies side by side. Your state's insurance department should have names of companies offering long-term-care insurance. Most states have begun to set minimum standards and consumer protection guidelines. Guides for evaluating policies may also be available from your state's insurance department or your local office on aging.

Keep in mind the following tips:

• Before you choose a specific policy, choose the company from which you will purchase it. Be sure that the company you choose will be around and solvent for a long time. Pick a company with a financial rating of B+ or better from financial-ratings services such as A.M. Best, Moody's, Standard & Poor's, or Weiss.

• Make sure your policy will pay benefits for all levels of care in a nursing home, including custodial care, as well as care in assisted-living facilities or other residential-care facilities.

- A good policy will pay benefits for home care and hospice care, including in-home personal care to help with activities of daily living.
- A variety of other benefits are increasingly common in policies, including respite care (to give family caregivers a break from caregiving); caregiver training; adult day care; the services of a care coordinator; home accommodations; and alternate plans of care. **Alternate plans of care** are any other services or supplemental items that effectively meet your care needs and that the insurance company approves. This can be an especially important policy feature over time, because systems for delivering long-term care may change significantly in the future in ways we can't anticipate today.
- Consider whether the amount of daily benefits provided by your policy will be adequate in the future. The average daily nursing home cost of over $190 a day in 2004 is increasing by a double-digit rate annually. Therefore, consider only policies with an **inflation adjuster** that increases benefits by a set percentage, compounded each year. Typically, the percentage available in long-term-care policies is 5 percent compounded annually. While this is less than the actual rate of cost inflation, it is far better than the alternative of no inflation adjustment.
- Do not assume that more years of coverage is always better. Very few people need nursing home care for five years or more. Four years is sufficient coverage for most. Three years may be acceptable if the cost of more coverage is simply too much for you. Consider, too, the amount of assets you have to protect. Even with long-term-care insurance, you are likely to deplete your assets over time. If your policy continues to pay benefits even after your remaining resources are gone, the policy may serve only to reduce the state's payments under Medicaid, rather than your costs.
- Six months is a reasonable exclusion period for preexisting conditions.
- Better policies allow payment of nursing home or home health benefits without requiring a prior period of hospitalization as a condition of coverage.
- Most policies impose waiting periods (commonly twenty to

ninety days after you begin receiving nursing home care or home care) before payments under the policy begin. First-day coverage will increase your premium. Consider self-insuring for the maximum waiting period, since utilizing the maximum waiting period will result in significant savings on premium payments. If you have to pay during the waiting period, the loss likely will not be catastrophic.

• Avoid policies that pay only for medically necessary care; that standard is too discretionary. Most good policies will cover care when the individual needs help with two or more **activities of daily living** (bathing, eating, dressing, toileting, transferring into or out of a bed or chair, or continence) or, alternatively, suffers a cognitive impairment. Be sure your policy covers Alzheimer's disease and other forms of dementia. More than half the residents of nursing homes suffer some form of dementia.

• Be sure that the premium remains constant over the life of the policy and that the policy is guaranteed renewable for life.

• Buy a policy only from a company that is licensed in your state and has agents physically present in your state. Out-of-state mail-order policies may leave you powerless to remedy problems if anything goes wrong.

• Consider a tax-qualified policy so that benefits received are not subject to federal income tax.

THE WORLD AT YOUR FINGERTIPS

• The Centers for Medicare & Medicaid Services (CMS) publishes a variety of helpful material relating to Medicaid at *www.cms.hhs.gov/home/medicaid.asp*.

• Medicaid rules differ from state to state. To find out what information is available about Medicaid in your state, contact your state or local agency on aging. Find them in your telephone book or call the Eldercare Locator at 1-800-677-1116. You can also search the database of the national Eldercare Locator online through its website at *www.eldercare.gov*.

- *Guide to Long-Term Care Insurance*, by America's Health Insurance Plans (AHIP), provides useful guidance and a checklist for comparing policies. This publication and other useful consumer information is also available on AHIP's website at *www.ahip.org*.
- The American Association of Retired Persons (AARP) also provides timely and useful information on the topic of private long-term-care insurance, which can be viewed online at *www.aarp.org/bulletin/longterm*.

REMEMBER THIS

- Medicaid is not the same as Medicare. The two are often confused. Medicaid is a medical assistance program for older or disabled persons, pregnant women and children, and parents with income below state financial-eligibility levels. You must meet both income and asset tests to qualify. Medicaid is managed by individual states, and benefits and eligibility rules thus vary from state to state.
- Despite serving mainly poor people, Medicaid benefits many middle-income individuals faced with the high costs of nursing home care or other long-term care.
- The rules for eligibility and coverage are complex, and professional advice is especially recommended when Medicaid is needed for nursing home care or other long-term care.
- Medicaid seeks recovery of costs from the estates of deceased persons who received long-term care and related services under Medicaid. However, there are many limitations on and exceptions to recovery. Again, professional advice is advisable.
- Private long-term-care insurance is still a relatively new and evolving insurance product to help individuals pay for the cost of long-term care. It is becoming increasingly important as a tool for financial and health planning, especially if you are in your fifties or early to mid-sixties, when policies are significantly more affordable.

• Because benefits under a long-term-care insurance policy may not be needed until decades after its initial purchase, it is important to evaluate and compare policies closely before buying, and to rely only on companies that are likely to be around for the long term. Use the list of tips provided in this chapter to evaluate policies.

CHAPTER 10

Elder Abuse, Guardianship, and Civil Commitment

Legal Protections for the Elderly

Donna's Aunt Jane can no longer pay her bills or make decisions about investments. She needs to sell her home but can't handle the transaction on her own. Donna just learned that her brother Tim, who has been helping Aunt Jane with the sale of her home, has been forging Jane's signature to pay her day-to-day bills. Donna can't get rid of the nagging feeling that something's not right. But is it elder abuse? What should she look for, and what can she do?

This chapter addresses three separate issues: elder abuse, guardianship, and commitment. While it may be necessary at times to consider guardianship or commitment as a last resort to protect a victim of elder abuse, the three issues are distinct.

WHAT IS ELDER ABUSE?

Elder abuse occurs when a family member, a caregiver (paid or volunteer), or another individual in a relationship of trust with an older person (such as an agent under a power of attorney) abuses, financially exploits, or neglects the older person. Examples of elder abuse vary from state to state, but generally include:

* physical abuse, such as hitting or shoving;
* sexual abuse, including fondling and sexual intercourse;
* emotional or psychological abuse, such as screaming and name-calling;
* neglect, such as withholding medications, food, or shelter; and

- abandonment, such as the desertion of an elder at a hospital or nursing home.

Additionally, some states consider **self-neglect**, which occurs when an older person fails to take care of him- or herself (or his or her home), to be a form of elder abuse. Examples of self-neglect might include failure to obtain needed medical treatment, poor personal hygiene, or the hoarding of animals or household items.

All states consider financial exploitation to be a form of elder abuse. Examples of financial exploitation include:

- cashing an older person's Social Security check and not using the money for the person's care;
- misusing credit cards and funds held in joint bank accounts;
- using a power of attorney for the agent's own benefit or advantage (e.g., to give gifts to oneself or others);
- tricking the elder into signing away property; and
- mortgage fraud.

Elder abuse occurs among people of all races, social classes, and economic levels, and it can happen to both men and women. Moreover, it can happen anywhere. Abuse in an individual's home is called **domestic abuse**. Abuse in a residential-care facility, nursing home, or other long-term-care setting is known as **institutional abuse**. Because there are no official national statistics on elder abuse, no one knows exactly how many older Americans are being abused, neglected, or exploited each year. But according to the National Elder Abuse Incidence Study, more than 500,000 Americans aged sixty and over were victims of domestic abuse in 1996.

More than two-thirds of abusers are family members, most often the victim's adult children or spouse. Research has shown that abusers are often financially dependent on the elder's resources and have problems with alcohol and drugs.

Recent research has shown that elder abuse victims usually experience more than one form of abuse. For example, a victim who is financially exploited may also experience physical or emotional abuse.

Some states have laws that treat elder abuse as a criminal

RISK FACTORS FOR ELDER ABUSE

Factors that may place an older person at risk for elder abuse include:

- history of domestic violence by the potential abuser;
- mental health or substance abuse problems on the part of the potential abuser;
- dependence of the potential abuser on the older person;
- isolation of the older person; and
- mental health or substance abuse problems on the part of the older person.

Source: National Center on Elder Abuse, *www.elderabusecenter.org/default.cfm?p=riskfactors.cfm,* 2005.

act. But even if a state has no such laws, the behaviors that constitute elder abuse (e.g., physically harming or sexually molesting an older person) are usually defined as criminal acts.

Warning Signs of Elder Abuse

An older person's statement that he or she is experiencing abuse, neglect, or exploitation should always be investigated, even if the older person has dementia or cognitive impairments.

According to the National Center for Elder Abuse, signs of physical abuse include:

- bruises, broken bones, abrasions, or burns;
- open wounds or untreated injuries;
- signs of restraints or punishment; and
- unexplained withdrawal from normal activities, sudden changes in alertness, or unusual depression.

Signs of sexual abuse include:

- bruising on the breasts or genital area; and
- unexplained vaginal or anal bleeding.

An older person may be displaying signs of emotional or psychological abuse if he or she becomes:
- emotionally upset or agitated; or
- withdrawn, noncommunicative, or nonresponsive.
  Signs of neglect include:
- bedsores, poor hygiene, or unusual weight loss; and
- untreated health problems.
  Signs of financial exploitation include:
- sudden changes in bank account balances or banking practices;
- lack of utilities or unpaid bills despite the availability of adequate finances;
- unexplained sudden transfers of assets to family members or others; and
- abrupt changes in a will, power of attorney, or other financial documents.

What Can You Do if You Suspect Abuse?

According to the National Elder Abuse Incidence Study cited above, only 16 percent of abusive situations are reported to adult protective services or other authorities. But we all have a moral responsibility to keep elders safe from abuse, and there may be a legal responsibility as well. Most states require certain professionals, such as doctors, home health-care providers, and others, to report suspected elder abuse. Some states require any person who suspects abuse, financial exploitation, or neglect to report their suspicions. Here's what to do if you suspect abuse:
- If someone you know is in immediate danger, call the police or dial 911.
- If the danger is not immediate but you suspect abuse, call the local adult protective-services office or law enforcement agency. Visit *www.elderabusecenter.org* for your state's adult protective-services reporting number or call the Eldercare Locator help line at 1-800-677-1116.

If you are or have been the victim of abuse, exploitation, or neglect, then you should consider telling your doctor, a friend, or a family member whom you trust, or calling your state's adult protective-services program.

GUARDIANSHIP

A guardian is an individual or organization appointed by a court to exercise rights and powers over the personal and/or financial affairs of a person (called the **ward** or **incapacitated person**) who is not able to make his or her own decisions. A **conservator** is an individual appointed by a court to manage a person's financial affairs, without control over that person's personal affairs. Because definitions vary from state to state, we will use the term "guardian" to refer to both guardians and conservators (and the term "guardianship" to refer to both guardianship and conservatorship).

A **limited guardianship** transfers powers to a guardian only in specific areas in which the ward is not able to make decisions. An **emergency guardianship** allows a court to appoint a temporary guardian quickly if the ward may be harmed during the time it would take for a regular guardian to be appointed. A **temporary guardianship** is an appointment for a limited period of time, after which the court order expires.

When Is Guardianship Appropriate?

A person may need a guardian when:

• he or she can no longer manage his or her affairs because of serious incapacity; *and*

• no other voluntary arrangements for decision making and management (such as durable powers of attorney) have been set up ahead of time, or when such arrangements are not working well; *and*

• serious harm will come to the individual if no legally authorized decision maker is appointed.

A person may also need a guardian if a power of attorney or trust has been misused.

A decision to seek guardianship should never be based on stereotypical notions of old age, mental illness, or disability. A person has a right to make foolish or risky decisions, and making these types of decisions does not necessarily indicate that a person lacks decision-making capacity. People often *choose* to run risks. However, an incapacitated person runs risks not by choice but by happenstance, and may not even be aware of the risks he or she is taking.

When is Guardianship Inappropriate?

If someone already has an agent under a durable power of attorney or a health-care advance directive, that person should not need a guardian unless a decision must be made that is outside the scope of the agent's authority or the agent is abusing his or her power. If the court appoints a guardian for a person who already has an agent, the court normally will determine whether the agent's authority should continue.

If the only real problem is management of a person's Social Security income or other public-pension-type payment, a **representative payee** may be able to take over management of the income. A representative payee can be established for an incapacitated beneficiary without going to court if the beneficiary is unable to manage income from Social Security, Supplemental Security Income (SSI), civil service, railroad retirement, the Department of Veterans Affairs, or some state pension funds. Someone must apply to the relevant administrative agency to be named as a representative payee (or **rep payee** for short). The agency will then determine whether appointment of a representative payee is appropriate, based on evidence of the beneficiary's incapacity. Medical and other evidence will be required. Once you are appointed rep payee for a beneficiary, you have the authority (and a fiduciary duty) to manage the relevant income for the benefit of that beneficiary. Your authority does not extend to any other income or assets. Under Social Security Administration (SSA) rules, you must also file fairly simple annual reports according to SSA instructions.

Note that the agent under a durable power of attorney cannot automatically act as a representative payee in managing a beneficiary's Social Security check. The agent will still have to complete the application. It is helpful if the durable power of attorney expressly authorizes your agent to act as a rep payee.

What Are the Advantages and Disadvantages of Guardianship?

The primary advantage of a guardianship is that, if it works like it should, it protects the incapacitated person and his or her property through judicial supervision and monitoring.

The primary disadvantage of a guardianship is the incapacitated person's loss of rights. Guardianship usually involves a tremendous encroachment upon fundamental rights, because the right to make decisions about one's own affairs is transferred to someone else. Because guardianship is a major intrusion into a person's life, it should be a last resort for decision making and management of personal and financial affairs, used only when a person is no longer able to understand the consequences of decisions or when there is no other way to stop an abuser.

Also, guardianship proceedings may be emotionally trying and embarrassing to the incapacitated person and his or her family. The proceedings are public, although judges and court staff typically try to protect the privacy of the people involved. Finally, guardianship can be cumbersome, expensive, and inflexible.

How Is a Guardian Appointed?

A guardian is appointed through the following steps:
- Guardianship is initiated through a formal petition to the court, with notice provided to all interested parties.

- The individual who is alleged to be incapacitated has the opportunity for a full hearing.
- The court may appoint a **guardian ad litem** to represent the best interests of the alleged incapacitated person during the proceeding. In some states the judge appoints a court visitor or a team of evaluators to investigate and report back to the court. In some states, a court-appointed lawyer may represent the rights and wishes of the alleged incapacitated person.
- Generally, the alleged incapacitated person must submit to an examination by a physician, psychologist, or other clinician.
- The judge weighs the evidence and crafts an order appointing the guardian and outlining the scope of the guardian's powers.

Once a guardian is appointed, a bond may be necessary. A bond is a kind of insurance policy. It guarantees that if the guardian mishandles the ward's funds, the bonding company will cover the ward's loss. The bonding company will then try to recover the losses from the guardian.

The guardian generally must file a periodic accounting of all transactions undertaken for the estate and a report on the well-being of the ward. However, sometimes the level of real protection is inadequate, and there is insufficient monitoring of the guardian's management of financial and quality-of-life decisions affecting the ward.

The discretion of the guardian is fairly restricted. Many transactions or decisions may require the guardian to go back to court for approval.

Who Serves as Guardian?

Many guardians are family members, and state laws frequently provide that family members be given preference for appointment as guardians. In addition, banks may serve as guardians when there is a need for financial management. Attorneys often serve as guardians, especially for wards who are longtime clients. A friend or neighbor may also be appointed as a guardian if he or she is willing and able, especially if he or she has known the ward for many years and understands the ward's values.

In addition, professionals and organizations provide guardianship services in many states. Guardianship agencies may be nonprofit or for-profit. A few states require certification for private professional guardians. In addition, many states offer local volunteer guardianship programs. As a last resort, most states and some localities offer public-guardianship programs to provide guardians in cases where no one else is willing or able to serve.

CIVIL COMMITMENT

Under extreme circumstances, a person can be compelled by court order to receive personal care and treatment in a mental institution. This process may be called **civil commitment, mental commitment,** or **involuntary hospitalization,** but throughout this chapter we will use the term "civil commitment." Since commitment is a drastic measure that restricts the liberty of the committed person, state laws establish very specific processes for commitment, with strict procedural safeguards.

How Does Civil Commitment Compare to Guardianship?

Civil commitment is used less frequently than guardianship to meet the needs of older persons who can no longer care for themselves. Civil-commitment standards focus on whether the person is a risk to himself or herself or others, whereas the standards for guardianship focus on whether the person has the capacity to make decisions about care and property. A judgment of incapacity is not sufficient grounds for mental commitment of a person under guardianship. Unlike the procedures for initiating guardianship, the interventions required for civil commitment are time-limited, and aim to treat and remedy specific mental impairments. An order for civil commitment does not necessarily mean that a person is incapacitated.

What are the Legal Criteria
for Civil Commitment?

The specific legal criteria for civil commitment differ by state. State law defines the types of mental conditions that warrant commitment, and generally requires a finding that the mental condition in question causes the person to be dangerous to himself or herself or others. Some states require satisfaction of other criteria, such as grave disability, inability to provide for one's own basic human needs, or the need for treatment essential to one's welfare.

A person subject to civil commitment has important rights, including the right to legal counsel, the right to a hearing, and the right to receive appropriate treatment in the least-restrictive setting possible.

Civil commitment is usually temporary. It can last anywhere from a few hours or days (in cases where emergency evaluation is necessary) to many months. Most state laws establish a period of time after which a court must redetermine the need for commitment.

THE WORLD AT YOUR FINGERTIPS

• In any emergency, call 911 to contact your local police department.

• Every state has an adult protective-services (APS) program responsible for protecting older adults from abuse, neglect, and exploitation. APS will investigate reports of abuse, and provide or arrange for services as necessary to alleviate or prevent further abuse. All states have established phone numbers at which suspected abuse may be reported. You can find those numbers by visiting *www.elderabusecenter.org/default.cfm?p=statehotlines.cfm*.

• The National Guardianship Association (NGA) provides education, training, and networking opportunities for guardians. NGA also provides an online directory of nationally certified

guardians and a list of state guardianship associations at *www*
.guardianship.org.

REMEMBER THIS

• Elder abuse occurs when somebody abuses, neglects, or financially exploits an older person. Abuse can be physical, sexual, or emotional.

• If you suspect abuse, contact your local adult protective-services office, long-term-care ombudsman program, or police department.

• Guardianship is a major intrusion into a person's life. It should be used only as a last resort for decision making and management of personal and financial affairs, in cases where a person demonstrates a serious inability to understand the consequences of decisions, or where there is no other way to remove an abuser from power.

CHAPTER 11

Housing and Long-Term-Care Choices

Ensuring That Your Needs are Met, Wherever You Live

Joe and Susan have lived in their home for thirty years, and they really don't want to move. The problem is, Joe has become rather forgetful and unsteady on his feet, and Susan isn't sure she'll be able to care for him for much longer without help. The house and yard work are becoming difficult to manage as well. They've seen the advertisements for retirement communities and assisted living, and wonder if maybe that would be the answer. Or maybe they could get some help at home. What should they do?

The range of housing options for older people is extensive—from staying in your own home, to sharing a home, to moving into housing designed for seniors. Where you live may depend on your health needs, your relationship to your family, your financial situation, and your ties to your current community. This chapter examines these housing options with an eye toward protecting your rights and ensuring that your individual needs are met.

Getting older does not necessarily mean losing your independence. However, many people begin to need some assistance as they age. You may choose to seek out supportive services available through agencies in the community, such as your local agency on aging. Or you may decide to move to housing where services are provided. But no matter where you live, you should be a careful consumer. Look into the risks and benefits of various options, and take time to learn about your legal rights.

OPTIONS FOR HOMEOWNERS

If you own your home and would like to remain in it, you may be eligible for some help. Some states sponsor property tax credit or deferral programs that give older homeowners a tax break by reducing taxes, or delaying payment until a house is sold, or freezing the tax rate when they reach a certain age. If your house is in need of repairs, or if you need to perform some minor renovations to accommodate a disability (i.e., build a ramp, widen a doorway, or install grab bars in the bathroom), the state may have a home repair program that provides funds to help you.

You may also wish to explore **accessory housing**, which consists of private rental units in or next to single family homes (either your own or someone else's home). Finally, your city or county may sponsor a home-sharing program, in which homeowners are matched with individuals who seek housing in exchange for rent or services. To find out more about these programs, call your local agency on aging.

A low income should not necessarily stop you from living in your own home. In fact, if you own your home, you may be able to use the equity in your home to fund the costs of your retirement, without selling your home. The sections below discuss some of the options available to homeowners, including reverse mortgages, sale-leaseback arrangements, and traditional home equity loans.

Reverse Mortgages

A **reverse mortgage** lets you borrow against the equity in your home, without having to repay the loan while you still live in the house. You can get the money in a lump sum, in monthly cash payments for life, or by drawing on a line of credit, or you can choose a combination of these options (e.g., monthly payments plus a line of credit for emergencies). The amount you can borrow, and the size of the loan installments, are based on several factors, including: your age, the value of the home and of your equity in it, the interest rate, and the kind of loan you select. Reverse mortgages can be costly, but the relative costs lessen over time, and you will never owe more than the value of your home.

Most reverse mortgages place no restrictions on how you use the money. The loan usually does not have to be repaid until you sell your home, move, or die. In years past, there were loans that had to be repaid at the end of a specified number of years. Very few, if any, of these types of loans still exist. Some lenders combine a reverse mortgage with an annuity that allows you to receive payments under the annuity even after you sell your home and move.

When you sell your home or move, or at the end of the term, you must repay the money you have borrowed plus the accrued interest and fees. The house can be sold to repay the loan, or the funds can be collected in some other way. The lender is not permitted to collect more than the appraised value of the house at the time the loan is repaid, even if the loan exceeds that amount.

The most widely available reverse-mortgage product is the federally insured Home Equity Conversion Mortgage (HECM). Under this program, the Federal Housing Authority (FHA) provides insurance for reverse mortgages acquired through private financial institutions. Another reverse-mortgage program available nationally through private lenders is Home Keeper Mortgage, which is backed by Fannie Mae. (Fannie Mae is a company chartered by the federal government to encourage home ownership.) Over the years, a few private companies have offered their own reverse-mortgage products. These tend to be more costly than the HECM or the Home Keeper Mortgage, because the lender must charge customers more in order to self-insure against potential losses. Federal law requires all reverse-mortgage lenders to inform you, before making the loan, of the total amount you will owe through the course of the loan. This enables you to compare the costs of different mortgages.

Eligibility for Reverse Mortgages

Eligibility for reverse mortgages depends on the individual product, but most programs have rules similar to those of the HECM

MANUFACTURED HOMES AND COOPERATIVES

Manufactured or factory-built homes may qualify for reverse mortgages if they meet certain requirements. Cooperatives may also be eligible for certain private reverse-mortgage programs.

program. Generally, the borrower and every other person whose name is on the deed must:

- be at least sixty-two years old; and
- own the property free and clear, except for liens or mortgages that can be paid off with proceeds from the loan.

In addition, the property must be:

- the borrower's primary residence (that is, not a vacation home); and
- a single-family home, or a unit in a one- to four-unit building. (Some condominiums are eligible; mobile homes are not.)

Will a Reverse Mortgage Affect My Government Benefits?

Income from a reverse mortgage will not affect your eligibility for Social Security, Medicare, or other retirement benefits, or for pensions that are not based on need. However, unless you plan carefully, reverse-mortgage payments may affect your eligibility for Supplemental Security Income (SSI), Medicaid, food stamps, and some state benefit programs. These benefits may be referred to as "need-based" because they are designed to meet basic needs, and recipients must meet strict financial guidelines that can include limits on income and resources (e.g., bank accounts, cars, and other property).

The general rule is that reverse-mortgage payments will not affect your eligibility for need-based benefits if you spend the money you receive from a reverse mortgage during the same month in which you receive it. If you do not spend the money during that month, and it carries over to the next month, it will be considered a resource (or asset) for purposes of benefit eligibility. If your total resources are greater than the allowable limit (for SSI, that limit is $2,000 total for a single person and $3,000 total for a couple), your benefits could be reduced or even eliminated. Some state need-based benefit programs follow the federal rules on this issue, but it is important to check the rules in your own state.

Federal eligibility rules for reverse-annuity mortgages are different from the rules for regular reverse mortgages. With a regular reverse mortgage, you can receive payments only while you are living in your home. With a **reverse-annuity mortgage**, payments can continue even after you move from your home. Reverse-annuity mortgage payments are considered income. As a result, they count toward the income limit for purposes of SSI, Medicaid, and similar need-based benefits, even if you spend the money in the month in which you receive it. These annuity payments could reduce the amount of need-based benefits you receive, and may affect your eligibility altogether. Annuities also receive less-favorable tax treatment than do loan advances.

Taxes and Reverse Mortgages

So far, the IRS has not taxed reverse-mortgage payments, as the money from such payments is considered a loan. However, a portion of reverse-*annuity* payments will be taxed. As to whether the interest on reverse mortgages is tax-deductible, the general rule is that interest cannot be deducted until it is actually paid. Since you do not pay the interest on a reverse mortgage until the loan comes due, it most likely will not be deductible until that time. Reverse mortgages may also have an effect on estate taxes. Consult a tax advisor if you have questions in this area.

Estate-Planning Considerations

Reverse mortgages allow you to spend your home equity while you are alive. This may result in you using up all of your equity and not having any left to pass along to your heirs. Some plans allow you to set aside some of the equity, so that it will not be used. You need to decide if this is what you want to do.

Reverse-Mortgage Counseling

The HECM program requires all potential borrowers to receive counseling from an agency certified by the U.S. Department of Housing and Urban Development (HUD). Fannie Mae products also require counseling. Some state laws require counseling for all borrowers, no matter what the product, but borrowers looking at private products generally are not required to undergo counseling.

Reverse mortgages are very complex, and involve difficult financial, legal, and personal decisions. Examine them carefully, and look for alternatives that may suit your needs. Talk to a lawyer who is familiar with the issues, and discuss your aims and concerns with your family.

Consumer information about reverse mortgages, including booklets, information about loan costs, and an interactive loan guide, is available from AARP at *www.aarp.org/revmort*. Additional information is available from the National Center for Home Equity Conversion at *www.reverse.org*.

Selling Without Moving

You can also put your home equity to practical use with saleleasebacks, life estates, and charitable annuities. Each of these options has significant consequences and should be used only with professional guidance.

Sale-Leasebacks

In a **sale-leaseback**, you sell your home, but retain the right to live there while you pay rent. The buyer usually makes a substantial down payment. You act as a lender by giving the buyer a mortgage. You get the buyer's mortgage payments, and the buyer gets your rent payments. You remain in the home, and can use the down payment and the mortgage payments as income. The buyer can deduct the mortgage interest payment from his or her income, and will also benefit if the value of the property increases.

In the case of sale-leasebacks, the IRS requires that both the sale price and the rental payments be fair market rate. Sale-leasebacks used to be good investments, especially for adult children, but today there are fewer tax advantages, so finding an investor may be difficult.

Life Estates

In a **life estate**, or **sale of a remainder interest plan**, you sell your home but retain the right to live there during your lifetime. The buyer pays you a lump sum, or monthly payments, or both. You are usually responsible for taxes and repairs while you live in the house. At your death, full ownership passes automatically to the buyer. This arrangement is used most commonly within families, as part of an estate plan. As with a sale-leaseback, it might be difficult to find an outside investor.

Charitable Remainder Trusts

In a **charitable-remainder trust**, you donate your home to a charitable institution in return for a lifetime annuity and possibly a tax deduction. You retain a life estate, and you remain responsible for taxes and maintenance. When you die, your home becomes the property of the charitable institution.

Home Equity Loans

A traditional **home equity loan** is very different from a reverse mortgage, and can be risky for an older person on a fixed income. As with a reverse mortgage, you borrow against the equity you have built up in your home. But in a home equity loan, you must make regular monthly payments, or you may lose your home.

Home equity loans do have tax advantages. It is no longer possible to deduct interest on consumer goods such as car loans and credit card bills. But with home equity loans, you can borrow up to 80 percent of the appraised value of your home, minus your current mortgage balance. In addition, you can deduct the interest on a home equity loan that exceeds $100,000 if you use the money for home improvements.

OPTIONS FOR APARTMENT DWELLERS

There are many different kinds of apartments available for older people, including federally assisted apartments, public housing, and private-sector housing. Apartment living frees you from most repairs and some other responsibilities, but you may not be permitted to keep a pet, and you may have to get permission to redecorate or remodel.

Some apartment complexes offer housekeeping services and one or more daily group meals. In some states these facilities are known as **congregate-care facilities**. Some congregate-care facilities are subsidized under federal housing programs. Personal care and health oversight are usually not part of such facilities' services, although they may be provided through community social services. Some federally assisted apartment buildings provide supportive services (help with necessary activities like housekeeping), and some offer a service coordinator on the premises. Most residents of privately owned buildings must make their own arrangements.

If you have a disability, you have special legal rights when it comes to housing. (See Chapter 12, "Living with Disability," for more information.)

OTHER RETIREMENT HOUSING CHOICES

Supportive Housing and Assisted Living

In the past few years, public- and private-housing options for older people have increased. These options vary from single-family homes that offer board and care to larger complexes, but they share one common characteristic: the availability of some combination of housing and supportive services. **Supportive services** may include:

- help with **activities of daily living (ADLs)**, such as eating, dressing, transferring from one position to another (e.g., sitting to standing), using a toilet, and bathing;
- help with **instrumental activities of daily living (IADLs)**, such as preparing meals, taking medication, walking outside, using the telephone, managing money, shopping, and house-keeping;
- oversight—for example, monitoring, reminding, or other supervision—particularly for someone with a cognitive impairment; and
- health services.

Depending on the state in which they are located, these facilities may be known as **board-and-care homes, residential-care facilities,** or **assisted-living facilities**. Some assisted-living services are generally provided in a continuing-care retirement community. (See the "Continuing-Care Retirement Communities (CCRCs)" section below.)

Assisted living is the fastest-growing living option for seniors. Assisted-living facilities usually offer personalized assistance, health care, recreation, and supervision. Depending on your state, facilities categorized as assisted-living facilities could range in size from mom-and-pop homes for fewer than five residents to apartment-style complexes housing several hundred persons. Providers include individuals caring for others in their homes, private for-profit corporations (including large hotel chains), not-for-profit organizations, and government entities. Fees vary according to the kind of residence and the type of service plan. Most states license assisted-living providers, although the definition of what constitutes assisted living and the state's oversight of the industry varies from one state to the next. Many states limit the extent of care that can be provided in assisted-living facilities.

ASSISTED LIVING PROFILED

- The term **assisted living** refers to a variety of residential settings offering a variety of services.

- Assisted living is the fastest growing segment of the senior housing industry.

- Assisted-living service models may be **all-inclusive** (meaning that you pay a flat monthly fee for all services); **basic/enhanced** (meaning that core services are included for a flat fee, with additional services available on a fee-for-service basis); **à la carte/fee-for-service** (meaning that all services except for rent are priced and charged separately); or **service level** (meaning that you are assessed and assigned a level of care based on need, with your cost determined by your level of care).

- Rates for assisted living range from several hundred dollars a month to more than $6,000 a month, depending on location, size, services available, and your service plan.

Source: American Association of Homes and Services for the Aging, *www.aahsa.org.*

Continuing-Care Retirement Communities (CCRCs)

Continuing care retirement communities (CCRCs) offer a range of options in one location, from independent-living apartments to assisted-living facilities (either in your apartment or in an assisted-living wing or unit) to skilled nursing care. Most CCRCs require a substantial entrance fee, as well as monthly fees, although some charge only monthly fees. A few CCRCs offer an ownership interest in your living unit (condo or co-op), plus a personal and health-services package. Ownership arrangements are complex and pose both special advantages and risks.

RETIREMENT HOUSING BY ANY OTHER NAME

Housing programs for older persons have many names. But for the consumer, the questions raised by these programs are the same: What will your living conditions be like? How much will the program cost? What will you get for your money? Will the program meet your health and safety needs? Who will be making the decisions? And how much independence will you have?

One type of CCRC, the **life care facility**, has virtually disappeared. In a life care arrangement, residents turn over all their assets or pay the total lifetime fee in advance in return for shelter, health care, and supportive services for life. These types of contract have largely gone the way of the dinosaur, because the assets and fees generally are not sufficient to keep up with rising health-care expenses.

CCRCs may be privately owned, government-supported, or sponsored by nonprofit organizations. In terms of the position they occupy on the housing continuum, CCRCs (along with nursing homes) are the opposite of independent living. The definition of a CCRC varies from state to state, and sometimes even within states. State law protections for CCRCs may also vary substantially.

What to Look For in a CCRC or Assisted-Living Community

Entering any kind of retirement community is a major commitment. Consider the decision carefully and seek professional advice from a lawyer or financial advisor before you make a commitment. If you change your mind, you may not be able to get your money back.

The questions provided in this section will help you to evaluate just about any kind of supportive-housing arrangement.

▶ ## CHOOSE A CCRC OR ASSISTED-LIVING COMMUNITY WISELY!

- Do not rely on advertisements.
- Visit the facility at length and talk to both staff and residents.
- Check with your state's office on aging to find out whether the facility is licensed and to see whether it has experienced any problems.
- Ask for a copy of the contract, read it carefully, and have it reviewed by a lawyer.

Questions Regarding the Solvency and Expertise of the Provider

1. *What is the provider's background and experience?* The **provider** is the person or entity legally and financially responsible for providing the housing. Some facilities advertise that they are "sponsored" by nonprofit groups or churches that in reality have no legal control or financial responsibility. Be wary if such illusory sponsorship is trumpeted.

2. *Is the provider financially sound?* Ask a professional to review the facility's financial, actuarial, and operating statements. Does it have sufficient financial reserves?

3. *Are all levels of care licensed or certified by the state?* Check with the state office on aging, and with the state licensing agency.

4. *How does the facility ensure the quality of its care and services?*

Questions Regarding Fees and Accommodations

1. *If there is an entrance fee, how much is it, and can you get a refund of all or part of it?* The facility should provide a formula for a pro rata refund based on the resident's length of stay, regardless of whether the facility or the resident initiates the termination. Some facilities offer fully refundable entrance fees.

2. *What is the monthly fee? When can it be increased, and by how much? What happens if you cannot afford higher fees?*

Some facilities give residents financial help if they become unable to pay.

3. *Do the fees change when the resident's living arrangements or level-of-care needs change?*

4. *How much say do you have in choosing where you live? How large is the living unit? Can you change or redecorate it?*

5. *What if your marital status changes? Will your payments change, or will you be asked to move if you marry, divorce, become widowed, or have a friend or family member move into the unit?*

6. *What if spouses require different levels of care?*

Questions Regarding Services and Health Care

1. *What services are included in your regular fees?* Ask about coverage, limitations (based on cost, time, or number of visits), and special charges for the following amenities and services:

Supportive/Social/Recreational Services

- Meal services—Is the schedule reasonable? Is it flexible?
- Special diets/tray service—What is the policy on eating in your room?
- Utilities—Are they included in the monthly fee?
- Cable television—Is it available? Who pays?
- Furnishings—Can you bring your own?
- Unit maintenance—Who is responsible for repairs?
- Linens/personal laundry—Is there an extra charge for laundry?
- Housekeeping—Is it included in the fees? What services are available?
- Recreational/cultural activities—What activities are available? Which activities are on-site?
- Transportation—To what types of destinations is transportation offered? Is there a limit on the number of trips you can take?
- Safety—What kind of security system and policies are in place? Is there a fire emergency plan?

Health and Personal Care

- Assessment and plan of care—What kind of assessment is conducted to determine your needs and a plan for meeting those needs? What are the qualifications of the person performing the assessment? Is a detailed plan of care developed? When and how is it reviewed?

- Physician services—Can you choose your own doctor?
- Medications—Who administers medications? How is medication coordinated with your physician?
- Nursing care facility services—Are they on-site? Who pays?
- Nursing services outside a nursing unit—Is assistance with medications provided?
- Private-duty nursing—Is it available? Are there limits on availability?
- Dental and eye care—Is it included in your fees? Is it available on-site?
- Personal-care services—Is assistance available with eating, dressing, bathing, toileting, and so forth?
- Homemaker/companion services—Are they available? Is there a limit on availability?
- Drugs, medication, and medical equipment/supplies—Who pays?
- Emergency call system—Is such a system available? Who pays?

2. *Are additional services always guaranteed?* If the facility provides a nursing unit, what happens if a bed is not available when you need it?

3. *Can services be changed?* To what extent does the facility have the right to cut back, change, or eliminate services, or change the fees?

4. *What about preexisting conditions?* Does the facility limit its responsibility for certain health conditions or preexisting conditions? Can the facility ask you to move if you become too sick or impaired to be cared for by the facility?

5. *Who pays for health care?* Can you receive Medicare and Medicaid coverage in the facility? Does the facility require residents to buy private insurance or participate in a special group insurance program for residents?

6. *Who decides that you need more care, and on what grounds?* What are the criteria and procedures for determining

when a resident needs to be transferred from independent living to assisted living, or to a nursing care unit, or to an entirely different facility? Who is involved in these decisions?

7. *What are the staffing levels?* What are the professional qualifications of the staff? Make sure that staff are professionally equipped to do their jobs. What kinds of emergencies are staff expected to handle, and how are they trained for them?

Questions Regarding the Rights of Residents

1. *Can residents participate in facility management and decision making?* What input do you have in activity and meal planning and house rules? Is there a resident council? How are complaints and disputes handled?

2. *What if you want the facility to make an exception to a policy or to routine scheduling?*

3. *What are the grounds for eviction?* Is there a right to appeal?

 THE CCRC INDUSTRY PROFILED

A study by the American Association of Homes and Services for the Aging reveals the following statistics:

- Five states (California, Florida, Illinois, Ohio, and Pennsylvania) are home to nearly 40 percent of CCRCs.

- More than 625,000 older adults live in an estimated 2,100 CCRCs.

- The median age of CCRC residents is eighty-three; the median age at which people enter such facilities is seventy-eight.

- Married couples make up 13 percent of all CCRC residents and 18 percent of independent-living CCRC residents.

Source: American Association of Homes and Services for the Aging, *www.aahsa.org.*

4. *Are the general operating rules reasonable?* What rules cover the facility's day-to-day operation? What happens if you break a rule? Can you appeal?

5. *What happens if you are injured?* Does your contract release the facility from liability for injury resulting from negligence? You should avoid agreeing to such waivers.

NURSING HOME CARE

What are your legal rights as a resident of a nursing home? What should you consider when looking for a nursing home? What can you do when problems arise relating to your quality of care? This section answers these and other questions.

When you are faced with the possibility of moving to a nursing home, be sure to read about the alternatives to nursing home care described throughout this chapter. Alternatives, in the form of home and community-based care and assisted living, are becoming more widely available every day.

The Nursing Home Industry

Nursing homes are big business. Seventy percent are for-profit businesses, and many are large multi-state chains. All nursing homes must be licensed under state law, and more than 90 percent choose to participate in Medicare and/or Medicaid, which requires them to meet federal certification standards on quality of care, quality of life, and residents' rights. Unfortunately, monitoring and enforcement of those standards varies substantially from place to place. There are good nursing homes out there, but there is often no easy way to identify them.

Nursing homes provide skilled nursing and medical care, rehabilitation services, custodial care, and other health-related services. **Skilled care** includes such services as administering intravenous injections, tube feedings, or changing sterile dressings. It may also include observation of a changing condition, evaluation, and patient education. The term **custodial care** refers to help with eating, dressing, bathing, using the toilet, and moving about. (See Chapter 8, "Medicare and Private Health Benefits," for information about Medicare coverage of nursing home services.)

Finding a Nursing Home

Many nursing home admissions occur under stress—for example, when a person can no longer live alone because of a sudden health crisis. Even when you have time for deliberation, choosing a good nursing home can be difficult, because limited information is available about how different facilities compare.

In hospitals, **discharge planners**, who are usually social workers, can help with your decision making. They can provide general information about the facilities in your area, but they probably will not know about the actual quality of care in those facilities. Guides on selecting a nursing home also cannot provide you with quick or simple answers. State and local long-term-care ombudsmen, described below, are probably your best source of information. Representatives from such programs visit facilities and respond to complaints from nursing home residents and families, so they get a sense of the strengths and weaknesses of each facility. However, they may not be willing to share their opinions, for fear of being accused of bias.

As a starting point for acquiring information, you can obtain a facility's inspection report. States usually inspect homes once a year. Inspection reports detail major and minor deficiencies in the operation of facilities. Virtually every facility, even the very best, will have some problems. After all, the job of caring for highly impaired individuals is difficult. But beware of facilities that have demonstrated serious deficiencies in administering medication, managing incontinence or bedsores, using restraints, or that repeatedly experience the same problems. Compare the facility's last three or four inspection reports. If the same problems never get resolved, then even minor deficiencies may constitute major shortcomings. Nursing homes are required to have their inspection reports available for you to read. If a home doesn't have its report available, or if the facility makes it difficult for you to examine the report, consider its reluctance a serious "red flag" that could indicate quality problems. State nursing home licensing agencies—usually part of the state health department—can also make inspection reports available to you; often state or local ombudsman programs will have them as well. Nursing Home Compare, a federal government website, posts inspection and other information about nursing homes around the country that are certified by Medicare or Medicaid. For more information, visit *www.medicare.gov/NHCompare/Home.asp*.

Visit the facility you are considering on more than one occasion at different times of the day. Observe mealtimes, resident activities, and the interaction between staff and residents. Be wary of administrators who make access difficult or evade your questions. Look for both positive and negative signs, including the following:

	Signs of Good Quality	**Signs of Poor Quality**
Staff	Numerous staff interact personally with residents in a friendly and respectful manner.	Few staff are on duty. Staff does not interact with residents, or does so in an impersonal or brusque manner.
Food/Mealtimes	The food is appetizing to you and served in a dining room that encourages people to socialize. Staff is available to help residents who need assistance. Residents needing help are integrated with other residents.	Food is unappetizing or cold and served in a setting that does not encourage socializing. Staff is not available to provide assistance. Residents needing assistance are fed elsewhere or at a different time than other residents.

Building Appearance	The most important rooms are residents' rooms. Rooms are personalized and homey.	Residents' rooms are drab and institutionalized looking, indicating that residents are not encouraged to personalize their rooms.
Resident Appearance	Residents are reasonably well groomed, clean, and appropriately dressed.	Residents are inappropriately dressed, dirty, or unkempt. (Indicates inadequate staffing.)
Restraints	Few (and preferably no) residents are restrained, physically or by medication. Ask the administrator how many residents are restrained, and why.	Many residents are in restraints, or the facility cannot give you a clear answer as to the number of residents who are restrained. (Indicates inadequate care planning or inadequate staffing.)
Bedsores	Preferably no residents suffer from bedsores, though you probably cannot gather this information during a brief visit. (Check recent state inspection reports and ask the administrator for numbers.)	Bedsores are more than a rare occurrence or facility cannot give you a straight answer regarding the incidence of bedsores. (Indicates inadequate care planning or inadequate staffing.)
Smells	Facility is generally free of offensive odors.	Lingering, offensive odors throughout building. (Indicates inadequate staffing.)
Activities	Substantial numbers of residents enjoy frequently scheduled activities.	The activity calendar is fairly empty or uncreative in its offerings. Most residents are sitting around in day rooms doing nothing.

TALKING TO A LAWYER

Q. I have read that many nursing homes are understaffed. How can I find information about a facility's staffing?

A. If a nursing home is certified to accept reimbursement from Medicare and/or Medicaid, the nursing home must post its staffing levels for nurses and nurse's aides. This posting must be made every day, at the beginning of each shift, "[i]n a prominent place readily accessible to residents and visitors."

Staffing information for every nursing home, along with national and regional averages, is available from Medicare's Nursing Home Compare website at *www.medicare.gov/NHCompare/Home.asp*.

—Answer by Eric Carlson,
National Senior Citizens Law Center, Washington, DC

Residents' Rights

You do not surrender your rights and privileges when you enter a nursing home. Although institutional care limits your lifestyle and privacy, you should nevertheless expect high quality care that is both compassionate and dignified.

The federal Nursing Home Reform Amendments of 1987, and corresponding state laws, protect residents. For residents who lack decision-making capacity, the resident's agent under a health-care power of attorney (or another legal surrogate recognized by state law, typically a family member) may exercise the resident's rights.

Federal law requires that nursing homes meet strong basic standards regarding each resident's quality of life and quality of care. Each home must provide services and activities aimed at attaining or maintaining the highest practicable physical, mental, and psychosocial well-being of each resident. This is accomplished for each resident through a required resident assessment and a written plan of care, which is prepared with the resident or the resident's family or legal representative. This process should occur just after admission, and then quarterly or after any significant change in the resident's physical or mental condition.

The law also guarantees the following specific rights:

Information Rights

Nursing homes must provide:

- written information about your rights;
- written information about the services included in their monthly fee rates, and any extra charges for additional services;
- advance notice of any changes in room assignment or roommate;
- an explanation of your right to create a health-care advance directive, and information about their policies on complying with advance directives (see Chapter 7, "Advance Planning for Health-Care Decisions," for more information); and
- information about eligibility for Medicare and Medicaid and the services covered by those programs.

Self-Determination Rights

Each resident has the right to:

- participate in an individualized assessment and a care-planning process that accommodates the resident's personal needs and preferences;
- choose a personal physician;
- voice complaints without fear of reprisal, and receive a prompt response; and
- organize and participate in resident groups (such as a resident council) and family groups.

Personal and Privacy Rights

Residents have the right to:

- participate in social, religious, and community activities of their choosing;

- privacy in medical treatment, accommodations, personal visits, written and telephone communications, and meetings of resident and family groups;
- confidentiality in the use of all personal and clinical records;
- access to long-term-care ombudsmen, physicians, and family members, and reasonable access to other visitors;
- freedom from physical and mental abuse, corporal punishment, and involuntary seclusion;
- freedom from any physical restraint or psychoactive drug, used for purposes of convenience or discipline, that is not required to treat medical symptoms; and
- protection of the resident's funds held by the facility, including the right to a quarterly accounting.

Transfer and Discharge Rights
A resident may be transferred or discharged only for the following reasons:
- the health, safety, or welfare of the resident requires it;
- the health, safety, or welfare of other residents requires it;
- nonpayment of fees;
- improvement of the resident's health, so that he or she no longer needs nursing home care; or
- the closing of the facility.

Under normal circumstances, residents must receive at least thirty days' advance notice of any transfer or discharge, with information about how to appeal the decision and how to contact the state long-term-care ombudsman program. The facility also must provide adequate discharge planning to prepare and orient residents for a safe and orderly transfer from the facility.

Protection Against Medicaid Discrimination
Nursing homes that participate in the Medicaid program must:
- have identical policies and practices regarding services to residents, regardless of the source of payment—in other words,

basic care and services must be the same for Medicaid residents as for private-pay residents (but remember that not all facilities participate in Medicaid);

- provide you with information on how to apply for Medicaid;
- explain the Medicaid **bed-hold policy**—that is, how many days Medicaid will hold the resident's bed or give priority readmission to the resident after a hospitalization or other absence;
- not require, request, or encourage residents to waive their rights to Medicaid; and
- not charge, solicit, accept, or receive gifts, money, donations, or other valuable consideration as a precondition for admission or continued stay under Medicaid.

Nursing homes that accept Medicare or Medicaid are not allowed to require a family member or friend to guarantee payment (i.e., be personally financially responsible), even if the individual resident's care is not going to be reimbursed through Medicare or Medicaid.

What to Do When Problems Arise

Different problems require different responses. Try these steps when problems arise. (The order may vary depending on the problem.)

- Keep a written log of the relevant details (When? Where? Who? What? Why?).
- Try to resolve the problem informally by talking to the supervising nurse, social worker, or administrator.
- If the resident's needs have changed or the care plan is inadequate, you have a right to a new assessment and care-planning conference. This should result in an individually tailored plan of care.
- Bring the problem to the attention of the resident council or family council. Better facilities have active councils of this sort.
- Contact your long-term-care ombudsman.
- Contact the state agency that licenses nursing homes. Usually, the state department of health has this responsibility.

• Contact a community legal-assistance program or other advocacy organization. For problems involving serious physical, mental, or emotional harm, consult an attorney experienced in long-term-care issues.

The Long-Term-Care Ombudsman Program

The federal Older Americans Act requires every state to operate a long-term-care ombudsman program. The ombudsman is responsible for advocating on behalf of residents of nursing homes, assisted-living facilities, board-and-care facilities, and other long-term-care facilities. The ombudsman can provide information about options and rights, and can resolve complaints.

Most states offer local or regional programs. Ombudsmen are usually effective partners in resolving problems. Federal law requires nursing homes to allow the ombudsman access to residents and facilities. In addition, the ombudsman usually has special authority under state law to inspect records and take other steps necessary to respond to complaints.

HOME AND COMMUNITY-BASED CARE AND SERVICES

In your state or community, you will probably find programs designed to meet the daily needs of older adults and to enable them to age in place—that is, to age at home and in the community. Some programs charge fees, but others are subsidized by tax dollars or private nonprofit agencies.

Agencies devoted to aging play a central role in subsidizing and administering these programs. Each state has a unit on aging that has responsibility for a comprehensive service system. In most states, units on aging are divided into a number of smaller **area agencies on aging** (**AAAs**). These AAAs may function as part of county governments, regional planning councils, city governments, or private nonprofit organizations. They plan services for older persons, coordinate the delivery system for these services, and advocate for the elderly. Most AAAs do not deliver services directly, but contract with local providers for social services such as those listed below. Together, state and area agencies on aging, service providers, and advocates comprise what is known as an **aging network** in each state.

Typical home and community-based amenities and services include:

- transportation;
- senior centers;
- outreach;
- legal assistance;
- information and referral;
- housing services;
- case management;
- respite care;
- home health care;
- personal-care services;
- protective services;
- homemaker services;
- employment services;
- chore services;
- counseling;
- home-delivered meals;
- volunteer programs;
- congregate-meal programs;
- residential repair;
- friendly visitors;
- crime prevention and victim assistance;
- adult day care;
- money management; and
- other supportive services.

THE WORLD AT YOUR FINGERTIPS

- The American Association of Retired Persons (AARP) offers information on a range of senior housing options online, at *www.aarp.org/families/housing_choices*.

- The National Center for Home Equity Conversion is an independent, nonprofit organization established to educate consumers about reverse mortgages. This organization publishes comprehensive consumer guides and a list of preferred lenders at *www.reverse.org*.

- For information about home modifications that can make living at home easier and safer, visit the websites of the National Resource Center on Supportive Housing and Home Modification at *www.homemods.org* and AARP at *www.aarp.org/families/home_design*.

- The American Association of Homes and Services for the Aging (AAHSA) is a membership organization for assisted-living providers. Useful publications include *Continuing Care Retirement Communities: A Guidebook for Consumers*. The guidebook profiles not-for-profit retirement communities around the country and provides an overview of CCRC types, terminology, and features; visit *www.aahsa.org*.

- *Nursing Homes: Getting Good Care There* is a very useful publication from the National Citizens' Coalition for Nursing Home Reform. It offers step-by-step guidance on how to make sure patients receive good care and enjoy a decent quality of life once they enter a nursing home; visit *www.nccnhr.org*.

- The National Senior Citizens Law Center (NSCLC) has also published helpful consumer publications on nursing home issues. The consumer manual *20 Common Nursing Home Problems—and How to Resolve Them* is available from the NSCLC website at *www.nsclc.org*.

REMEMBER THIS

- No matter where you live, you should be a careful consumer by knowing the risks and benefits of various housing options, as well as your legal rights.

- Entering any kind of retirement community is a major commitment. Consider the decision carefully and seek professional advice from a lawyer or financial advisor before you make a commitment. If you change your mind, you may not be able to get your money back.

• There are good nursing home facilities out there, but no easy ways to identify them—so do your research.

• You do not surrender your rights and privileges when you enter a nursing home.

CHAPTER 12

Living with Disability

The Americans with Disabilities Act and Other Legal Protections

Mary lives in an apartment. In recent months, she has become unsteady on her feet. She fell twice, and now uses a walker when she goes out. She is anxious about slipping in the shower. She still drives during the day, but can rarely find a parking space close to her building. She does not want to ask for special help, because the building manager is already hinting that Mary should move. Mary's daughter wants Mary to move so that they can be closer to one another, but Mary's life is centered around her current home. Is there a way to make Mary's life a bit easier, without requiring her to move?

We all age differently. Although we are now living longer and are in better health than ever before, we have a higher likelihood of suffering from a disability as we age. A third of us over the age of sixty-five have a physical disability, as do half of us over the age of eighty-five. But a disability does not mean that you must give up the places, activities, and livelihood to which you have become accustomed. Three important federal laws—the **Rehabilitation Act of 1973**, the **Americans with Disabilities Act of 1990 (ADA)**, and the **Fair Housing Amendments Act of 1988 (FHAA)**—protect people with disabilities from discrimination. In addition, these laws require employers and providers of housing or services to make reasonable modifications to their rules to meet the needs of persons with disabilities.

The Rehabilitation Act, the ADA, and the FHAA protect qualified individuals with physical or mental impairments that substantially limit one or more major life activities, such as:

- seeing;
- walking;

- learning;
- hearing;
- breathing;
- caring for yourself;
- speaking; and
- performing manual tasks.

Examples of impairments that substantially limit major life activities include paralysis, mental retardation, substantial vision or hearing loss, severe arthritis, respiratory difficulties, AIDS, alcoholism, diabetes, heart disease, mental illness, and other disabling chronic conditions. The laws also protect you if you have a record of such an impairment or if you are *perceived* as having such an impairment.

These laws do not protect people who threaten the safety or health of others, or whose behavior would result in substantial damage to the property of others. Nor do the laws protect current users of illegal drugs.

It is important to note that these laws do not protect people on the basis of age, but they do protect older people with disabilities that arise *because* of their age.

THE REHABILITATION ACT

The key provision of the Rehabilitation Act of 1973 is **Section 504**, titled **Nondiscrimination under Federal grants and programs**. Section 504 prohibits discrimination against qualified individuals with disabilities by any program or activity that receives federal funds. Section 504 was designed to place individuals with disabilities on an equal footing with nondisabled people in regard to such programs and activities.

The Rehabilitation Act covers all "programs or activities" operated by departments or agencies of the federal government and departments of state or local governments that receive federal funds. In addition, the following organizations and places are covered by the Rehabilitation Act *if* they receive federal funding:

- public schools, including colleges and universities;
- entities principally engaged in providing education, health care, housing, social services, or parks and recreation; and
- other businesses, any part of which receive federal financial assistance.

Examples of covered operations include post offices, courthouses, city halls, hospitals and nursing homes that receive Medicare or Medicaid payments, and senior centers that are supported by federal money.

Section 504 provided a model for the Americans with Disabilities Act, which expands on Section 504 to include private businesses, public accommodations, and state and local governments, regardless of whether they receive federal funding.

THE AMERICANS WITH DISABILITIES ACT (ADA)

The ADA aims to provide equal opportunity for persons with disabilities in:

- employment;
- state and local government programs and services;
- places open to the public, such as restaurants, theaters, stores, banks, or senior centers;
- public transportation; and
- telecommunications services.

The ADA does not apply to private clubs or religious entities, except when they sponsor public events. Also excluded are employers with fewer than fifteen employees. Two areas not covered by the ADA are housing and insurance. The Fair Housing Amendments Act imposes similar requirements on housing. However, no other federal laws cover disability discrimination in the insurance arena.

Employment

If you are a qualified person with a disability, then private employers with fifteen or more employees, state and local governments, employment agencies, and labor unions with fifteen or more employees cannot discriminate against you on the basis of your disability in any matters related to employment. You are considered qualified if you are able to perform "essential functions" of the job, with or without reasonable accommodations.

A **reasonable accommodation** is a modification that makes it possible for you to do a job for which you are qualified, and that does not cause an employer undue hardship. Some examples of reasonable accommodations include:

- changing work schedules;
- modifying examinations or training materials;
- making facilities accessible;
- restructuring jobs;
- providing equipment or devices (such as text telephones for the deaf or special computer software); and
- providing qualified readers or interpreters.

An employer does not have to provide an accommodation that would cause an undue hardship—that is, an accommodation that would entail significant difficulty or expense. Some factors to consider in deciding whether an accommodation would create significant difficulty or expense include: (1) the nature and cost

 AGE VS. DISABILITY DISCRIMINATION

Age is not considered a disability under the ADA. If you are forty or older and have experienced employment discrimination because of your age, you may have a claim under the Age Discrimination in Employment Act (ADEA), which is discussed in Chapter 13, "Age Discrimination in Employment." If you are an older person with a disability, you may have claims under both the ADA and the ADEA. If you suspect that you have a claim under either law, you should file a charge of discrimination with the Equal Employment Opportunity Commission (EEOC) if the problem involves an employer.

of the accommodation; (2) the financial resources of the employer; (3) the number of people employed by the employer; and (4) the impact on the business of making the accommodation. For example, it would be considered reasonable to expect an employer to widen a doorway and lower a desk to accommodate an employee who uses a wheelchair. But it likely would be considered an undue hardship to require the employer to build a new wing on an office building in order to accommodate the same employee. In addition, it would not be considered reasonable to require an employer to transfer the essential functions of a job to another employee.

Access to Programs, Services, and Facilities

The ADA promises individuals with disabilities equal access to state and local government services, programs, and facilities, such as schools, senior centers, and courts. It also provides that disabled individuals should have access to the services of private businesses and commercial facilities, such as law offices, banks, and grocery stores. The ADA calls for three major actions by these providers of services. Under the ADA, they must:
 • make reasonable modifications to policies, practices, and procedures as necessary to ensure access by disabled people;
 • ensure the opportunity for effective communications; and
 • make newly constructed physical facilities accessible to people with disabilities, and remove barriers to accessibility when such removal is "readily achievable."

Only truly private clubs and religious organizations are exempt from the ADA requirements concerning public accommodations.

What Constitutes a Reasonable Modification to a Policy, Practice, or Procedure?

Under the ADA, a reasonable modification to a policy, practice, or procedure is a change in rules or practices that is enacted in order to avoid discrimination. For example, if a restaurant has a no-pets rule, it must make an exception for service animals that accompany blind customers. However, modifications that fundamentally change the nature of a service are not required. Thus, a museum would not be required to allow blind persons to touch art objects if touching would damage the art.

What Constitutes an Effective Communication under the ADA?

State and local governments and public accommodations must ensure that their communications with disabled individuals are as effective as their communications with nondisabled individuals, and they must make available appropriate auxiliary aids and services. For example, if you have a hearing impairment and are called for jury duty, the court must provide an interpreter or an assistive-listening device if necessary to enable your participation as a juror. Actions that would change the nature of a service or constitute an undue burden on the provider are not required.

How Can Providers Make Facilities Physically Accessible?

The ADA provides that all new buildings must meet certain design standards of accessibility. In existing buildings, private businesses must remove architectural barriers and make modifi-

---

 ### EXAMPLES OF AUXILIARY AIDS AND SERVICES

Examples of auxiliary aids and services for persons who are deaf or hard of hearing include qualified interpreters, notetakers, computer-aided transcription services, written materials, assistive-listening systems, TDDs (text telephones for the deaf), and the exchange of written notes. Examples of aids for individuals with vision impairments include qualified readers, taped texts, audio recordings, braille or large-print materials, and assistance in locating items.

cations (such as installing wheelchair ramps, widening narrow doorways, aisles, and restroom doors, and lowering drinking fountains and pay telephones) if such barrier removal is readily achievable—that is, able to be carried out without significant difficulty or expense. If a barrier cannot be readily removed, such services must be provided in another way. State or local government entities such as courts or libraries must ensure that their programs as a whole are accessible, either by removing barriers or taking other actions. In a courthouse without an elevator, for example, the court must schedule a trial on the first floor if a person who cannot climb stairs is involved in the trial. Similarly, library staff must retrieve books from an upper floor if necessary to assist a disabled patron.

Enforcing Your Rights under the ADA

In order to enforce your rights under the ADA, you may wish to take the following steps:

1. First, talk to the business, service, or employer from whom you require assistance. Explain your needs and the requirements of the ADA; perhaps you can resolve the problem informally.

2. Try mediation. Check with your local court or bar association for referrals to a mediation program in your community.

3. File a complaint with the Department of Justice if your complaint concerns state or local government programs and services. You must file within 180 days after the discrimination occurs.

4. If you think a potential or current employer is discriminating against you because of a disability, file a complaint with the Equal Employment Opportunity Commission (EEOC). Again, you must file your complaint within 180 days of the discriminatory act. (See Chapter 13, "Age Discrimination in Employment," for more information.)

5. If these steps have not been successful, file a lawsuit. Contact an attorney familiar with employment or disability law for advice and representation. If your complaint relates to an

employment matter, you must file a complaint with the EEOC before going to court.

HOUSING AND DISABILITY

Sometimes landlords refuse to rent to older people because they think older people are too frail to live alone; sometimes they evict older people with disabilities because disabled people need assistance with certain activities. Renters may find protection in one of two federal laws: the Fair Housing Amendments Act of 1988 and the Rehabilitation Act of 1973. These laws also protect against discrimination by assisted-living and continuing-care retirement communities; however, these cases can be complicated because such facilities also provide health-care and other services, and may also be licensed. (See Chapter 11, "Housing and Long-Term-Care Choices," for more information.)

Section 504 of the Rehabilitation Act applies to housing programs that receive federal funds, such as public housing or federally subsidized housing for older persons. The Fair Housing Amendments Act prohibits discrimination in housing matters against people with disabilities. It does not apply to single-family rental properties if the landlord owns fewer than three homes and rents them out without using a realtor, or to buildings with four or fewer rental units if the owner also lives in the building. Newly constructed (post-1991) multifamily housing comprised of four or more units must provide access for persons with disabilities.

Examples of prohibited discrimination include:
• refusing to rent to a family with a member who suffers from mental illness;
• requiring an applicant for senior housing to provide a doctor's letter stating that he or she is in good health;
• denying a resident who uses a wheelchair or a walker access to a communal dining room; and
• evicting a tenant because he or she is receiving homemaking help or other services.

What is Required of Landlords

A landlord must make reasonable accommodations to provide a tenant with a disability equal opportunity to use the residence. Reasonable accommodations are reasonable changes in rules or procedures, such as:

- in the case of a person with a mental disability who is afraid to leave his or her unit, changing a policy that requires rent to be paid in person at the rental office;
- providing large-print notices for a tenant with vision impairment;
- waiving a no-guest rule for a tenant needing live-in help;
- waiving a no-pet rule for a tenant with a service animal; and
- allowing a tenant to bring in supportive services such as meals or housekeeping.

Accommodations for disabilities often can be worked out informally. However, there is a limit to the accommodations that a landlord is required to make. Landlords are not required to provide services that would change the nature of their business. For example, a landlord might be required to allow a tenant to continue living in an apartment even though he or she receives various support services from the county, but the landlord is not required to provide those services. So if a tenant needs housekeeping assistance or help in preparing her meals, a landlord would not be required to perform those tasks.

Landlords must also permit reasonable physical modifications to existing buildings in order to provide a tenant with disabilities equal access to the residence. Examples of such modifications include:

- installation of grab bars in a bathroom;
- replacement of doorknobs with lever handles;
- widening of doorways to allow wheelchair access;
- installation of a ramp; and
- replacement of small floor numbers with larger numbers so that tenants can read them more easily.

The major distinction between private rental housing and federally funded housing arises in the area of reasonable modifications. The Fair Housing Amendments Act grants tenants of *private* rental housing the right to make reasonable modifications to apartments and common areas of their property, but these changes must be made *at the tenants' own expense*. Common areas include hallways, or even the entrances to buildings. If you make modifications to your private rental property, you may be required to restore the premises to the original condition when you move out. Tenants in housing that receives *federal* funding have additional protections. Section 504 requires landlords to bear the cost of reasonable modifications, whether such modifications are made inside the apartment or in common areas.

There is one situation in which a renter of private housing may not have to bear the expense of certain modifications to common areas. If you live in a building that has space open to the public, such as a rental office, a senior center, or a meal site, that space could fall under the requirements of the Americans with Disabilities Act because a rental office or senior center is a public accommodation.

For new construction—specifically, construction completed after 1991—the obligations of landlords and builders are much

 LIMITS ON LANDLORDS

The Fair Housing Act prohibits a landlord from asking a potential tenant about his or her health or medical history. As a general rule, a landlord may require only information that establishes an applicant's ability to meet the terms of a lease—i.e., to pay the rent, care for the unit, and not interfere with the rights of others. There may be exceptions to this general rule if the apartment is available only to tenants with certain disabilities, or if an applicant with a disability requests an accommodation. In those cases, a landlord may be permitted to ask for verification of the disability.

clearer. Builders must meet specific design standards that provide accessibility for persons with disabilities. To find out what buildings are covered and the standards that apply, contact the Fair Housing Complaint Hotline of the Department of Housing and Urban Development (HUD) at the number listed below.

Enforcing Your Housing Rights

The Department of Housing and Urban Development (HUD) has the authority to enforce Section 504. The Fair Housing Amendments Act also can be enforced by HUD, by state or local human relations commissions and fair-housing agencies, or by individuals through the courts. If you believe you have been discriminated against, you can file a complaint with HUD. Call HUD's Fair Housing Complaint Hotline at 1-800-669-9777, or file a complaint online on the HUD website, at *www.hud.gov/ complaints/housediscrim.cfm*.

DRIVING AND DISABILITY

Cars are such a vital part of American life that giving up driving can signal the beginning of dependence on others. Although they have fewer accidents per driver than drivers of any other age group, older drivers have more accidents per mile driven than do middle-aged drivers. Moreover, older drivers are at greater risk than other drivers of dying from accidents. Many older drivers are perfectly capable of driving, but key driving skills tend to decline with age. Vision, hearing, and mobility may be impaired. In addition, reaction times in older drivers may also diminish.

Many older drivers recognize their declining skills and limit their driving accordingly—by not driving at night, on highways, or on unfamiliar roads. However, some drivers—especially those with dementia—may not be aware of their limitations. Drivers should be aware of any declining driving skills and look for ways to compensate. In addition, drivers should:

WARNING SIGNS OF DECLINING DRIVING SKILLS

Drivers should begin to limit driving or stop driving altogether when they have trouble doing any of the following:

- staying in one lane of traffic or judging gaps in traffic;
- reading road signs or pavement markings;
- responding to unexpected situations;
- moving their foot from the gas to brake pedal, or pressing the correct pedal; or
- turning around to check over their shoulder while backing up or changing lanes.

Drivers should also limit their driving accordingly when they experience an increase in the number of:

- "close calls";
- warnings or tickets issued by the police;
- dents or scrapes on their car or garage door;
- other drivers honking or yelling at them; or
- situations in which they find themselves angry with other drivers.

Source: "When to Stop Driving," by AARP, available online at *www.aarp .org/families/driver_safety/driver_safetyissues/a2004-06-21-whentostop .html* (November 2005).

- get regular eye examinations;
- check with a doctor about the effects on their driving ability of any medications;
- adjust driving habits to cope safely (e.g., by avoiding unnecessary left turns and rush hour traffic);
- combine errands more efficiently, or enlist another person to act as a "copilot";
- take a refresher course in driving techniques, such as the AARP Driver Safety Program; and

• look for other ways of getting around in addition to driving. Many communities offer special transportation resources for older persons, senior-friendly public transportation, or volunteer driver programs. Check with your area agency on aging and your public transportation agency for more information.

The right or privilege of holding a driver's license is based on state laws, which are enforced by state motor vehicle departments. In determining whether a driver's license will be granted, revoked, or restricted, some states try to balance the need for public safety with the driver's need for independence and mobility, while others make the decision based on cost.

License Renewals

All states require driver's-license renewal on a regular basis. In some states, license renewal procedures are different for older drivers than for younger drivers. For example, drivers above a certain age may be required to take a vision test, or even a knowledge or road test. The renewal period may be shorter after a certain age. However, age itself should never be the reason for denial of renewal.

When Can They Take Your License Away?

This depends on state law. A driver's skills may be reevaluated and his or her license revoked if:
• he or she fails to pass a license renewal test;
• his or her accident rate indicates that he or she may be an unsafe driver; or
• a police officer, physician, family member, or other person reports him or her to the licensing agency as an unsafe driver.

In some cases, medical-review boards may administer or review the results of tests. Researchers are exploring new and better ways for doctors, review boards, motor vehicle departments, and older drivers themselves to assess driving performance and decide when a license is no longer warranted.

Fighting a License Revocation

In most (if not all) states, drivers have the right to appeal a revocation of their license. Each state has different procedures for reviewing license revocations. Some states may provide an opportunity for a hearing or other administrative review. A medical-review board may be involved. Drivers may also have the right to have a licensing agency's decision reviewed by a court. Check with your state's licensing agency to find out your rights.

Restricted Licenses

States also provide for specific restrictions on the right to drive. The most common restriction requires drivers to wear glasses or contact lenses if they have experienced vision loss. Some states are beginning to allow limited licenses for older drivers who have a history of accidents or traffic violations, or who have failed their driving tests. A **restricted** or **graduated license** might allow a driver to drive during daylight hours, at restricted speeds, with special outside mirrors, within city limits, only on non-freeway roads, or only after passing yearly tests.

The increasing issuance of restricted licenses could mean that licensing is no longer such an all-or-nothing option. For example, a driver may no longer be able to drive safely in dense urban traffic or at high speeds, but may be very capable of getting to the grocery store or the post office on less-traveled roads.

 AUTO INSURANCE DISCOUNTS

Depending on the state where you live and your insurance company's policies, you may be eligible for an automobile insurance premium reduction or discount just for completing an approved driver refresher course. Check with your insurance company for more information.

THE WORLD AT YOUR FINGERTIPS

• You can contact the U.S. Department of Justice, Civil Rights Division, Office of the Americans with Disabilities Act by phone at 1-800-514-0301, and ask to speak with an ADA specialist. Information is also available online at *www.usdoj.gov/crt/ada/cguide.htm*.

• The Department of Housing and Urban Development (HUD) handles housing complaints in several categories. If your discrimination complaint involves housing, contact the agency toll-free at 1-800-669-9777, or online at *www.hud.gov/complaints*.

• Each state has its own disability rights agency called a Protection and Advocacy Agency. These agencies provide legal representation and advocacy on behalf of persons with disabilities. To find the agency in your state, call the National Disability Rights Network at (202) 408-9514 or visit their website at *www.ndrn.org*.

• The Centers for Independent Living (CILs) are private non-profit self-help organizations that help people with disabilities live independently in the community. There are more than four hundred CILs across the country that can provide you with information, make referrals for services, and assist you in finding accessible housing. A listing of independent-living centers can be found online at *www.ilru.org*.

• The Job Accommodations Network provides information on accommodations for workers with disabilities at *http://janweb.icdi.wvu.edu*.

• AARP sponsors the AARP Driver Safety Program, aimed at improving the driving skills of older drivers, and publishes a number of useful materials at *www.aarp.org/families/driver_safety*.

• The American Automobile Association (AAA) Foundation for Traffic Safety also publishes useful guides, which can be ordered online at *www.aaafoundation.org/home*; click on "Products."

REMEMBER THIS

• Three important federal laws—the Rehabilitation Act of 1973, the Americans with Disabilities Act of 1990 (ADA), and the Fair Housing Amendments Act of 1988 (FHAA)—protect people with disabilities from discrimination.

• These laws do not protect people on the basis of age, but they do protect older people with disabilities that arise because of their age.

• Key driving skills—including vision, hearing, mobility, and reaction time—tend to decline with age; communities may offer special transportation resources for older persons or refresher driving courses in driving techniques.

CHAPTER 13

Age Discrimination
in Employment

Your Rights in the Workplace

John, age sixty-two, has worked as a marketing representative for ABC Corporation, a large manufacturing company, for twenty-five years. This week, John's supervisor informs him that ABC is undertaking a reduction in force and that John is among the group to be laid off. The main reason, the supervisor says, is that John lacks some of the high-tech skills the company thinks will be essential for its future financial success—for example, proficiency in using the Internet, newer data management software, and automated telemarketing systems. John responds that the reason he lacks some of these skills is that he has not been offered training in many of these areas, whereas younger employees either already have these skills as part of their education or are more likely to be offered training by ABC. Upon further inquiry among his coworkers, John finds out that fifteen of twenty-five marketing employees are to be laid off; of those fifteen, ten are over the age of fifty-five. John thinks that age is a big reason why he is being laid off—not qualifications or skills, as his supervisor told him. What can he do?

Protection of the rights of older workers has been a national policy reflected in the law for many years. In the early 1960s, employers commonly discriminated against older workers because of negative stereotypes about aging and faulty assumptions about the costs and productivity of older workers. In response, Congress passed the Age Discrimination in Employment Act (ADEA) of 1967. This federal law attempts to secure fair and equal treatment for workers age forty and over by:

• promoting the employment of older persons based on their ability rather than age;

- prohibiting arbitrary age discrimination in employment; and
- encouraging employers and workers to find ways of solving

problems arising from the impact of age on employment.

The ADEA is even more important today than it was when it was passed. Corporate streamlining in the form of downsizing has become the norm—through layoffs, production cutbacks, plant closings, corporate mergers, restructurings, and techno-

---

 ## HOW WIDESPREAD IS AGE DISCRIMINATION IN EMPLOYMENT?

The chart below reveals the number of age discrimination charges that were filed with the Equal Employment Opportunity Commission (EEOC) from 1999 to 2004. Of course, there were likely many more instances of age discrimination than are represented below. The process of filing a charge is discussed in more detail later in this chapter, in the section titled "How to Enforce Your ADEA Rights."

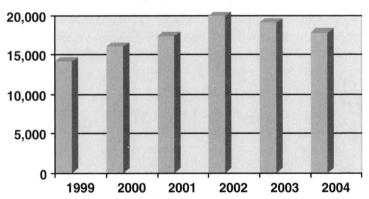

Age Discrimination Charges Filed Nationwide with the EEOC

Source: U.S. Equal Employment Opportunity Commission.

logical change. Older workers are more likely than others to face discrimination relating to hiring and layoff policies, and sometimes not-so-obvious discrimination relating to early-retirement incentives or severance benefit offers.

In the example described above, John may very well be a victim of unlawful age discrimination. Determining whether discrimination has actually taken place will require a closer examination of the facts of his case, and a careful understanding of the substance of the ADEA.

WHO IS COVERED BY THE ADEA?

The Age Discrimination in Employment Act applies to most (but not all) workers age forty and over. The most significant exclusion is of small businesses employing fewer than twenty workers. However, the Act does apply to:

- private employers with twenty or more employees;
- all state, federal, and local government employers;
- private and public employment agencies; and
- labor organizations with twenty-five or more members.

Previously, the Act did not protect workers over the age of seventy, but the age cap was removed in 1987. The ADEA protects you even if you work in a foreign country for an American corporation or its subsidiary, so long as the ADEA does not directly conflict with the law of the country in which you work.

WHAT DOES THE ADEA PROHIBIT?

Generally, the ADEA prohibits:

- discrimination against workers age forty and older in all aspects of employment (such discrimination may range from the telling of offensive age-related jokes to the use of age as a factor in decisions relating to hiring, firing, layoff, promotion, demotion, training opportunities, compensation, benefits, or working conditions and hours);

• the use of age-related preferences in notices or advertisements for employment;

• retaliation against employees for complaints about age discrimination or for assisting government investigations of alleged age discrimination; and

• age-based discrimination in matters relating to membership activities and referrals by labor organizations and employment agencies.

The ADEA prohibits age-based discrimination even if such discrimination favors members of the age group the law was designed to protect (i.e., those forty and older). For example, an employer cannot favor a forty-five-year-old over a sixty-year-old.

Can an employer discriminate against you if your age is only one of several reasons that an employer discriminated against you? As long as age is one determining factor for the discrimination, you are protected by the ADEA; age does not have to be the sole factor. Other unlawful forms of discrimination, based on factors such as race or sex, are covered by other laws.

EXAMPLES OF UNLAWFUL DISCRIMINATION

The goal of this section is to provide you with a better sense of the breadth of the ADEA.

Mandatory Retirement

You cannot be forced to retire when you reach a certain age. Nor can your employer penalize you for continuing employment at a certain age by forcing you to take a job that entails less responsibility or a lower salary.

Naturally, however, there are exceptions to this rule. Three groups are not protected by the ADEA from mandatory retirement:

1. Public appointees in policy-making positions, and their immediate advisors.

2. Persons who have been in "bona fide executive" or "high policy-making" positions for at least two years and whose retirement benefits (i.e., benefits from pension, profit-sharing plans, savings, and deferred compensation) add up to at least $44,000 a year, not including Social Security. (Yes, $44,000 is a ridiculously low amount in light of today's levels of executive compensation, but the ADEA provides a fixed figure that is not adjusted yearly.) Earning a salary greater than $44,000 is not sufficient to cause an employee to fall within the exception. Rather, the exception is intended to apply to the relatively few top-level employees in an organization who exercise substantial authority over a significant number of employees. If you fall within this group, you may be subject to mandatory retirement at age sixty-five. However, the ADEA's other antidiscrimination protections will still apply.

3. Public-safety officers, such as firefighters and police officers. The ADEA permits their mandatory retirement at any age specified by state or local law; it also specifies upper age limits on hiring.

Discrimination in Hiring: The "Overqualified" Worker

Discrimination can be hard to detect. Sometimes it can even take the form of a thinly veiled compliment. For example, older workers with a great deal of experience are often denied jobs on the grounds that they are "overqualified."

Whether this is legal depends on the nature of the job and the surrounding circumstances. Sometimes it might be reasonable for an employer to deny you a job because you have too much experience or education. For example, someone with a PhD in education could be legitimately overqualified for a teacher's-aide position that requires only two years of college education. In other cases, however, a court might decide that an employer deems an older worker "overqualified" simply as a way to avoid giving him or her a job.

TALKING TO A LAWYER

Q. My company says that its mandatory-retirement policy applies to me because I am a vice president, and therefore an upper executive not subject to the ADEA. Is this correct?

A. Perhaps not. The ADEA provides an exception to the prohibition against mandatory retirement for "bona fide executive or high policy-making employees," but the burden is on the employer to prove that all requirements of the exception are met.

The exemption applies only to employees who are at least sixty-five years old, have been employed in their positions for at least two years immediately before the compulsory retirement, and are entitled to an immediate annual retirement benefit of at least $44,000 under a pension or other plan of their employers. Only if you meet these requirements will your employer's claim of exemption be given consideration.

The mere fact that you have been given the title of "vice president" will not by itself establish that you are covered by the bona-fide-executive exemption. The exception is very limited, and is intended to apply only to a very few top-level employees who exercise substantial executive authority over a significant number of employees and a large volume of business. Typically this might include the head of a substantial local or regional operation of a business organization, but not the head of a minor branch, warehouse, or retail store. You do not mention that you hold any high-level responsibilities within your company, and it thus seems quite possible that you would not fall within the bona-fide-executive exemption.

The term "upper executive," which your employer used to refer to you, has no precise counterpart in the ADEA; indeed, the term does not appear in the statute at all. But perhaps your employer's use of the term suggests that it believes you are a high-level policy-making employee of the type to which the exemption would apply. Again, whether you fall within that exemption will be determined by careful consideration of your actual job duties—not just your title. Generally speaking, for purposes of the ADEA a high policy-making position is a position held by an employee who has little or no line authority (i.e., direct supervisory authority), but who plays a significant role in the development of corporate policy, and who effectively recommends implementation of policies.

—Answer by Ed King, Executive Director,
National Senior Citizens Law Center, Washington, DC

Be wary of a potential employer who says to you, "I'm sure that with your extensive experience, you wouldn't be interested in this entry-level position." This type of rejection could be a subtle form of discrimination.

Layoffs or Downsizing by Employers

The ADEA prohibits employers from using age as a factor in layoffs or **reductions in force** (downsizing). Employers may make layoff decisions based on reasonable factors other than age, such as objective performance evaluations, skill level, or seniority (i.e., "last hired, first fired"). However, sometimes employers' reliance on these other factors simply serves to mask age discrimination. For example, if an employer lays off only its highest-paid employees, it may be unlawfully discriminating against older employees, because higher pay often correlates with older age. Determining whether this type of layoff constitutes age discrimination requires further investigation into the employer's motives. Even layoff decisions that are age-neutral on their face can be challenged if they disproportionately affect older workers. This kind of claim, based on **disparate impact**, is permissible under the law, but is difficult to prove.

EVIDENCE OF AGE DISCRIMINATION: DISPARATE TREATMENT AND DISPARATE IMPACT

Disparate-treatment evidence is evidence that shows you were treated differently *because* of your age. Such evidence may be direct or inferential, but it must show that, but for your age, you would have been treated differently. You must show that the motive of your employer was discriminatory. Any policy that refers to age may be suspect under this approach—for example, a policy of not training workers who are over the age of fifty. Providing evidence of disparate treatment is the most common approach to proving age discrimination.

Disparate-impact evidence is evidence that a policy or practice that appears neutral on its face is nonetheless discriminatory against older persons. For example, a seemingly neutral employee evaluation process could be administered in a way that consistently downgrades all older workers without reasonable justification. If this is the case, then the impact of the evaluation process is *disparate*, to the disadvantage of older workers. Disparate-impact cases often rely heavily on statistics rather than evidence of motivation, but are more difficult to prove than cases of disparate treatment.

When a layoff does occur, the ADEA explicitly prohibits an employer from reducing an employee's severance benefits or other layoff benefits just because he or she is eligible for a pension or pension-related benefit, except in certain narrowly defined circumstances.

Compensation and Fringe Benefits

Wage discrimination based on age, in which older employees are paid less than younger employees, is clearly illegal, and probably rare. A more common scenario is discrimination in connection with job-related fringe benefits, such as insurance or health care.

The general rule is that employers must provide the same benefits to all age groups, or provide benefits that cost the same for all age groups. For example, if it costs an employer more to provide a life insurance benefit to older workers than to younger workers, then the employer may provide older workers with a smaller insurance benefit, as long as the cost of the benefit to the employer is the same as the cost of the benefit offered to younger workers.

With respect to health insurance, employers must cover older workers and their spouses under the same conditions as younger workers. While you are employed, your benefits cannot be lowered simply because you become eligible for Medicare. In fact, your employer's insurance must remain your primary insurance; Medicare will become your secondary insurer.

Training and Promotions

Older workers must be given the same privileges of employment as younger workers. Training opportunities and promotions are two examples of privileges that employers must administer fairly.

An employer cannot argue, for example, that younger workers are likely to be with the company longer and should thus receive more opportunities for promotion than older workers. Older workers must be given the same chance to receive promotions as all other workers. However, age does not *entitle* an older worker to a promotion; an employer may have a valid reason, apart from age, for promoting a younger person rather than an older one.

Job Assignments, Demotions, and Working Conditions

Employers cannot demote older workers based on age. Such demotions can sometimes occur indirectly, when an employer gradually shifts more and more responsibilities from an older worker to other workers without adequate justification. If working conditions, hours, or other elements in the working environment change for the worse, these changes may violate the ADEA if they are based on age, or if they are motivated by a desire to make the work so unpleasant that the older worker is forced to quit.

Performance Evaluation

Performance evaluations cannot be age-biased in terms of their content or the way in which they are applied. Be wary of any job performance system that is applied differently to older workers than to younger workers. A legitimate performance evaluation system should be objective. It should also be age-neutral in terms of its content and the way it is administered, and it should have "teeth"—that is, it should have real consequences in terms of your continued employment.

Harassment

All harassment related to age is illegal. Managers cannot harass you or make fun of you because of your age, nor can they permit others to do so. For example, older workers should not be made to feel uncomfortable because they are labeled as "old-fashioned," "out of synch," "set in their ways," or "old dogs" who cannot learn "new tricks." As a practical matter, a finding of harassment requires a significant pattern of harassing activities, rather than just a single act or event.

Advertising

Advertisements may not exclude or discourage older workers from applying for a job, unless age is a **bona fide occupational qualification (BFOQ)** for that job. For example, an age limit would be permissible in an advertisement seeking a person to model teen clothing, since the clothing in question is designed to be worn by teens. But an age limit would not be permissible in an advertisement for a clerk position that merely involved *selling* teen clothing. A general rule is that advertisements may not imply that only people of certain age groups are wanted for a job.

BONA FIDE OCCUPATIONAL QUALIFICATION

A **bona fide occupational qualification** is an employment qualification that, although it may prove discriminatory, relates to an essential function of a job and is considered reasonably necessary to the operation of the business in question.

Retaliation for Making an ADEA Complaint

It is illegal for an employer to retaliate against an employee for filing a complaint under the ADEA. This means that if you've made a claim under the ADEA, and your employer directly or indirectly withholds expected resources or work assignments from you, or your working conditions obviously decline, or if you are subjected to a hostile attitude by supervisors, then the employer has engaged in an additional violation of the ADEA. This could be grounds for another ADEA-based claim. Because these types of behaviors can be subtle, you should keep careful notes about your employer's behavior as evidence for your claim.

Discrimination Based on Disability

The ADEA protects you only from discrimination based on age. If an illness or disability prevents you from performing your job satisfactorily, the ADEA does not prevent your employer from requiring you to retire, regardless of your age. However, other federal and state laws, including the Americans with Disabilities Act (ADA) of 1990, forbid discrimination against persons with disabilities or handicaps, including those associated with certain illnesses. If you are the victim of discrimination but the ADEA does not apply to your situation, consider whether you are being treated unfairly because of your disability. Your protections under the ADA are described in Chapter 12, "Living with Disability."

Early-Retirement Incentives

More and more employers are using **early-retirement incentives** to reduce their work forces. Common examples of such incentives include:

• payment of full retirement benefits to workers who retire early;

• supplementation of retirement benefits with additional cash (**bridge payments**) for a limited period of time in order to assist former employees until they become eligible for Social Security benefits; and

• addition of age and/or service credits to employees' work records to enable them to meet pension eligibility provisions at an earlier age, or an increase in the benefits such employees would otherwise receive at their age.

The ADEA permits voluntary early-retirement incentive plans such as those described above, as long as they are part of bona fide employee benefit plans and are consistent with the purposes of the ADEA. Thus, a simple lump-sum bonus for employees over fifty-five who choose to retire would be acceptable. But if the bonus had an upper-age cap, say sixty years old, then the plan would be discriminatory, because sixty-one-year-olds would be denied the same benefit being offered to the younger age group. Early retirement plans can provide substantial benefits if you are willing to retire early. However, giving up employment also has great economic and personal disadvantages, such as loss of income, loss of regular activity, loss of health benefits, and loss of professional status. Your employer should provide you with sufficient information and plenty of time to consider an early-retirement offer. Review your options with a financial advisor if possible. You should not receive threats of layoff or demotion if you do not choose early retirement. This kind of pressure, express or implied, should raise doubts about whether the retirement would be truly voluntary.

Waiving Your ADEA Rights

Some companies ask employees who accept an early-retirement offer or other exit incentive to sign a waiver of their rights under the ADEA, including the right to sue the employer. Waivers are legal only if they are "knowing and voluntary" and the employer follows specific procedures required by the ADEA, such as fully disclosing all relevant information, providing employees with extensive notice, and giving employees sufficient time to make an informed decision.

LAWFUL EMPLOYER ACTIONS
UNDER THE ADEA

Some employer practices that may adversely affect older workers are lawful.

Bona Fide Occupational Qualifications (BFOQs)

If an employer can prove that age is a bona fide occupational qualification (BFOQ) for a given job, then age-based discrimination is allowed under the ADEA with respect to that job. One obvious example in which age constitutes a BFOQ is a situation in which an employer must hire an actor to play the role of a child in a movie. (Obviously, only a child could effectively play the role of a child; it would thus be permissible to discriminate against middle-aged candidates for the job.)

It can be difficult to prove that age is a BFOQ for a given job, and the burden of proof is on the employer. In order for the BFOQ exception to apply, an employer must show two things. First, that the job qualifications in question are reasonably necessary to the essence of the employer's business. And second, that most persons outside the specified age limit cannot perform the job safely, efficiently, or effectively, or that it is impossible or highly impractical to assess the fitness of each candidate for the job on an individualized basis (which makes establishing an age limit the only practical way to hire employees).

Use of Reasonable Factors Other Than Age

Employers may base decisions about hiring, firing, or other actions on reasonable factors other than age, even if those decisions adversely affect older workers, if the decisions are justified by business necessity. This is a common-sense exception to the ADEA. A simple example is the basing of decisions on performance evaluations and physical exams, which is a perfectly acceptable practice as long as the same factors are applied fairly to workers of all ages. In all cases, the reasonable factors other than age must be related to the job in question. Age itself may *not* be a factor in the decision.

Actions Based on Good Cause

In another common-sense exception to the ADEA, employers may take adverse action against employees based on good cause, even if those actions adversely affect older workers. The term "good cause" usually refers to poor job performance. For example, a discharge due to tardiness or proven deficiencies in performance constitutes a good-cause discharge.

Actions Based on Seniority Systems

An employer may observe the terms of a bona fide seniority system, even if doing so has an adverse effect on older workers. Seniority systems seldom cause a problem under the ADEA, since they normally favor long-term workers over those with shorter tenure.

HOW TO ENFORCE YOUR ADEA RIGHTS

In order to enforce your rights under the ADEA, there are two steps you can take. The first is to file a charge or complaint with the state or federal agency responsible for enforcing the ADEA. The second is to file a lawsuit, usually in federal court.

Step 1: Filing a Charge

If you have been fired, forced to retire, or otherwise discriminated against by your employer because of your age, you (or someone on your behalf) can file a charge by mail or in person at the nearest office of the Equal Employment Opportunity Commission (EEOC). You can find the nearest office by consulting your local telephone directory (under "United States Government") or calling 1-800-669-4000 (voice) or 1-800-669-6820 (TTY).

To file your complaint, you will need to provide:
- your name, address, and telephone number;
- the name, address, and telephone number of the employer, employment agency, or union that is alleged to have discriminated against you, and the number of employees (or union members) employed by that employer, if known;
- a short description of the alleged violation (the event that caused you to believe that your rights were violated);
- the date or dates of the alleged violations; and
- if relevant, any employment contracts, brochures, or similar documents that demonstrate the policy that you allege to be discriminatory.

The EEOC is the federal agency that has authority to investigate and file lawsuits based on claims of age discrimination, as well as claims of discrimination based on race, sex, disability, and other grounds. Your local EEOC counselor will advise you in writing of your rights and responsibilities during the EEOC process, such as the right to a hearing before an administrative judge. Your counselor will also inform you that, under the ADEA, you have the right to proceed directly to court.

Many state and local governments have passed antidiscrimination laws and established antidiscrimination agencies. The EEOC refers to these agencies as **Fair Employment Practices Agencies (FEPAs)**, and has agreements with these agencies to coordinate enforcement.

BE AWARE OF TIME LIMITS!

Normally, you have 180 days from the date of the violation, or the date on which you received reasonable notice of the violation (whichever occurs first), to file a charge with the EEOC. For example, if you receive notice of a layoff on January 1 that will take effect on March 1, then you must file within 180 days of the earlier date—the date on which you received notice, *not* the date of the actual layoff.

If your state has an age discrimination law and enforcement agency, the time limit may be extended to 300 days. Nonetheless, just to be safe, you should make every effort to act within 180 days. Ideally you should contact the EEOC or local age discrimination agency as soon as you suspect any discrimination.

If you file a charge with a FEPA and the charge is also covered by federal law, then the FEPA automatically "dual files" the charge with the EEOC to protect your federal rights. The charge usually will be handled by the FEPA. Be aware that some state laws offer more protection against discrimination than the ADEA.

If you file a charge with EEOC that is also covered by state or local law, the EEOC "dual files" the charge with the state or local FEPA, but ordinarily retains the charge for handling.

Once you file a charge with the EEOC or your state agency, the agency is required to contact the discriminating party and attempt conciliation between the parties. If the problem is resolved to everyone's satisfaction at this point, the case is closed. If not, either you or the EEOC can proceed to the next step by filing an age discrimination lawsuit.

While the EEOC has the power to file a lawsuit to enforce your rights, it does so only in a small percentage of cases. The EEOC does not make any formal findings of guilt or innocence on your charge; only a court can do that.

FILING A CHARGE VERSUS FILING A COMPLAINT

If you file a **charge**, your name will be disclosed to the employer. If you wish to remain anonymous, you can file a **complaint** instead. A complaint may initiate an EEOC investigation; however, the government gives complaints much lower priority than charges. In addition, even if EEOC action leads an employer to correct its discriminatory practices, your own unfair treatment may not be remedied if you have only filed a complaint. Consequently, it is usually more effective to file a charge.

Step 2: Filing a Private Lawsuit

Before you can file an age discrimination lawsuit in federal or state court, you must have filed a charge with the EEOC as described above. After sixty or more days from the date you filed the charge, you have a right to file a private lawsuit under the ADEA, if the EEOC has not filed a lawsuit on your behalf (it seldom does). You do not have to wait for a right-to-sue notice from the EEOC, as is required in other types of discrimination claims. Your own lawsuit will be a private one, and you must bear the court costs and attorney's fees. An advantage when the EEOC decides to file a lawsuit on your behalf is that you would not be

 ## FEDERAL EMPLOYEES, LISTEN UP!

The procedures for enforcing your rights under the ADEA are somewhat different for federal employees or applicants for federal employment than for other employees or applicants. For more information, read the fact sheet entitled *Facts About Federal Sector Equal Employment Opportunity Complaint Processing* at *www.eeoc.gov/facts/fs-fed.html*.

AGAIN, BE AWARE OF TIME LIMITS!

There is a limit to how long you can wait before suing an employer for discrimination. The federal statute of limitations is two years from the time you knew or should have known about the violation. If the violation was willful, you have three years to file a lawsuit.

required to pay its costs. If the EEOC files a suit either on its own or on your behalf *before* you do, the Commission enforces your rights and you can no longer file a private lawsuit.

If a lawsuit has already been filed against your employer for age discrimination, you may be able to join it. The ADEA allows class-action lawsuits. A **class action** is a lawsuit in which a single person or a small group of people represents the interests of a larger group. However, unlike many other class-action cases, in an ADEA case you are not automatically part of the subject class just because the alleged discrimination affects you. Rather, you must opt in to the case by consenting in writing.

If you have suffered significant loss as a result of age discrimination and you are willing to invest substantial time and money, filing a private lawsuit may be worthwhile. But weigh the costs of such a lawsuit realistically. ADEA cases can involve a great deal of legal analysis, effort, and **discovery** (the disclosure of documents and information between the parties before trial). Generally, attorneys do not take ADEA cases for a **contingent fee**, an arrangement in which the lawyer only charges for his or

 JURY TRIALS

The ADEA entitles all litigants to a jury trial on any issue of fact. If you desire a jury trial, you must specifically ask for one. If you fail to request one, your right to a jury trial is automatically waived.

her services if the lawsuit is successful or is favorably settled out of court. However, if your lawsuit is successful, the ADEA permits you to obtain attorney's fees from the discriminating party.

If you win your case, the court will order the employer to pay damages or provide other remedies to make up to you what you lost through discrimination, thus making you whole again. This might include:

• awarding back pay for salary you did not receive while unemployed;

• awarding future pay, or **front pay** (not all courts have been willing to do this);

• paying or reinstating lost benefits, such as seniority rights, health or insurance benefits, sick leave, savings plan benefits, expected raises, stock bonus plan benefits, and lost overtime pay;

• reinstating your former job, with your former salary and benefits; and

• awarding punitive damages if it is proven that the employer acted with malice or reckless indifference.

If you win your case, the employer that discriminated against you will usually have to pay for your lawyer and other expenses, as well as for court costs.

THE WORLD AT YOUR FINGERTIPS

• Equal Employment Opportunity Commission (EEOC) offices are listed in the telephone directory under "United States Government." The EEOC publication *Federal Laws Prohibiting Job Discrimination: Questions and Answers* and other general-information booklets produced by the EEOC are available at no charge. To order, visit *www.eeoc.gov*.

• The American Association of Retired Persons (AARP) offers a variety of free booklets and articles on age discrimination online at *www.aarp.org*.

• The U.S. Administration on Aging (AoA) produces a fact sheet, "Age Discrimination: A Pervasive and Damaging

Influence," that can be accessed at *http://library.findlaw.com/ 1999/ Mar/2/126569.html*. The AoA also publishes "Aging Internet Information Notes: Workforce and Aging," available online at *www .aoa.dhhs.gov/prof/notes/notes_workforce.asp*.

REMEMBER THIS

- The ADEA protects you from age discrimination if you are an employee or job applicant age forty or older.
- The ADEA covers most employers with twenty or more employees. It also covers employment agencies and unions. Most states and some local governments have laws that offer even more protection than the federal law.
- The ADEA requires employers to make all employment decisions based on a worker's qualifications and not on age. This includes any aspect of employment—hiring, firing, layoffs, promotion, demotion, working conditions and hours, training opportunities, compensation, benefits, and even forms of expression (for example, ageist attitudes and jokes are not allowed).
- The enforcement of your rights under the ADEA begins with the filing of a charge with the Equal Employment Opportunity Commission or your state or local government's Fair Employment Practices Agency. You have 180 days from the date of the alleged discriminatory action to file such a charge.
- After sixty or more days from the date you file a charge, you have the right to file a private lawsuit under the ADEA, if the EEOC has not filed a lawsuit on your behalf. If you succeed in your lawsuit, you will usually be entitled to attorney's fees from the other party in addition to damages.

CHAPTER 14

Consumer Protection

The Lowdown on Common Consumer Scams

John and Mary had always been careful with their money, so when unauthorized charges appeared on their credit cards, they knew something was wrong. But what they didn't know was where to turn for help—and what to do to prevent this type of fraud from happening again.

This chapter will describe a few common consumer scams to which older people often fall prey. It will suggest ways in which you can protect yourself, and recommend steps you can take if you fall victim to a scam.

TELEMARKETING FRAUD

Any crime in which the telephone is used to further a scam is an example of **telemarketing fraud**. In instances of telemarketing fraud, scam artists might call with offers of free vacations, income opportunities, prizes, and preapproved loans. Fraudulent telemarketers may reach you in several ways: through cold calls (i.e., unsolicited calls to persons with whom they have had no prior contact), direct mail, or broadcast and print advertisements.

Telemarketers can get your number from the phone book, a mailing list, or a so-called sucker list. A **sucker list** contains the personal information of consumers who have previously responded to telemarketing solicitations, including information about how much money they have spent. Such lists are bought and sold by telemarketers. They are very useful to scam artists who believe that consumers who have been scammed once are defenseless against additional scams.

Telemarketers can even lure consumers into calling *them*. For example, you can fall victim to telemarketing fraud when placing a call in response to a television or magazine advertisement. Letters or postcards stating that you have won a prize or contest may also lure consumers into calling telemarketers. Such letters and postcards often instruct you to call a certain number in order to claim a prize. If you do, you may be subjected to persuasive sales pitches, scare tactics, and false claims. Remember: The fact that you initiate a call does not mean that the business you contact is legitimate, or that you should be less vigilant about buying or investing over the phone.

The federal **Telemarketing Sales Rule (TSR)** requires that all telemarketing calls be made only between the hours of 8:00 A.M. and 9:00 P.M., and that such calls begin by providing:

- the identity of the caller;
- the nature of the goods being sold and the total cost of the goods being offered;
- details on refund policies or a disclosure that all sales are final; and
- if a prize is offered, a statement that the consumer does not have to purchase anything in order to win the prize, as well as the odds of winning prizes, and any restrictions involved with obtaining such prizes.

Another practice targeted by the TSR involves **recovery room operations,** in which companies promise to provide assistance with repairing poor credit ratings or obtaining loans, or in recovering money lost by the consumer to illegal telemarketing operations. However, some of the companies offering these services are actually the same companies that defraud unsuspecting consumers in the first place. The TSR prohibits payment for such services until after the services are performed.

What Can You Do to Protect Yourself?

If a telemarketer calls you with a suspicious offer, say "no" and hang up the phone. It's best not to talk to telemarketers at all, but if you are interested in what they propose, ask them to send you more information before committing to anything over the phone.

The most basic rule of thumb is to avoid giving personal or financial information to strangers over the phone, *unless* you initiate the call to a number you are sure is legitimate. Do not provide your credit card number if it is requested to "verify" who you are for some other purpose, such as for receipt of a so-called prize, and do not give out your checking account number or authorize the seller to take money from your bank account without providing your signature on a check.

Check your bank and credit card statements monthly for unauthorized charges. If you notice unauthorized charges, notify your credit card company immediately by following the procedures set forth on your bill, and do not pay the contested amount.

If you receive merchandise that you did not request, Federal Trade Commission rules and many state consumer laws permit you to treat the merchandise as a gift and keep it free of charge.

It is illegal for a telemarketer to call you if you have asked to be placed on the company's do-not-call list, or if you have signed up for the National Do Not Call Registry. However, there are some exceptions to this rule for certain types of calls, including:

- calls from organizations with which you have established a business relationship;
- calls for which you have given prior written permission;
- calls that are not commercial or that do not include unsolicited advertisements; and
- calls by or on behalf of tax-exempt nonprofit organizations.

Signing up for the National Do Not Call Registry is easy, and registration is free. Sign up by visiting *www.ftc.gov/donotcall* or calling 1-888-382-1222 (voice) or 1-866-290-4236 (TYY) from the number you wish to register. Most telemarketers must stop calling within three months after you have registered or they will be subject to a fine. If you continue to receive unsolicited telephone calls, hang up and report the calls to your state's attorney general's office, the Federal Trade Commission, or the National Fraud Information Center. To file a complaint with any of these offices, document the name and phone number of the company that called and the date of the call.

TALKING TO A LAWYER

Q. I got a call from a man who said I need credit card loss protection insurance. Isn't there a law that limits my liability for unauthorized charges to $50? He told me that the law had changed, and that now consumers are liable for all unauthorized credit card charges on their accounts. Is this true?

A. No. You are protected from unauthorized use of your credit card. Under the law, your liability for unauthorized use of your credit card is limited to $50. Thus, if someone steals your card, your credit card lender can charge you a maximum of $50, no matter how much the thief has charged on your card.

As soon as you know of the unauthorized use of your credit card, call the lender to make a report. If you call before unauthorized charges are incurred, you cannot be charged anything, even the $50 maximum, since the lender can take steps to cancel your card and send you a new one.

If a charge unexpectedly appears on your bill for something you did not authorize, you can also use billing error procedures to dispute the charge. Some credit card lenders have been telling consumers that they can only report unauthorized use by sending a written billing error notice within sixty days of receiving a bill with an unauthorized charge. *This is not true.* You can report unauthorized use over the telephone. You also are not required to do so within sixty days—although the sooner you report unauthorized charges, the better.

After you report an unauthorized charge, the credit card lender must conduct a reasonable investigation of your claim, unless it simply decides to remove the charge from your account. A reasonable investigation might include analyzing the signature on the credit card slip, obtaining a copy of a police report, or comparing the site of a disputed purchase with the location of your home.

—Answer by Deanne Loonin,
National Consumer Law Center, Boston, MA

MAIL FRAUD

Mail fraud is any crime in which the U.S. mail is used to further a scheme. Criminals often target consumers through fraudulent sweepstakes, work-at-home schemes, merchandise misrepresentations, vacation or real estate scams, and investment schemes.

While most mail solicitations are for legitimate products, services, and charities, others are not. Many are scams, perpetrated by con artists to take advantage of your financial situation

 PRIZE SCHEMES

Be skeptical of all prize offers. Many have long strings attached. For example:

- You may have to purchase something in order to get the "prize."

- You may be required to pay shipping and handling (typically at an inflated rate).

- The value of the prize (i.e., its "estimated retail value") may be greatly overstated.

- You may be obligated to make future purchases under a subscription plan.

- You may be required to sign an acceptance that, in small print, authorizes a company to switch your long-distance phone service to another carrier.

- You may be required to attend a sales orientation for some product or property. This, of course, sets you up for further high-pressure sales tactics.

- You may have to call a 1-900 phone number (a call for which you will be charged).

- You may be asked for your credit card number or bank account number for verification or payment of shipping costs.

or dreams of striking it rich. Telling the difference between a legitimate offer and a scam is not easy. Scam solicitations are carefully written and often appear authentic. However, most scam solicitations are merely variations on old themes. Scam artists repeatedly target consumers with promises of easy money or guarantees of valuable prizes.

What Can You Do to Protect Yourself?

To spot mail fraud, look for the following warning signs:
- envelopes dressed up to look like official notifications (e.g., "Award Claim Number 88-7906");
- mail designed to look like it was sent by the government;
- chain letters featuring promises of money;
- first-class or express deliveries from companies with which you are not familiar;
- mail from companies with official-sounding names (e.g., "National Prize Center" or "Federal Audit Bureau");
- mail from an out-of-state company whose only listed address is a post office box; and
- small print tucked away in the midst of glossy notification materials. If it is hard to read or understand a mailing, this is generally an indication that the sender does not want you to understand it.

To avoid becoming a victim, remember that you can simply throw away mail notifications that appear to be scams. If you are interested in an offer, check out the company by contacting your state's attorney general's office, the National Fraud Center, or your Better Business Bureau before agreeing to anything.

DOOR-TO-DOOR SALES

Older people tend to be at home more often than younger people, and are therefore more likely to encounter door-to-door salespeople. Door-to-door salespeople sell everything from vacuum cleaners to home repair services.

(i) FEDERAL DECEPTIVE MAIL PREVENTION AND ENFORCEMENT ACT

The federal Deceptive Mail Prevention And Enforcement Act requires mailings that advertise contests or sweepstakes to clearly display:

- rules and order forms;

- a statement that no purchase is necessary to enter the contest;

- a statement that a purchase doesn't improve your chance of winning;

- the terms and conditions of the sweepstakes promotion, including rules and entry procedures;

- the name of the sponsor or mailer of the promotion and its principal place of business, or other contact addresses of the sponsor or mailer; and

- the estimated odds of winning each prize, the estimated retail value and nature of each prize, and the schedule of any payments made over time.

Most companies that sell door-to-door are legitimate and responsible. However, problems can arise in some situations. Fraudulent door-to-door sales typically involve deceptive salespeople who obtain entry into your home, high-pressure sales tactics, and misrepresentation of the price or quality of products or services.

Door-to-door salespeople use a variety of approaches to scam you. They may say they are taking a survey or conducting research and need to ask you a few questions. Some may claim they are testing a pilot educational plan or new product, and want you to participate by trying it out. Others may offer you a "free" gift just for taking the time to speak with them. Once these salespeople have your attention, high-pressure sales techniques are often used to get you to buy.

What Can You Do to Protect Yourself?

To avoid becoming a victim of door-to-door scams, follow a few simple steps. First, protect yourself by not letting anyone you do not know into your home. Always ask to see the person's credentials. Many localities require door-to-door sellers to have permits. Contact your local business permit office to verify the permit.

Second, never say, "yes" on the spot. Ask for all the relevant information in writing, including information about price, warranties, conditions, additional fees, and financing. Tell the seller you will review the material and get back to him or her.

Third, if you are interested in an offer, thoroughly evaluate the offer and the company. Check out the company through the local Better Business Bureau or consumer affairs office. Compare the salesperson's prices to those of local merchants. Be sure you know exactly what the price includes—for example, does it include delivery and installation? Make sure that any agreement is in writing and includes the seller's address (not just a P.O. box)

 COOLING-OFF PERIODS

All door-to-door sellers should clearly inform you that you have the right to cancel any door-to-door contract within three business days after the contract is signed. This is called a **cooling-off period**. Federal and most state law requires that the seller provide you with a written notice of cancellation, including a cancellation form. You need only sign, date, and mail the cancellation form in order to cancel the contract. Send it by certified mail, return receipt requested, and keep a copy of the form and the return receipt so you can verify your cancellation. The three-day right to cancel may be extended in some circumstances. For example, if the notice to cancel is defective, you may have more than three business days to cancel the contract. Check with a lawyer to see if your state's law provides for an extension of your right to cancel.

---

and the signatures of both parties. Never sign a contract with spaces left blank, and never sign a contract you do not understand.

INTERNET AND E-MAIL FRAUD

Any crime in which the Internet is used to further a fraudulent scheme is an example of **internet fraud**. Internet fraud most

 NIGERIAN LETTER SCAMS

Watch out for advance-fee solicitations, also known as **Nigerian letter scams**. Perpetrators of such scams frequently use the following tactics:

- Con artists claiming to be Nigerian businesspeople, government officials, or the surviving spouses of former government officials offer to transfer millions of dollars into your bank account in exchange for a small fee.

- If you respond, you may receive documents that look authentic.

- You may even be encouraged to travel to Nigeria or a neighboring country to complete the transaction.

- You may then be asked to provide blank letterhead, bank account numbers, and a small amount of money to cover transaction costs and attorney's fees.

- Inevitably, an emergency will arise requiring more of your money and delaying "transfer" of funds to your account.

In the end, there aren't any profits to share and the scam artist has vanished with your money. If you have fallen victim to a scam like this, call your local Secret Service field office. Local field offices are listed in the Blue Pages of your telephone book, or you can find listings online at *www.secretservice.gov/field_offices.shtml*.

commonly occurs when an individual wins an Internet bid in an auction, but the seller sends an inferior product or never sends the item at all.

E-mail is another new medium for fraud. Some con artists use e-mail to reach large numbers of people with promises of extravagant earnings, while others break into consumers' modems and cram large long-distance charges onto their phone bills.

Phishing is another increasingly common scam. In this scam, the victim is lured into revealing his or her personal information. Messages that appear legitimate may in fact be connected with phishing scams. Be on the alert if you receive a message containing a statement that resembles either of the following examples:

• "We suspect an unauthorized transaction on your account. To ensure that your account is not compromised, please click on the link below to confirm your identity"; or

• "During our regular verification of accounts, we couldn't verify your information. Please click here to update and verify your information."

Even a message that appears to be from your bank may in fact be the product of a sophisticated fraud. If you receive e-mail messages asking for personal information that appear to be from your bank, contact your bank personally to ensure that the messages are legitimate.

What Can You Do to Protect Yourself?

If you receive an e-mail or pop-up message that asks for personal or financial information, do not reply or click on the link in the message. Also, protect your computer using up-to-date antivirus software and a firewall. Never send personal or financial information via e-mail, and always review credit card and bank account statements as soon as you receive them to check for unauthorized charges. Always use a secure Internet site when divulging your personal information over the Internet—for example, when making an online purchase. The appearance of a small "lock" symbol in your Web browser, and a Web address that begins with *https://* are indications that you are using a secure connection. If you believe you have been scammed, file a complaint with the Federal Trade Commission.

PREDATORY LENDING

Victims of **predatory lending** can lose their homes and their investments because of predatory lenders who take advantage of borrowers' failure to understand extremely complicated transactions, and who make loans that borrowers cannot afford.

Predatory lending almost always involves very high-cost credit and a wide array of abusive practices, including:

• knowingly lending more money than a borrower can afford to repay;

• using false appraisals to sell property for much more than it's worth;

• convincing borrowers to accept higher-risk loans, such as "balloon" loans, which have a large amount (a "balloon" payment) due at the end of a scheduled payment period;

• pressuring borrowers to lie about details of their financial situation, including income, expenses, or cash available for down payments; and

• encouraging homeowners to refinance over and over again, even if such refinancing creates no benefit for the homeowner.

What Can You Do to Protect Yourself?

Every year, consumers fall victim to predatory lenders. Such lenders usually target consumers who are short of money or have poor credit records. In some cases even borrowers who are eligible for prime loans fall victim to the high-pressure sales tactics of a predatory lender and are forced into predatory or subprime loans. The following tips can help to protect you from falling victim to these types of practices:

• Do not agree to anything simply because you feel pressured by a salesperson.

- Shop around for the best deal by calling other lenders.
- Remember: If it's too good to be true, it probably is.
- Check out any lender's references and status with the Better Business Bureau.
- Ask questions, read everything carefully, and make sure you understand all the terms of any loan.
- Avoid balloon payments.
- Consider a reverse mortgage as an alternative to a home equity loan. For more information on reverse mortgages, see Chapter 11, "Housing and Long-Term-Care Choices."

 REDUCE YOUR RISK OF FORECLOSURE

If you have fallen victim to predatory lending and are worried about making your mortgage payments, there are a number of things you can do to reduce your risk of foreclosure, including:

- obtaining legal advice;
- keeping current on home payments;
- applying for income maintenance, tax abatement, and public-assistance programs;
- negotiating a temporary delay in payments;
- negotiating a permanent loan restructuring;
- refinancing home debt; or
- filing for bankruptcy.

Source: "Consumer Concerns for Older Americans: Steps That Advocates Can Take to Help Prevent Foreclosure," by the National Consumer Law Center, available online at *www.nclc.org/initiatives/seniors_initiative/content/advforcl_content.html.*

HOME REPAIR FRAUD

Home repair fraud occurs when a consumer either pays for a service he or she never receives, or pays for an inadequate home repair. Victims of home repair fraud can even lose their homes if they agree to financing agreements that give con artists an interest in their home.

Con artists appeal to consumers by offering estimates that are significantly lower than those offered by other companies. But don't be fooled. Remember: If an offer sounds too good to be true, it probably is.

What Can You Do to Protect Yourself?

Do not commit to a project, sign a document, or turn over money on the spot. Do not believe that an offer is available "today only" because a contractor happens to be in your neighborhood. If you are interested, take the time to research the offer and the company. Call your local Better Business Bureau, office of consumer affairs, or state attorney general to find out if any problems have been reported about the contractor. Make sure the contractor is insured and licensed in your county or city. You can usually find the phone number to verify this information under "Licenses" or "Business" in your local government's telephone listings.

Demand that any contracts include a detailed description of the work to be done, the materials to be used, and the date on which the project is to be completed. Avoid contracts with blanks that are not completed, or contracts that use the term "work per agreement" or similar nonspecific language. If a contractor makes any type of guarantee, make sure the guarantee is in writing. Better yet, have someone familiar with these types of home repair agreements review the contract. Never sign a contract that is vague or that includes wording you don't understand.

Get other estimates, or at least call a local contractor and

INDICATORS OF HOME REPAIR SCAMS

Watch out for the following indicators of home repair scams:

- workers cruising through the neighborhood knocking on doors, claiming that they are doing other work in the neighborhood or have leftover materials from another job, and offering to give you an extra-low price if you act immediately;

- workers driving an unmarked truck or a truck with out-of-state tags;

- workers demanding cash payment for their work;

- workers who cannot provide any references;

- companies that offer money for referring potential clients;

- workers who make exaggerated claims and lavish promises; and

- workers who insist that you are qualified for a home equity loan, regardless of your credit.

---

ask if the proposed work and price are comparable to what the local contractor would offer.

Avoid financing arrangements that give the contractor a mortgage or security interest in your home as part of the financing arrangement. This creates a lien against your home and could even result in foreclosure. And always arrange to hold back a portion of payment until all of the work is completed to your satisfaction.

CHARITY FRAUD

Charity fraud is a crime perpetrated by scam artists who either misuse funds donated to a legitimate charity, or convince consumers to donate to a fraudulent or nonexistent charity.

Most charitable solicitations are honest, but unfortunately Americans lose millions of dollars to fraudulent charities each

GIVE GENEROUSLY

When you are asked to donate to a charity, remember these six smart tips:

1. Look for an identification badge or other formal identification that indicates the solicitor's connection to the charity in question. Ask for background literature that explains: (1) the charity's purposes; (2) how it accomplishes its purposes; and (3) its financing, including how much of your contribution actually goes to the cause and how much goes to fundraising and administration.

2. Check with your state's attorney general's office to determine whether the charity is registered and in good standing.

3. Do not judge a charity based on the emotional appeals of the person contacting you, or upon a charity's impressive-sounding name or cause. Do not be pressured by guilt tactics.

4. Ask how much of your contribution is tax-deductible. Remember that political contributions are never tax-deductible.

5. Always contribute by means of a check made out to the charity. Cash contributions are too easy for someone to pocket.

6. Use caution when a charity offers a prize or gift to encourage you to donate. If a charity sends you a gift, remember that you do not have to pay for it.

year. Before you give, find out more about the organization to which you are giving.

INVESTMENT FRAUD

Investment scams are among the most serious examples of consumer fraud, because they can place your entire life savings at risk. Perpetrators of such scams promise amazing benefits if you act quickly—of course, by giving them your money. You may think you can spot a phony scheme a mile away, but it's not always easy. Perpetrators may work patiently to win your confidence over time with friendly conversations that have nothing to do with investing. Then one day, after earning your trust, they'll offer you "the deal of a lifetime."

As an example, one common investment scheme involves a con artist calling several senior citizens during the same period of time. Half the seniors are told that the price of gold (or some other commodity) is going to rise, and the other half are told that the price is going to drop. The salesperson carefully avoids pressuring the seniors to invest. Whichever way the price actually moves, the salesperson later calls those who received the "correct" prediction to boast about his accuracy. After building up a good track record with some of the group, the scam artist then announces that "now is the time to invest," and urges the victims to invest big money.

Some con artists have even represented themselves as fraud investigators who are seeking the cooperation of consumers to catch perpetrators of investment scams. Consumers are persuaded to permit a transfer of funds in order to catch the criminals. But in these situations, it is the quack investigators who are the real criminals.

What Can You Do to Protect Yourself?

The easiest way to protect yourself from this form of fraud is to never respond to investment offers. If you are interested in investigating an opportunity, request all information in writing, as in the form of prospectuses, brochures, and corporate reports. Most investments are securities or commodities. Companies and brokers that deal in securities or commodities must be registered with the Securities and Exchange Commission, the Commodity Futures Trading Commission, and probably your state's commerce department or corporation commission. If securities are sold through telemarketing, the Federal Trade Commission is also involved. These agencies can help you research the back-

INVESTMENT SCAM WARNING SIGNS

To avoid becoming a victim of investment fraud, watch out for the following warning signs:

- Unsolicited phone calls from someone you do not know who attempts to sell you an "investment opportunity." Some of the more common examples of this type of scam involve penny stocks, or commodities such as oil and gas leases, coins, and precious metals.

- Promises of high or "guaranteed" profits. All investments entail risk.

- Out-of-state companies that list only a P.O. box as an address.

- Instructions to send money quickly. Perpetrators may even offer to provide express delivery from your home or bank. Do not fall for these tactics. U.S. mail fraud laws may not cover private delivery services, such as courier services, overnight-delivery systems, or money transfer services.

- Small "investment opportunities" or advice that promises success on a small scale. These types of promises may be a setup designed to convince you to invest a large amount the next time around.

ground of any individual or company attempting to solicit your investment. Keep in mind that registration with any of these agencies does not guarantee the honesty of a firm or individual, nor does such registration constitute a recommendation. The responsibility to investigate a firm or individual solicitor ultimately rests with you.

HEALTH CARE FRAUD

Americans spend billions per year on products that have no proven medical value, but that are nonetheless promoted as modern cures for age-old problems. Aging Americans are a prime target for health quackery that accomplishes little more than the draining of their wallets. This type of fraud can even cause harm by keeping people in need of treatment from obtaining appropriate medical assistance.

What Can You Do to Protect Yourself?

To avoid falling for health-care scams, remember these seven tips:

1. Do not believe advertisements that promise a "secret cure" or "miracle drug." And ignore testimonials from unidentified users of a product. Typically, false advertisements look like legitimate news stories.

2. Do not buy a product based on a seller's claim that Medicare will pay for it. Check first with your Medicare insurance carrier to confirm coverage.

3. Check with a medical doctor before buying any medical device or product.

4. Be especially wary of products that promise dramatic weight loss or restoration of youth and vigor.

5. If you are considering buying a hearing aid, obtain a prescription or recommendation from a physician or audiologist first. Do not be pressured into buying a particular hearing aid. Review the hearing aid contract before buying. It should be written using plain language and should clearly spell out all guarantees, all servicing and repair costs and procedures, and your right to cancel and to receive a refund.

6. Do not trust claims of official government endorsement or hints that the federal government is blocking use of a product that has cured thousands in other countries.

7. Before purchasing any health-care-related product, check with voluntary health associations such as the American Cancer Society or the American Diabetes Association. These organizations offer reliable information about legitimate health resources and treatment options.

If you have purchased a product of questionable medical value, report your experience to your state's attorney general's office. State attorneys general have the authority to prosecute sellers that engage in deceptive sales practices. You can also contact the Federal Trade Commission, which has authority to prosecute the deceptive advertising of foods, nonprescription drugs, medical devices, and health-care services. If you suspect that the seller of a questionable product might bill Medicare, notify your Medicare carrier or call the Medicare hotline at 1-800-MEDICARE (1-800-633-4227). If a substantial amount of money is involved, get help from a lawyer to get your money back.

LIVING-TRUST SCAMS

Living trusts, also known as **inter vivos trusts**, may be an important part of an estate plan for some seniors (see Chapter 5, "Estate Planning and Probate"), but they are not right for everyone. In recent years, the marketing of living trusts has become a common consumer scam. Official-sounding companies promote living trusts as a surefire way to save thousands of dollars in attorney's fees, taxes, and probate costs, and to protect privacy and avoid court delays. These scams use misrepresentation, scare tactics, and high-pressure techniques to persuade seniors to purchase prepackaged living trusts at inflated rates.

What Can You Do to Protect Yourself?

Be suspicious of operations using names that could easily be confused with those of legitimate organizations, such as the American Association for Senior Citizens or the American Association for Retired Citizens. The similarity of these names to that of the American Association of Retired Persons (AARP) is no coincidence. These operations often rely on home visits by salespeople to make their high-pressure sales pitches.

To avoid becoming the victim of a living-trust scam, watch out for the following:

• **Fake claims of affiliation.** Do not necessarily believe that a company has some connection to an established organization such as AARP, or that its product is endorsed by such an organization—call the organization and check.

• **Cost traps.** Be wary of solicitors who exaggerate the costs of writing and probating a will. A living trust might be less expensive than a will, but this is by no means always the case. Talk to a local attorney to find out the typical cost range in your area for preparing and probating a will. Learn how long it generally takes to probate a will in your state.

• **Exaggerated benefits.** Understand that a living trust does not guarantee that you will be able to avoid probate proceedings. Nor do living trusts protect you from the claims of creditors, or protect your assets if you enter a nursing home, or enable you to avoid death taxes. Moreover, some companies charge more to create living trusts than a local attorney would charge. To make their costs seem lower, some companies avoid disclosing the necessary cost of transferring your property to a trust. Remember that a trust does you no good if none of your property is transferred into it. Be suspicious of "maintenance fees" or other additional costs.

• **Boilerplate products.** Sales representatives typically are not attorneys. They may claim that an attorney prepares your documents, but this may mean only that an attorney drafted the boilerplate (i.e., standardized) language used in the company's documents. Trust documents need to be tailored to your specific needs in compliance with *your* state's law. The attorney, if any, who is involved with living-trust documents purchased from a company may not even practice within your state. In addition, a lawyer who is employed by a company selling trusts will not be able to give you truly independent legal counsel. Do not decide to create a living trust until you have sought advice from an independent attorney, experienced in estate planning and licensed to practice law in your state. If a living trust is appropriate for you, an attorney representing you (and not a company) should draft the instrument.

• **Package deals.** The sale of a living trust may be part of a "membership" package that includes discounts on various products or services. Be wary of these kinds of deals, especially those sold door-to-door by companies with which you are not personally familiar. Contact your Better Business Bureau and state attorney general's office to find out if there have been problems reported with the company.

- **Time limits.** Do not be pressured. If a salesperson tells you that a deal is good "only today," then it is probably no good at all.

FUNERAL ARRANGEMENTS AND PREPAID FUNERAL PLANS

Funeral planning generally occurs at a time of emotional upheaval. Time constraints add to the difficulty of funeral planning. Consequently, you may rely too heavily on the advice of funeral directors, sometimes to your detriment.

To avoid the stress and financial burden of funeral planning during mourning, many adults prefer to make funeral arrangements ahead of time through prepaid funeral plans. Prepaid options may be a legitimate choice for some consumers, but they also have serious pitfalls.

There are two general types of prepaid plans:

1. **Insurance-funded plans.** Under these plans, the consumer chooses caskets, funeral plots, or other goods or services, and buys an increasing-benefit life insurance policy from the funeral director or cemetery owner. The price of the goods and services is usually guaranteed. Upon death, the policy proceeds are paid to the funeral director or cemetery.

2. **Pre-need trusts.** Instead of purchasing an insurance policy, the buyer of a pre-need trust pays the funeral director or cemetery an amount for guaranteed goods or services to be provided at the time of death. The seller holds the money in a trust fund.

Each of these types of plan has serious pitfalls, and consumers should obtain all of the relevant information before purchasing a plan of either type. Pre-need trusts are regulated in many states, yet many problems still arise. The worst involve funeral trusts that have been squandered or gone bankrupt, leaving aggrieved consumers without any benefits and remedies.

Other problems include substantial penalties for cancellation, hidden expenses, a lack of earnings on money placed into the trusts, high-pressure sales tactics, and a limited selection of funeral homes and cemeteries.

What Can You Do to Protect Yourself?

The Federal Trade Commission's Funeral Rule and some state laws enable you to obtain the information you need to make informed decisions. For example, under the Federal Trade Commission's Funeral Rule, you have the right to obtain information about the cost of individual items and services over the telephone. And when you inquire in person, a funeral home must provide you with a written price list of goods and services. For example, if you want to purchase a casket, the funeral provider must supply you with a list that describes all the available selections and their prices. You can purchase individual items or buy an entire package of goods and services. You also have the right to choose the funeral goods and services; the funeral provider must state this right in writing on the general price list. The provider may not require the consumer to buy a casket or an urn, and the funeral provider cannot refuse, or charge a fee, to handle a casket or urn you bought someplace else.

When planning a funeral, do not fall into the trap of thinking that the money you spend is a measure of your love for the deceased. Your budget and values should guide you. Comparison shop using the general price lists available from funeral directors, and get help with the planning from others, such as a responsible family member, friend, or advisor.

IDENTITY THEFT

The term identity theft is used to refer to all types of crime in which someone wrongfully obtains and uses another person's personal data in some way that involves fraud or deception,

IDENTITY THEFT FACTS AND FIGURES

- There were 9.3 million victims of identity theft in 2004.

- On average, victims spent twenty-eight hours resolving credit, financial, and other problems caused by identity theft.

- Family, friends, and neighbors comprise half of all known identity thieves.

Source: 2005 Identity Fraud Survey Report, Javelin Strategy & Research.

typically for economic gain. For example, victims have reported unauthorized persons removing funds from their bank accounts. Many other victims have reported having their identities stolen by criminals who incur large debts and commit crimes while using the victims' names.

Dumpster diving is one way for scam artists to steal your identity. **Dumpster diving** occurs when scam artists physically sift through your trash and take items containing your personal information. To protect yourself from Dumpster diving, follow these important steps:

• Try to put your garbage out on garbage day, instead of the night before.

• Don't throw anything in the garbage that contains your personal information, unless it has been shredded. You can purchase an inexpensive shredder for use at home, or your community center or library may offer shredding services. Shred all bank statements, credit card statements, credit card offers, free checks, bills, and any other documents that contain your personal information.

In addition to Dumpster diving, thieves may also obtain your personal information and steal your identity in many other ways. For example, thieves can steal your outgoing mail or mail that has been delivered to your home. Thieves may also obtain personal information by looking over your shoulder when you are entering your ATM pin number. This practice is known as "shoulder surfing." Thieves may also obtain your personal information by listening to your cell phone conversations or by posing as an employee of your bank calling to obtain personal information. Thieves may also send e-mails from addresses that resemble those of companies you recognize. Once you open their e-mails, they can gain access to your personal information. Of course, thieves may also steal your purse or wallet.

What Can You Do to Protect Yourself?

To reduce or minimize the risk of becoming a victim of identity theft or fraud, there are some basic steps you can take. The Fraud Section of the U.S. Department of Justice tells people to remember the word **SCAM**:

- **S**—Be **S**tingy about giving out your personal information to anyone, unless you are absolutely sure the person or company is legitimate.
- **C**—**C**heck your financial information regularly. Look for what should and should not be there.
- **A**—**A**sk for a copy of your credit report at least once a year.
- **M**—**M**aintain careful records of your banking and financial accounts.

One of the most important things you can do to protect yourself from identity theft is keep a close watch on your credit report. A federal law enacted in December 2003 gives consumers the right to obtain one free credit report every twelve months from each of the three national consumer-reporting companies: Equifax, Experian, and TransUnion. Because you have the right to three credit reports a year (one from each of the three national consumer-reporting companies), you should request a report from a different company every four months. If you see any unusual activity, or accounts with which you're not familiar, you may have been a victim of identity theft.

SELLING YOUR LIFE INSURANCE POLICY FOR CASH

If you are ill with a limited life expectancy, you may be able to sell your life insurance policy to an investor (usually through a broker), and get cash out of the policy now. Such sales are sometimes called **viatical settlements** or **life settlements**.

Suppose, for example, that James, age eighty-two, has a life insurance policy that will pay $100,000 after death. A broker offers to arrange the sale of the policy to an investor for $50,000. Of this amount, the broker says James will get $25,000 and the broker will get $25,000. The investor will pay the premiums on the policy until James's death and will then collect $100,000.

Should James accept this offer? It sounds awfully good, especially if James has expenses he cannot meet, but there are many dangers for both James and the investor. These types of settlements have often been the subject of investment scams. How does James know that he is getting a fair price? Is the broker taking advantage of James's age or illness? What effect will the proceeds from the sale have on public benefits that James may receive? Can James be held liable if the insurance company or the investor challenge the arrangement later on? Will James's survivors be without needed financial support because James sold the policy? Because of the many risks involved, James should proceed only after evaluating his options with a legal professional.

THE WORLD AT YOUR FINGERTIPS

• Every state has an office of the attorney general that enforces laws against most consumer scams described in this chapter. These offices rely on consumer complaints to identify fraudulent operations. So no matter how foolish you feel for "being taken," complain to your local attorney general's office.

Many such offices also provide helpful consumer protection information. Look for your state attorney general's number under the state or local government listings of your phone book.

• The National Fraud Information Center provides consumers with answers to questions about telephone or mail solicitation, how and where to report fraud, referral services, and filing complaints. Visit *www.fraud.org/welcome.htm*.

• The Federal Trade Commission (FTC) is responsible for enforcing federal regulations dealing with telemarketing, door-to-door sales, mail order operations, and funeral arrangements. The FTC also maintains a Consumer Information page on seniors' issues at *www.ftc.gov/bcp/menu-seniors.htm*.

• The National Consumers League is the nation's oldest consumer organization. It provides a variety of publications for consumers at *www.nclnet.org*.

• The Identity Theft Resource Center at *www.idtheftcenter.org* seeks to broaden consumer awareness and understanding of identity theft issues, and to decrease the potential victim population by increasing access to information. It distributes numerous consumer and victim resources as well as scam and consumer alerts.

• The Annual Credit Report Request Service will provide you with one free credit report every twelve months from each of the three national consumer-reporting companies: Equifax, Experian, and TransUnion. Visit *www.annualcreditreport.com*.

REMEMBER THIS

• As a general rule, you should avoid giving personal or financial information to strangers. If you receive an e-mail or phone call from your bank, double-check with your bank to make sure it is legitimate.

• If an offer sounds too good to be true, it probably is.

• Never sign up on the spot for an offer you receive over the phone or from a door-to-door salesman. If you wish to investigate an offer, request all information in writing.

• Shred all bank statements, credit card statements, credit card offers, free checks, bills, and any other documents that contain your personal information.

• Check your bank and credit card statements every month for unauthorized charges, and obtain a free copy of your credit report every four months to ensure that you have not fallen victim to identity theft.

CHAPTER 15
Finding Legal Help

When You Need to Call In the Professionals

Bob and Irene are thinking about retiring, selling their home, and moving to Florida. They think they should hire a lawyer to help them make these major decisions. But with so much at stake financially and personally, they want to make sure they find the right lawyer. How can they find the legal help they need?

This book can help you answer some of the legal questions you may encounter, but sometimes you will need to consult with a lawyer. How do you know when to call in the professionals? This chapter contains some guidelines.

DO YOU NEED A LAWYER?

With a basic knowledge of the law and how to use it, you can handle many of the tasks and challenges you face as an older American. However, major decisions can require a lawyer, especially if they involve complex facts or significant amounts of money, property, time, or personal freedom. In areas such as estate planning, where decisions can have both financial and personal consequences, you should be sure to seek competent legal advice.

If you are not sure whether you need legal help, ask your clergyperson, a counselor, a social worker, a financial advisor, or a trusted friend to help you decide whether you may need legal assistance or another expert's help. If a dispute is involved, determine whether resources exist in your community to help you resolve problems on your own or through the use of services such as mediation. And when in doubt, it's probably a good idea to call a lawyer.

RESOLVING DISPUTES ON YOUR OWN

If you encounter problems with consumer goods, services, or a public agency, you may be able to resolve the dispute on your own. Self-advocacy requires good negotiating skills, which we all possess to varying degrees.

Representing yourself requires time, energy, and knowledge of the law. Public service websites such as *www.lawhelp.org* can help you find information about the law in your state. Some bar associations or government agencies publish consumer guides to legal issues. Check your library or bookstore. Be sure that whatever guide you read describes the law in your state, and remember that laws change, so books may be out of date. If you need to go to court—whether to file papers to begin a case or to respond if you have been sued—you will need to use certain documents and forms. In some states, the court provides forms that you can use. Some courts also help people who want to handle legal matters by themselves.

MEDIATION

Many disputes can be addressed through mediation or other means of dispute resolution. In **mediation**, a trained neutral person helps parties come to an acceptable agreement. Each side tells his or her story, and the mediator helps them think of ways the problem could be solved. If mediation does not work, you can still bring a legal action in court.

Many localities have court-based dispute resolution programs. Some have community dispute resolution centers or private mediation offices. Check the telephone book or ask the local court clerk's office, bar association, or consumer affairs office.

HOW DO I FIND THE RIGHT LAWYER?

There is no surefire way to locate the best lawyer. Many legal problems directly related to your age are best addressed by a

EIGHT TIPS FOR RESOLVING DISPUTES WITHOUT A LAWYER

If you decide to resolve a problem on your own, without a lawyer, keep in mind the following eight tips:

1. If you call someone to make a complaint or seek more information about a problem, always find out and record the name and position of the person with whom you are speaking.

2. Go up the chain of command. Ask the name, title, and means of contacting the person who has the authority to do what you are asking.

3. Bring a friend. Sometimes there is strength in numbers, and it is easier to record and remember information if two people are present. Decide ahead of time the role that each of you will play.

4. Get and keep copies of everything: letters, receipts, records, your own notes, and other documents. Make written notes of any contact.

5. When speaking to another person involved with your case, ascertain the exact law, regulation, contract provision, or other authority on which that person is relying. Ask for a copy of the materials in question. Do not assume that the other person's interpretation is always correct.

6. Find points of compromise. Try to clarify the primary issues and identify the areas in which agreement can be reached.

7. Get any agreement or determination in writing! In disputes involving public benefits, you almost always have the right to a written determination, and a right to a formal appeal.

8. Remember the importance of attitude:

    • Focus on issues, not personalities.

    • Be honest.

    • Start with the assumption that the other person is interested in a fair and efficient resolution.

    • Do not lose control. Controlled, genuine anger can be effective, but a blowup usually stops communication.

LEGAL HOTLINES CAN HELP

As of August 2005, at least twenty-three states, plus the District of Columbia and Puerto Rico, operate toll-free legal hotlines for seniors. Legal hotlines provide information and advice on simple matters directly over the phone; they refer callers who need more extensive help to free or reduced-cost legal assistance or to local attorneys.

lawyer who specializes in elder law, but lawyers who do not call themselves elder law specialists may also be able to meet your needs. Older people frequently face the same legal problems as other adults, and simply need to find a lawyer skilled in that area of the law. You'll probably need to do some research. Some people rely on their own or a friend's contacts. Others find referrals through churches, local organizations, and support groups. The resources described below are a good place to start.

Most communities offer some form of legal assistance for older people, funded by the Older Americans Act or other public funds. These free programs are staffed by lawyers, paralegals, and other advocates who specialize in the rights of older persons. Your state or local agency on aging can refer you to these programs, or to a legal-aid office offering more general help.

The National Academy of Elder Law Attorneys (NAELA) is a membership organization of lawyers who specialize in representing older people.

State and local bar associations have referral programs, and they may also sponsor **pro bono** programs. These are programs that operate for the good of the public and provide free legal help to people who meet certain income guidelines. Local courts may also provide information and assistance to people who are proceeding without a lawyer.

If you are homebound and want to speak to a lawyer, your local area agency on aging might be able to provide help in finding a lawyer who can come to your home. If you live in a nursing home, you should speak with the long-term-care ombudsman.

(See Chapter 11, "Housing and Long-Term-Care Choices," for more information.) The listing at the end of this chapter provides information about how to contact these programs.

WHAT QUESTIONS SHOULD I ASK WHEN SELECTING A LAWYER?

No matter what specialization a lawyer has or advertises, it is best to verify for yourself whether he or she will be able to meet your needs. During your first call, you should ask the lawyer (or the lawyer's secretary or office manager if you prefer):

• How long has the lawyer been in practice?

• What percentage of the lawyer's practice is devoted to your type of legal problem?

• If the lawyer is a specialist in the area of law you are seeking, how long has the attorney specialized? What specialty memberships or certifications does he or she have?

• Is there a fee for the first consultation, and if so, how much is it? Is the fee negotiable?

• Can the lawyer provide you with references to clients he or she has served with similar needs?

• If an appointment is made, what information should you bring with you to the initial consultation?

• Does the attorney carry malpractice insurance?

Once you have an appointment, come prepared to summarize the facts of your situation briefly and accurately. Providing a written summary really helps. After you have explained your situation, ask:

• What will it take to handle the matter and how long will it take? Are there alternative courses of action? What are the advantages and disadvantages of each?

• What experience does the lawyer have in handling this particular type of matter? (This is the same as the initial inquiry, suggested above, but this time it is based upon your particular circumstances, which the lawyer now knows in detail.)

• If the matter involves a dispute, what outcomes does the

lawyer expect (including time involved, costs, size of awards, and burdens on you personally)?

- Exactly who will be involved in working on your case and how? What experience and expertise do these people have?
- What will it cost, and how will you be billed?

Finally, consider your "comfort level" with the lawyer. This involves personal style or personality, physical environment, office organization and staffing, and convenience (e.g., convenience of office hours, availability by phone, staff helpfulness, and the lawyer's willingness to visit you at home if necessary).

WHAT TYPE OF AGREEMENT SHOULD I CONSIDER?

There is no standard fee or fee arrangement for most legal cases, so you should discuss fees openly and fully on your first meeting with an attorney. Some attorneys charge a flat fee for all or part of their services, especially if the service is relatively routine. If a flat fee is charged, ask whether incidental costs (such as photocopying, long-distance telephone calls, court filing fees, or delivery fees) are included. If not, get an estimate of these expenses.

Many attorneys charge an hourly fee, with different rates for different kinds of work (e.g., in-court versus out-of-court) or for work performed by different personnel (e.g., attorneys, paralegals, or secretaries). Again, incidental or out-of-pocket costs are often charged separately. Ask for a fair estimate of time and expense.

Contingency fees are common when money damages are sought, such as in personal-injury cases. **Contingency fees** are fees that are only charged if the lawsuit is successful or is favorably settled out of court. If you win, the attorney receives an agreed-upon percentage of the recovery, commonly one-third. If you lose, the attorney gets no fee, although you will still have to pay expenses, such as filing fees, deposition expenses, and other incidental costs.

The attorney also may ask for a **retainer fee**. This is money paid up front and usually placed in a trust account. The attorney debits the trust account each time he or she bills you.

Find out the billing procedure and the amount of detail you can expect. In how much detail will the bills itemize work done, time spent, personnel involved, and the nature of incidental expenses?

Make sure the arrangement is clear and reasonable. Get it in writing with sufficient detail so that you know exactly what to expect. Most lawyers use a written agreement, called a **retainer agreement** (even if no retainer fee is required up front). This agreement should be adapted to your specific situation.

WHAT HAPPENS AFTER I HIRE A LAWYER?

Good communication is the main factor that determines how positive your experience will be. Good communication begins with you asking the kinds of questions described in this chapter, and continues with you and your lawyer keeping each other adequately informed and involved. The lawyer is ethically bound to defer to you as the decision maker in all major decisions regarding outcomes or objectives, and to keep you reasonably informed of progress. It is helpful to educate yourself about the general area of law or the particular task the lawyer is handling for you. This will help you to understand the decisions you must make and help you to assist your attorney more effectively.

If your lawyer's style or specific actions are unacceptable, discuss your concerns immediately with him or her. If you cannot work it out, you may be better off ending the relationship. You will still have to pay for work actually completed, but doing this sooner rather than later will limit your costs and grief in the long run. If a problem arises that involves possible misconduct by your lawyer, and it cannot be informally resolved to your satisfaction, you can file a complaint with the disciplinary division of your state bar association.

THE WORLD AT YOUR FINGERTIPS

• The website of the American Bar Association (ABA) Commission on Law and Aging contains numerous links to resources that can help you locate a lawyer. Visit *www.abanet.org/aging.*

• State bar associations can provide information regarding lawyer referral services available in your state, and lawyer discipline and complaint procedures should you have a serious complaint about your attorney. The ABA Lawyer Referral Services website (*http://findlegalhelp.org*) provides direct links to the websites of state and local bar associations. Some states, including California, Florida, New Mexico, North Carolina, South Carolina, and Texas, certify lawyers in specialty areas such as estate planning.

• The ABA Section on Dispute Resolution publishes a directory of over 450 community dispute resolution programs at *www.abanet.org/dispute/home.html.*

• The National Academy of Elder Law Attorneys (NAELA) publishes a directory of elder law attorney members, including those certified in elder law by the National Elder Law Foundation; visit *www.naela.com.*

• Your local area agency on aging should be able to inform you about the availability of free or reduced-fee legal assistance available to persons sixty years of age and older in your community. Call the national Eldercare Locator at 1-800-677-1116 or visit *www.eldercare.gov* to find the agency on aging nearest you.

• The Administration on Aging (AoA) funds legal hotlines that provide legal counseling and advice to older Americans. Access *www.aoa.gov/eldfam/elder_rights/legal_assistance/legal_hotline .asp* for a list of these legal hotlines.

REMEMBER THIS

• With a basic knowledge of the law and how to use it, you can handle many of the tasks and challenges you face as an older

American. However, major decisions can require a lawyer, especially if they involve complex facts or significant amounts of money, property, time, or personal freedom.

• There is no surefire way to locate the best lawyer, but there are some good places to start. Ask friends and neighbors for recommendations, or use a referral service provided by your local bar association.

• No matter what specialization a lawyer has or advertises, it is best to verify for yourself whether he or she will be able to meet your needs.

• There is no standard fee or fee arrangement for most legal cases, so you should discuss fees openly and fully on your first meeting with an attorney.

• Good communication with your lawyer is essential. Good communication begins with you asking the kinds of questions described in this chapter, and continues with you and your lawyer keeping each other adequately informed and involved.

CHAPTER 16

Where to Go for More Information

Recommended Books and Websites

Throughout this book, we've provided you with resources for finding more information on a variety of topics associated with legal issues facing people over the age of fifty. You can build on your knowledge by checking out the websites, books, and other helpful suggestions we offer in this chapter. Some of these resources may have been mentioned earlier, but we still think they're your best places to start. This chapter is broken up into the following subsections:

- Heard It on the Telephone
- Take It Easy: Eleven Websites to Get You Started
- Read All About It: Check Out These Books
- Don't Forget . . .

HEARD IT ON THE TELEPHONE

The U.S. Administration on Aging (AoA) funds legal hotlines that provide legal counseling and advice to older Americans. A list of legal hotlines for people over 60 in the states that presently have them is provided at *www.aoa.gov/eldfam/elder_rights/legal_assistance/legal_hotline.asp*.

TAKE IT EASY: ELEVEN WEBSITES TO GET YOU STARTED

These sites cover everything from your pension to your grandchildren, and are good sources for other information as well. Some of these websites are housed within larger sites, but they all contain lengthy sections on topics associated with law and aging. You're bound to find what you're looking for at one of these sites, or from one of their links. (Note: These are not arranged in any order of preference.)

AARP

www.aarp.org

The American Association of Retired Persons' website is chock-full of information for those aged fifty and older. Here you'll find information on such topics as money matters, insurance, Medicare, advocacy, caregiving, and much, much more.

FirstGov for Seniors

www.firstgov.gov/Topics/Seniors.shtml

This government portal site features information on a variety of topics, including Social Security, the foster grandparents program, veterans, health care, retirement, leisure, and much more. It also features links to other government sites including those of the Department of Health and Human Services and the Department of Housing and Urban Development.

U.S. Administration on Aging

www.aoa.dhhs.gov

The Elders and Families section includes resources on elder abuse and legal assistance, among other topics. Other sections cover money, health, housing, services for seniors, and more.

National Institute on Aging

www.nia.nih.gov

The "Health Information" section of this site includes links to publications and a link to NIHSeniorHealth.gov, a website of the National Institutes of Health. Many publications are free; some are available in Spanish. Publication titles include: "Medicines, Use Them Safely;" "Older Drivers;" "Shots for Safety;" and "Caregiving Resources."

National Center for Assisted Living

www.ncal.org

This site is sponsored by the American Health Care Association. It includes consumer information on topics such as long-term care and finding a facility; news about assisted living; and links to others sites of interest.

Eldercare Locator
www.eldercare.gov
This government site from the Administration on Aging of the U.S. Department of Health and Human Services connects older Americans and their caregivers to state and local information on senior services.

MyZiva.net: The Complete Nursing Home Guide
www.myziva.net
This free resource allows people (whether prospective residents, health-care professionals, or caregivers) to find and compare nursing homes. Resources include tips on finding nursing homes, tips on preparing for admission to a nursing home, and links to the websites of elder law attorneys. The site is also available in Spanish and includes a glossary.

CNN/Money Retirement
money.cnn.com/retirement
At this site you can find practical information, articles, and tips to help you plan for your retirement. Features include an archive of related news articles and online calculators.

SeniorHousing.net
www.seniorhousing.net
Part of Realtor.com, this site offers information about types of senior housing (ranging from independent living to continuing care, assisted living, and more), as well as an online tool to help you discern which housing option may be best for you or your loved one. The site also offers information about financing, and a "Health and Wellness" section.

National Center on Elder Abuse
www.elderabusecenter.org
This site features frequently asked questions (FAQs), publications, information on laws and legal issues, and more.

Nolo.com
www.nolo.com
Topics addressed on this site include health-care and elder law, wills and estates, powers of attorney, and other issues of interest.

READ ALL ABOUT IT:
CHECK OUT THESE BOOKS

Wisdom comes with age, but it can also be gained from reading the following books. But don't stop with these; you can find many more at your local library, as well as at Amazon.com and other online bookstores.

The New Rules of Retirement: Strategies for a Secure Future—*Robert C. Carlson. John Wiley & Sons. (November 2004)*

Social Security, Medicare & Government Pensions: Get the Most of Your Retirement and Medical Benefits—*Joseph L. Matthews, Dorothy Matthews Berman, J.L. Matthews. NOLO. (February 2005)*

AARP Crash Course in Estate Planning: The Essential Guide to Wills, Trusts, and Your Personal Legacy—*Michael T. Palermo. Sterling. (December 2004)*

Grandparents' Rights, 4th Edition—*Traci Truly. Sphinx Publishing. (December 2005)*

DON'T FORGET . . .

Check local venues for courses, lectures and seminars, or expert panels related to issues affecting aging, including Social Security, elder law, Medicare, wills and estates, retirement, and other topics. Start with your local library, bar association, colleges, and senior citizens' centers to see what's in the works, or suggest topics for upcoming events. Area hospitals may also feature programs or seminars. Your local radio and TV stations also feature experts on health care, pension planning, and aging, so get with the programs. Don't forget that shows on many cable networks (as well as public and local channels) also offer special programs geared towards aging Americans; many of these programs also sponsor websites that offer a variety of resources. And your local newspaper might also include tips and tricks regarding financing, housing, and consumer protection laws.

The Internet is also a great resource; countless posting boards, user groups, mailing lists, and chat rooms exist in cyberspace—many of these could help you in your quest for knowledge and/or provide a "been there, done that" perspective on issues that you're facing. Communicating with others who have been in your position is a great way of learning about other avenues to explore, and what pitfalls to avoid.

That's about all we have for you now, so we invite you to begin checking out the resources above. We also welcome your comments and suggestions for future editions of this book. Please visit us on the Web at *www.abanet.org/publiced* or drop us a line via e-mail at *abapubed@abanet.org*.

INDEX

ABOUT THE AUTHORS

This book was written by the staff of the ABA Commission on Law and Aging. Charles P. Sabatino, Director of the Commission, wrote several chapters; chapters were also contributed by staff members Erica Wood, Stephanie Edelstein, Leslie Fried, Lori Stiegel, and Ellen M. VanCleave Klem. The Commission also wishes to thank Paul J. Buser, of the Paul J. Buser Law Offices in Scottsdale, Arizona for his assistance.

The fifteen-member ABA Commission on Law and Aging is composed of lawyers, judges, physicians, academics, and advocates, who bring an interdisciplinary perspective to a wide range of legal issues. The mission of the Commission is to strengthen and secure the legal rights, dignity, autonomy, quality of life, and quality of care of elders. It carries out this mission through research, policy development, technical assistance, advocacy, education, and training. The Commission also provides more than ninety publications and videos to professionals and the public.